The Hidden Truth

A logical path through compelling evidence to discover the nature of reality and the meaning of life

Wade C. Wilson

The Hidden Truth: A logical path through compelling evidence to discover the nature of reality and the meaning of life

Copyright © 2012 by Wade C. Wilson

ISBN-13: 978-0-9857284-0-3

Published by Wade C. Wilson
Contact information: thehiddentruth.book@googlemail.com
www.thehiddentruth.us

Printed in USA

Permissions:

Grateful acknowledgement is made for permission to reprint material copyrighted by:

The Case for Reincarnation by James Dillet Freeman (Unity Village, MO: Unity Books, 1986). Used with permission of Unity, www.unity.org

Table of Contents

Tables

Chapter One

Introduction

Before we get started with a discussion of the nature of reality, I think you deserve to know who I am, why I embarked on a study of the nature of reality that resulted in this book and what I hope you might be able to get out of it.

As an infant, I was baptized in the Catholic Church but to be honest, like many "Catholic" families I spent virtually no time at church as a child. My parents were burnt out on organized religion from their own childhood experiences and did not feel the need to impress upon us the same strict upbringing. My brothers, sister and I were raised to believe there was a God and Jesus was the Son of God who died for our sins. It sounded like a nice, feel-good story and I was curious enough in the matter that of my own volition I read and reread the Gospels and much of the rest of the Bible before I began to think that something was wrong with the entire concept of organized religion. However, as a young child, one's misgivings are not easily rectified with logic. Neither was there an easy way to seek alternative information for a broader understanding to answer my questions, so the matter was relegated to limbo for most of my childhood as I pondered.

One of my most vivid memories as a young child was walking outside and suddenly wondering, "What if life were but a dream?" What if there was a greater being out there and I was but a figment of his imagination? Now, that is an odd thing for a child to ponder!

It either sounds like fantasy or is so ridiculously deep in philosophical implications that assuredly such a thought was not dreamt up in the mind of a child. But it fostered in me a feeling of curiosity about life that stuck with me. I was certain my existence did not begin with life as a child, but I could not fathom from whence I came or why. As it would turn out, that farfetched childhood idea remained with me, in the back of my head, for more than two decades. As a child I was not ready to tackle this philosophical challenge, but as an educated adult I gained the tools to reconsider this problem and address it with a deliberated purpose that was both logic-based and analytical. That journey took a decade to complete as I gathered wide-ranging evidence across many diverse genres to support answers to the questions that haunt us all, and would eventually result in a personally acceptable answer, manifested in the form you see as this book.

Along my search for answers, I considered many other problems I had with organized Western religions. Of course the easiest conundrum was the one that vexes man almost daily: If God loves us, then why does he make us suffer with floods, earthquakes, tornados and a plethora of other natural disasters? Alternately, if God is perfect, then why would he put us on a world where human conflict and competition leads us to commit war, rape, and pillage against our common brethren? The answer to these questions and many more, I'm happy to say, are in this book, since the typical answers provided by most preachers, Imams, Fathers, deacons, etc. in the world's organized religions were simply not satisfactory to me.

Similarly, I wondered: Why are some people ridiculously rich or beautiful or famous while the vast majority is poor, hungry, or quite simply mundane? How is there justice in a world where slavery and famine still exist; or where murderers and thieves still lurk in the dark no matter how many are placed in overcrowded, inhumane jails? If a child lives but a few days, months or years, how can one say God loves us all equally when someone else lives past 100? And why must there be disease, cancer and accidents that result in death well before our time? Where is the fairness? The answers are in this book, and quite logically satisfying, unlike the so-called answers I heard from organized religion.

There have been many books written on the subject of, 'What is the purpose of life?' Unfortunately, many point to their own religion as containing *the* -- "one and only" -- answer, but again as I read the theories proposed in those books I knew deep down that the books were either partially or completely wrong. They were often mere feel-good books that had underlying motivations: their particular religion was the *only* answer so one should listen to that particular author, or face the wrath of a vengeful God at death should the message be ignored. I was troubled that it seemed odd how many preachers and sects of Christianity thought their particular interpretation of the Bible was *the only one* that was right, and must be followed implicitly in order to 'thread the eye of the needle' to enter Heaven. This is not to say that these self-help and religious books did not have many good points. Yes, it is important to love your neighbor as yourself and one *should* love God, but how can that be the summation of the whole purpose of creation? Surprise, it's not! Again, organized religion does not hold a logically sound answer for the question concerning the purpose of life, but I'll help you learn your own purpose herein.

I think the one thing that upset me most about organized religion was the absolute insistence that each religion has claimed to have *the* answer, and only the followers of that particular religion could claim a hold on the truth and the way to "salvation," if indeed there is even a need for salvation; an answer that I think might surprise many readers. Consider the implications if that religion were but the smallest subset of a larger belief, such as and probably most especially Christianity. Then only that church's "true believers" could hope for salvation and the rest of the seven-plus billion people in the world were simply out of luck. I'm sorry but that to my mind is the ultimate counter-argument for their religion's own validation because I cannot fathom how a loving God could create a universe some 12-14 billion years ago to reach its current state, so that mankind could evolve on Earth over the most recent one million-year period, all for the sole prospect of saving a few thousand to a million-plus of that religion's followers – who follow a particular subset of a religion or preacher, and tithe to the "appropriate" church or cause. Doesn't that strike anyone else as counterintuitive at best? It struck me as asinine.

There must be an answer, and I was going to find it. So in my spare time I started reading, researching and postulating; a process that would last more than a decade. There was no one book to go to that could provide all the answers I sought. If there was, I certainly wouldn't need to write this book. It took years because one book was as likely to provide a half-dozen more leads to follow as have nothing of use in it at all, and only a few of those leads would ultimately prove productive. It was a grueling effort to separate the wheat from the chaff in order to find consistency on issues that indicated solid, evidential support of basic underlying truths. But there were a few books that asked some thought provoking questions, and other books that helped me start an internal dialogue, or provided studies on information that led me down yet more tangents, or provided bibliographic clues as to where else I should look. The search resembled a scavenger hunt, to say the least, in my quest to find and then assemble all the pieces into one cogent theory of reality and meaning of life.

I've read many dozens, if not hundreds of books on the subject by this point, and I've found that many needed to be re-read a second or third time because without a clear guide to follow to assemble the understanding I needed, I was not ready to understand and assimilate all of the information in each of the most important works at the times I initially read them. Many glossed over highly important information because such might be tangential to the main discussion but when I returned to the piece a second time, a minor point or sentence hidden within a larger thought often times suddenly seemed to be a key to understanding or helping corroborate important information somewhere else completely – sometimes in an entirely different genre of study. For example, near-death or out-of-body experiences might provide information of amazing import within the context of understanding principles of quantum physics.

Now at this point you probably need to know a little more about me. I am not a new age hippy, living off the land and making sure I have a zero carbon footprint – though I certainly have nothing against living a responsible, sustainable lifestyle. I have been a Soldier most of my adult life, and like many Soldiers, I'm probably more conservative than I am liberal, though I cannot be typecast so limitedly.

I am a very cerebral-type person. I have a Master's degree in Strategic Intelligence and a Liberal Arts B.A. in Natural Sciences and Mathematics. I found my niche in the Army in the intelligence field because I liked the mental challenge of the specialization, including analyzing unknowns and assessing how best to discern means to acquire information for or otherwise overcome strategic challenges. Obtaining a master's degree was an easy choice and accomplishment for me: I like to read and write, and assembling papers that proved a thesis statement was hardly a challenge; it was a pastime and something I did most every day at work anyway.

And thus, the challenge of determining for myself the true nature of reality was a massive but feasible endeavor for a goal-oriented, highly motivated "student" of knowledge. The process simply took a lot longer than completing a college degree, but the basic work path was an old familiar one: research information that was most readily available, take notes, make assumptions, follow leads to obtain information that was less readily available, assess and compile ideas, assemble/modify a working outline and thesis, and repeat.

So what you will find herein is a thinking man's examination of the nature of reality. I would like you to know that I was a skeptic who did not accept most of what I read on any subject until I had massive amounts of corroborating evidence in hand, especially if that evidence was merely anecdotal. I have an ingrained preference to insist on argumentative agreement from multiple sources across completely separate fields of research before lending weight to any proposed ideas. Thus this guide, if it does the job I hope to do, should help fellow skeptics understand the path I took to discovery and the reader can then decide whether the presented logic is sound and transferable to their own experience-set and level of acceptance.

Historically, I have found it very hard to read most new age-type, spiritual books because the authors tended to discuss various, possibly harebrained concepts as if they were a given truth – with no intention of convincing a skeptic to believe those points, and expecting every reader to already exist on their same baseline of understanding. I hope not to repeat those mistakes.

Even after writing this book, I am still a skeptic and if I have not experienced something personally or had it proven to me logically, then the item of interest still resides in potential fantasyland for all intents and purposes. I'm sure that many readers and personal growth explorers have been similarly turned off from the new age-genre because of that disconnect, so it has been my intention not to make the same mistake here. With this book, I hope to break down those stereotypical walls and create a methodology that engenders general acceptance from the common man.

This book can be considered a study guide – a path of research that I walked over many years time to come to a greater understanding of the nature of reality and the meaning of life, and the peace of mind that knowledge brings. However, one should be aware that this book is not presented in the same order by which I eventually came to these conclusions. Writing a book that mimicked my own path of discovery would have resulted in a disjointed sequence, so I needed to impose some logic and structure on the thesis ideas so a beginner could more quickly come to their own decision on the logical merits of my work.

This work will mostly concentrate, therefore, on presenting the body of evidence for each listed topical area. The reader is invited and encouraged to research further by exploring the references used in each chapter as those authors – mostly scientists, doctors and professional researchers – have all done exhaustive research in their own specialty. I could not possibly do justice to their work by presenting all of their collective ideas, evidence and work in my own summarized, analytical piece, so those references are an excellent continuation point for a reader's own exploration of truth. The cited bibliography of this work is also by no means exhaustive on the topical areas, but merely a starting point that is stilted towards my own experience and research path in the search for the truth. It does not include every important work on the covered research topics because I simply could not reference or cite all of the thousands of books and academic papers written on each topical area of research. Also, many works that I did read are not referenced herein, for one reason or another. Many were secondary sources providing information that would be better cited in my work by primary sources, or otherwise did not offer substantive information necessary for this book. Nevertheless, many more sources contributed to my search for the truth as I sought an overwhelming consensus from the body of available evidence and information.

The following chapters then provide a cross reference of corroborating evidence between the various genres of research I explored. The study begins with the most scientifically sound evidence available and moves down a continuum of esoteric, though solid anecdotal evidence within increasingly metaphysical genres. This includes the fields of quantum physics, near-death experiences, out-of-body experiences, reincarnation, hypnosis-studies, including inter-life sessions and spirit guide interviews, and finally channeling. The evidence is intended to convince even skeptical readers to reach similar conclusions to my own on the true nature of reality and the meaning of life. The evidence leading up to the conclusion is obviously the most important component of this book as without it, my conclusions would make little sense to the reader, and indeed the journey to the conclusion is most of the enjoyment of the experience anyway. Still, I ask you not to take my word for any of the ideas presented herein, but to consider the evidence provided, read the material referenced throughout for further information, and then come to your own conclusion.

I hope you enjoy the journey.

Chapter Two

Quantum Physics

Introduction:

Of all the diverse fields I researched on the subject of the nature of reality this one was the most divergent and the most scientifically sound. Information provided in this genre sets the stage early for whether or not a skeptic should even consider plausible, anecdotal or less scientifically sound evidence discussed in the rest of this book. The reader will also note through the later chapters that topics highlighted here are then repeated in so many other genres of evidentiary study, ideally lending weight to such evidence given their consistency of agreement. Therefore it made sense to me to place this weighty chapter at the front.

In order to aid understanding and enjoyment of this chapter, I will include virtually no mathematical equations so as to try not to lose anyone's interest or compromise their full understanding. I caveat this endeavor with a warning that this amounts to a matter of translating one imprecise language – mathematics – for another: English. Translating reality as scientists have observed it at subatomic levels into mathematical formulas is imprecise in itself and may never achieve what Einstein had proposed was the ultimate goal of physics: an equation that defined all of reality. Unfortunately, without the perfect equation that defines all of reality, the process of translating pieces of observed reality into mathematics results in an inexact representation of that reality. Therefore, translating those imprecise mathematical equations into simple English for the common reader's enjoyment further clouds that reality but provides a close approximation that should help most people understand the implications of this astounding field.

As I compiled my thoughts on the nature of reality, aimed at eventually winning over skeptics like myself, it was clear that some of the most important evidence for that goal would be found in quantum physics, a highly technical field contributed to by such eminent personalities as Albert Einstein, Max Planck, Niels Bohr, and many others. As might be expected, none of these celebrated personalities embarked on their groundbreaking work as physicists with any intention their efforts would be utilized to forward a theorem on the existence of a universal spirituality. Indeed, some among them were ardent atheists who could not conceive of a God-personality or even life after death. It is quite ironic, therefore, that some of the best proof on the true nature of reality derived of quantum physics would end up, decades later, leading others in their field to acknowledge an unexpected truth – that there must be something behind that which mankind perceives in the physical world that allows 'reality' to function. Indeed, there is.

Modern physics is not the sterile, boring discipline some might perceive it to be. It is a rich, profound venture that has become inseparable from philosophy; an amalgamation blending the hardest of hard physical sciences with the softest science of academia. However, delving into the philosophical tenets underlying the meaning of some modern discoveries of physics is not generally encouraged in the field of physics. A pseudo-agreement known as the Copenhagen Interpretation provided the interpretation of Quantum Theory accepted by the bulk of the scientific community in the early 20th century. This agreement stated the proper goal of science was to provide a mathematical framework for organizing and expanding life's experiences, rather than seeking to provide a picture of some reality that could lie behind those experiences.[1] From the Copenhagen point of view, quantum theory was satisfactory as it was; i.e. as impersonal mathematical equations concerning the behavior of subatomic structures. Thus, the Copenhagen Interpretation found the effort to understand the philosophical and spiritual implications underlying hard science theories was not productive for the betterment of *science*. My aim herein is to show that an understanding of quantum physics is an integral beginning for setting the stage for the philosophical and spiritual basis of the nature of reality.

Classical Physics:

Quantum mechanics is important because it took cutting edge research in physics from a literal dead end, following Newton's classical ideas of mechanical physics, to a nearly boundless new field with findings that have eerie similarities to statements by spiritualists, mediums, and Eastern and new age religions. In the age of Newton, physics was seen as a field of defining life's processes as cogs within a massive machine. If one could understand how or why the smallest parts functioned as they did, then – the theory presumes – it should be possible to extrapolate how all the larger parts of the universe, seemingly connected to it directly through physical, chemical or gravitational connections, would function in turn. Thus, like Einstein, they hypothesized it might be possible to create a physics equation that would define not only how everything in the universe functioned, but to extrapolate that function forward to determine what would occur at any point in space and time in the future. They saw life as preordained, following a regimented course that was begun as required by the 'equation of life' since the Big Bang initiated the forward movement of time. Every future event thereafter was predestined to occur.

Newton's great work showed that the Earth, moon and planets were governed by the same laws as falling apples – gravity. The French mathematician, Rene Descartes, invented a way of drawing pictures of relationships between different measurements of time and distance, known as analytical geometry. Analytical geometry is a wonderful tool for organizing a wealth of scattered data into a meaningful pattern; for example, combining huge tracts of apparently unrelated experience into a rational framework of simple concepts like the laws of motion. The starting point of this process was a mental attitude that initially perceived the physical world as fragmented and different experiences as logically unrelated. Newtonian science, then, was the effort to find the relationships between these pre-existing separate parts.[2]

The problem with Newtonian, *classical relativity*, physics was that exceptions to the rules kept popping up in the equations. Mercury's cycle around the sun, for example, did not follow the standard equations defining other planets' gravitational relationships with the sun. Classical physicists also followed Newton's line of thinking in that matter could be broken down into its smallest constituents – essentially small, indestructible 'balls' or atoms – and therefore there either was matter or there was a void. The Newtonian model of physics also provided for the conservation of matter, and claimed matter was essentially passive.[3] These classical assertions were contradicted, however, by new discoveries in quantum physics. Thus 19th century physicists were reaching a dead end trying to make old theories fit modern observations of both macroscopic and sub-atomic reality.

Newton's mechanistic worldview – i.e. the classical laws of physics – was appropriate for most macroscopic observations of the world, but became completely insufficient and contradictory at the sub-atomic level. This forced twentieth century physicists like Albert Einstein, Neils Bor, and many others to create new laws, theories and mathematical languages in order to explain their observations of these new phenomena. These laws became known as quantum theory.

Whereas classical science started with the assumption that separate parts worked together to constitute physical reality – thus the parts determined actions and events of the whole – quantum mechanics was based on an opposite epistemological assumption: the whole could influence actions and events of the smallest parts.[4] Indeed, the 'smallest parts' – the void – was not a void at all, but rather constantly in a state of flux of sub-atomic particles coming into and going out of existence in microseconds, based on mathematical probabilities.

A fundamental difference between Newtonian physics and quantum theory was that Newtonian physics predicted events and quantum mechanics predicted the probability of events. According to quantum mechanics, the only determinable relation between events was statistical – that is, a matter of probability, but those events could not be stated with absolute certainty as Newton had tried to claim.[5] These observations showed another surprising truth about sub-atomic particles: they could not be isolated as independent entities. They may exist for a period of time, but they could not be isolated or confined to a specific location at a specific point in time. Rather, scientists found probability relationships that certain sub-atomic phenomena might occur within a given set of parameters, but they could not be definitively described as having an independent reality with a specific energy at a given time and location, as will be further described shortly. For centuries, scientists tried to reduce reality to indivisible entities. Imagine how surprising and frustrating it must have been for them to come so close, only to discover that elementary particles did not have an existence of their own! Thus, there were profound differences between Newtonian mechanics and quantum theory.

These generalities may seem confusing in a broad brush stroke, so we will spend a little more time considering each of these points in isolation.

Quantum Mechanics:

A quantum is a specific amount of energy or action, and first entered the physics lexicon when Max Planck discovered a specific amount of energy was realized depending on the amount of light that hit photographic plates. The amount of energy could never be divided into fractions smaller than that amount provided by a single photon, but always presented itself in whole numbers, or specific amounts – i.e. quanta – of energy. This discovery further led to Einstein's discovery that light photons displayed characteristics of both waves and particles. The problem with this association was that previously items were either waves or particles, but they could not be both. Waves seemingly lacked physical mass, and particles seemingly had no reason or ability to move as waves. And yet a photon apparently had both energy and mass but still moved like a wave, providing it a duality characteristic that would extend into the realm of sub-atomic particles and help reshape physicists' understanding of the nature of reality.

Quantum theory would demonstrate that subatomic particles like electrons were not the indestructible particles of classical physics: they also exhibited both wave and particle characteristics – similar to light. Rather than being permanent entities or independent particles with definite and enduring mass, sub-atomic matter reacted according to waves of interconnectedness; spider-web-like relations where the part was dependent upon and connected to the whole. Thus, nature was impossible to break into its constituent parts to consider how it might react according to the behaviors suggested by its building blocks but rather must be considered as a whole where the whole directed the manner in which the 'building blocks' would behave. This was the exact opposite conclusion suggested by classical physics.

The wave phenomenon added another aspect to modern physics, identified by Einstein as probability waves. An atomic event could never be stated or anticipated with any certainty but rather could only be predicted as a probability wave that showed how likely something was to occur. When given a beam of electrons, for example, quantum theory can accurately predict the probable distribution of those electrons over a given area in a given amount of time, but quantum theory cannot predict, even in principle, the course that a single electron will take along that path.[6] Because they are neither tangible nor permanent, subatomic particles demonstrate only *tendencies* to exist and *probabilities* to behave, move or be located in any particular area at any point in time. The idea that matter might wink in and out of existence in microseconds or less was certainly not a concept considered by Newton.

When two subatomic particles collide with high energies, they generally destroy themselves by breaking into pieces, but these pieces are **not** smaller than the original particles; nor are they components of the original from which the original is always made! The new particles are merely **different** sub-atomic particles based on the energies available during the collision. In this way, matter can be divided again and again, indefinitely, but we never obtain smaller pieces because we just create new particles out of the energy involved in the collision process. Subatomic particles are thus destructible and indestructible at the same time.[7]

Sub-atomic particles should not be thought of as basic building blocks, but rather as waves that exist as stable entities based on probabilities of the 'quanta,' or amount of energy present in the wave. Excited states may exist for short periods of time before excess energy is released and a more enduring and stable probability state is then realized. Expanding upon these ideas, Louis de Broglie dropped a bomb on the physics community that demolished what was left of the classical view of physics. He showed that not only were waves particles as Einstein had proven, but he claimed that particles were also waves![8] De Broglie's equation determined the wavelength of 'matter waves' that corresponded to matter. It says simply that the greater the momentum of a particle, the shorter is the length of its associated wave.

This explains why matter waves are not evident in the macroscopic world. De Broglie's equation tells us that matter waves corresponding to even the smallest object that we can see are so incredibly small compared to the size of the object that their effect is negligible. However, when we get down to something as small as a subatomic particle, like an electron, the size of the electron itself is smaller than the length of its associated wave. Under these circumstances, the wave-like behavior of matter should be clearly evident, and sub-atomic particles should behave different than 'matter' as we are used to thinking about it.[9] Only two years after de Broglie presented this hypothesis, Clinton Davisson at the Bell Telephone Laboratories verified the hypothesis experimentally. Both were awarded Nobel Prizes for their work.

Atom:

In Newtonian physics matter was understood as being physical objects which could be broken down to ever progressively smaller items until the smallest solid, physical component was finally realized. A mountain, for example, might be composed of boulders, composed of rocks, composed of dust, composed of silicate molecules, composed of silicone and oxygen atoms, etc. As scientists came to understand atoms, they realized atoms were not the solid particles envisioned by classical physicists. Atoms, measuring on the order of a billionth of an inch in diameter, are composed of a nucleus and outer electron shells. Protons, neutrons and electrons comprise the main subatomic particles that make most stable atoms, and in turn are a hundred thousand times smaller than the atom itself.

Imagine a baseball blown up to the size of the Earth. Each of the baseball's atoms would then be about the size of a grape, each placed snuggly against the others. In order to better understand an atom's structure, one would need to imagine that grape-sized atom further blown-up to the size of a football stadium. As such, the nucleus of the atom would measure no larger than a grain of rice and electrons would be dust particles flying around the stands at unimaginable speeds near the speed of light. Matter is indeed mostly empty, ghostly space, as the early twentieth-century British physicist Sir Arthur Eddington characterized it. Or to be a little more precise, it is closer to 99.9999999 percent empty space.[10]

One might wonder then why it is not possible to walk through a wall if it is in fact almost purely empty space. The answer lies in the powerful atomic attractions that keep electrons moving in a stable 3-dimensional orbit around the nucleus of the atom at near the speed of light. Imagine a fan spinning its blades, creating the impression of a circle. One realizes logically it would be impossible to stick your hand through the spinning fan without getting cut even though there is more open space than solid fan blades between oneself and the goal of the other side. Similarly, the speed at which electrons are spinning around the nucleus creates an impenetrable shell through which most other particles cannot normally pass. Atoms may be tightly packed against one another, but they are not intermingled and do not pass through one another. Their electron orbits behave as if they were solid objects.[11]

Inside the atom are the three primary sub-atomic particles: protons, neutrons and electrons. Scientists had theorized that these sub-atomic particles would in turn be comprised of other sub-atomic particles but the surprising answer to this theory caused the field to develop an entirely new line of study within quantum physics. Scientists learned how to smash these sub-atomic particles against one another in such a way that they divided into yet new sub-atomic particles. Interestingly, different sub-atomic particles were created after each collision based on probabilities, and not because a proton was comprised of distinct, ever smaller sub-atomic pieces. Indeed, collisions between a proton and another sub-atomic particle always create even **larger** particles. For example, a collision between a proton (mass 1836) and a negative Pion (mass 273) may create a neutral Kaon (mass 974) and a Lambda Baryon (mass 2183). These two new particles are each larger than the original particles from which they were derived, and are themselves highly unstable; each existing for less than a billionth of a second before decaying into more stable forms: the neutral Kaon into positive and negative Pions (mass 273 each); and the lambda decays into the original two particles, a negative Pion and a proton(!), thus creating more mass out of nothing but the energy of the original collision.[12]

It is evident here that one of the first classical physics laws broken in this example is the law concerning conservation of mass. In the above example, two lighter particles created two heavier particles, which in turn created four lighter particles, all of which were heavier than the two originals. Some mass was seemingly created out of thin air for the first transformation, and then lost into the nothingness again for the 'final' decay. The answer to this conundrum is that matter is not actually made of matter![13] Any search for the ultimate 'stuff' of the universe from which all other 'stuff' is derived ends with the discovery that *there isn't any*. What we've found is that if there is any ultimate 'stuff' of the universe, that 'stuff' is pure energy. More specifically, subatomic particles are not actually made of energy they simply are energy. This amazing find was already apparent to Einstein when he theorized it in 1905.[14]

Einstein's famous equation, E=mc², where e stands for energy, m stands for mass, and c stands for the speed of light, shows that there is a direct relationship between energy and mass. As an item's energy increases, so does its mass and vice versa. How could this be possible, if classical physics claimed atoms were made of ever-smaller pieces and thus must somehow gain even more of those pieces as they increased their energy? Remember, it is possible to increase one's energy in a variety of means, most commonly visualized by moving faster. Quite simply, the old Newtonian physics could not account for this observation. Realizing that everything is made of energy because everything simply is energy – in some form of stabilized state – made sense to Einstein. It also helps to explain how mass changes can occur with impacts between sub-atomic particles. Protons moving at a high rate of speed acquire more energy with their increasing rate of speed, thus providing sufficient energy needed to create heavier, albeit unstable, subatomic particles upon impact. When the heavier particles seemingly lose mass to decay into smaller particles, they may actually be shedding energy to reach a more stable form; energy that may be in another form altogether, such as light or heat.

What we have termed matter is actually constantly being created, annihilated and created yet again. This occurs both as particles interact with one another and also, quite literally, out of nowhere. Within a vacuum, particles may appear and vanish again in nanoseconds and faster. Thus, in particle physics there is no technical distinction between empty, as in the vacuum of space, and not empty, or even between something and not-something. The world of particle physics could be described as a world of sparkling energy forever dancing with itself as particles twinkle in and out of existence, collide, transform and disappear yet again.[15]

Newton's void was summarily rendered all but obsolete. What one might perceive as the great emptiness of outer space was merely a perception, albeit a false perception.

Perceptions of physical reality:

Our life is full of false perceptions, but those perceptions are designed to help us deal with life in a physical reality. As a quantum physicist-philosopher might note, physical objects observed by a human may or may not exist as perceived by the human conscious. A simple example of this philosophical challenge would be to consider colors. Colors are simply an impression made on the human eye, relayed to the human consciousness, but are actually a subjective quality of a light-wave's specific frequency. There is no color green for example – simply a light-wave which is translated in the human conscious to help humanity deal with the physical world surrounding it. Thus, the color green exists as a subjective experience perceived only in one's mind.[16]

This provides the barest impression that there is some level of disconnect or separation between physical reality and human consciousness. One could note we never actually see light itself. When light strikes our eye we only become aware of this fact through the energy that is released on contact. This energy is then transmitted to the brain and is in turn translated into a visual image in the mind. Although the image our mind interprets appears to be composed of light, the light we 'see' is actually an interpreted quality, appearing in our consciousness. However, because of this disconnect we can never actually directly see or know what light is.[17]

Returning to the earlier discussion about sub-atomic particles moving into and out of existence based on probability factors and wave functions, one could extend the implications of this observation. Particles also do not seem to have an independent existence. Particles are represented in mathematical theory only by wave functions, and the meaning of the wave functions lie only in their correlations with other macroscopic things.[18] This idea is astounding because it implies that seemingly 'solid' objects like chairs and tables are macroscopic objects that are simply organizations of energy that merely provide some means by which our consciousness gains an impression of what physical reality must be like.

These impressions are such that we can believe that physical objects have a persisting existence in our reality, and have a well-defined location in space-time that is logically independent of other physical objects. Nevertheless, the concept of independent existence disappears when we zoom down to the level of individual particles. The limitation of the concept of independent existence at the level of particles emphasizes that even chairs and tables are, for us humans, but tools for correlating our experience in physical reality.[19]

The problem can be rectified by understanding the simplicity of the human mind when interpreting life in physical reality. In other words, the real problem is that humans are used to looking at the world in the simplest terms possible. We are accustomed to believing that something exists or doesn't simply because we can or cannot see it, touch it, hear it, taste it, smell it, etc. Whether we can look at it or not, for example, we immediately reach a conclusion in our mind that it is either there or it is not there based on the results of our physical senses. Our experience in this regard has taught us that the physical world is solid, real, and independent of us. However, quantum mechanics asserts that this conclusion is incorrect.[20]

Indeed, the implication that colors do not exist is expanded by quantum mechanics to imply that even light photons themselves do not exist *independently*. Rather, all that exists in physical reality is an unbroken Unity that presents itself to us as webs of relations, according to quantum mechanics. Individual entities become idealizations, which are then correlations made by us to better experience the *illusion* of physical existence.[21] The implication here is that nothing can exist without consciousness to intend and then realize a physical reality wherein independent entities are perceived. The implication could be further expanded such that what consciousness expected to perceive might then be realized as a result. The Cartesian partition between one's self and the surrounding world, between the observer and the observed, or the scientist and the observed particle, cannot be made when dealing with atomic matter.[22] One interacts with and affects the other! These ideas have been proven in the lab by quantum physicists, and will be further described shortly. In the meantime, we will continue our discussion on perceptions.

Geometry, or more specifically, Euclidean geometry was developed by Greek mathematicians more than two thousand years ago to help describe relationships in space. Geometry was considered a proven mathematical discipline, but unfortunately its two-dimensional rules do not translate to a three-dimensional world. Consider the rules of a square or parallelogram: four 90-degree angles connecting straight lines. Now consider a person standing at the North Pole and beginning a trek south. At the equator the person turns right ninety degrees and walks westward some distance. The person then turns right ninety degrees and walks north again. Eventually that person will reach the North Pole again, thereby creating a triangle, though the "rules" of a triangle prevent it from having two ninety-degree angles, and the 'rules' of a parallelogram required it to have four sides, not three. Two-dimensional geometry was thus insufficient to fully and accurately describe reality in three-dimensional space. But mathematicians like Henry Margenau have noted that geometry is a construct of the intellect but is not actually inherent in nature.[23] This was a central precept of Einstein's Theory of Relativity. Distance, or space, is naught but a mode of particularization for the benefit of a particularizing consciousness, but has no real existence of its own.[24] This idea can be proven experimentally through the concept of super-luminal thought, further described below. However, perhaps even more astounding is that this assertion similarly applies to our concept of the idea of time.[25]

Space-time continuum:

Einstein developed the idea that space and time were **NOT** separate, independent concepts, but were inexorably linked in a four-dimensional reality called the space-time continuum. In the space-time continuum, events do not proceed from one moment to the next, they just are. In other words, if we could observe our reality in a four-dimensional way, we would see that everything that now seems to happen before us, seemingly because of the passage of time, already exists *in toto*, as if it were painted on the fabric of space-time. From that outside vantage point, we could see *all*: the past, present, and future exist at once.[26] While Einstein's four-dimensional space-time continuum has been proven mathematically, even physicists cannot visualize it. Humans live in a three-dimensional reality wherein consciousness seems to flow through time thus allowing human senses to experience what appears to be causality and the development of events based on cause and effect over the passage of time.

Hermann Minkowski conducted much work on the mathematical explorations of space and time, developing a simple diagram that showed the mathematical relationship between the past, present, and future. Amongst the wealth of information contained in this diagram, one of the most striking details was that all of the past and all of the future, for each individual, forever meets at a single point, '*now.*' Furthermore, individuals can never experience anything other than *now*, and that point will never be found in any other place than *here*.[27] The implication of this finding will become more astounding as we begin to consider the philosophical and spiritual aspects of this work – an area normally not considered by mathematically-minded scientists.

The Phenomenon of Light:

When Gallileo developed *classical relativity* he postulated the laws of physics were the same in all uniformly moving frames of reference. Consider, a ball dropped inside a steadily flying airplane would appear to a passenger in the airplane to bounce straight down and up, and would not slam into the back of the airplane at 500 mph. Similarly, a car moving at 60 mph that passes a truck moving at 55 mph would appear to be moving ahead of the truck at only 5mph, the difference in their respective rates of velocity. The problem with classical relativity was that it did not apply to light.

The speed of light is 186,282 miles per second. So under classical relativity, a speeding electron moving at 186,281 miles per second would be passed by light at a relatively slow 1 mile per second (the difference between the two), but in actuality, light from the perspective of the electron would be seen to be moving at 186,282 miles per second! This was the basis of Einstein's Special Theory of Relativity – light moves at the same speed in all frames of reference. This theory has been proven experimentally though the idea defied 'common' sense. Einstein reasoned where common sense and experimental findings were in violent disagreement then common sense must be wrong.[28] Obviously this puts light in a special category all by itself since it does not behave like a common physical phenomenon.

Indeed, as previously noted, light behaves with a dual nature, with characteristics of both a wave and a particle.[29] But light has a uniqueness that separates itself from matter. Experimentally and mathematically, it has been shown that objects increase in mass as they increase in speed, ultimately reaching infinite mass at the speed of light. Of course this conundrum seems impossible: it would require infinite energy to move an infinite mass. Thus, nothing could ever attain the speed of light – except, that is, for light itself.

Another interesting item about light's uniqueness is that time seems to slow with increased speed – a phenomenon that has also been proven experimentally. Mathematically it has been shown that time would slow to a complete standstill at the speed of light. This might make one wonder if time cannot move forward at light speed, how does light continue to flow – at the speed of light – regardless of the speed of the frame of reference? Some physicists have concluded that whatever light is, it seems to exist outside of space-time, in a realm where there is no past or future; there is only *now*.[30] Einstein's theory of relativity and quantum theory both suggest that light transcends the physical world, and indeed is beyond the entirety of space-time; it just *is*.[31]

Energy and mass:

Einstein's relativity theory showed that mass has nothing to do with any physical, tangible substance, but was a form of energy in his famous equation, $E=mc^2$. Energy is a dynamic quantity associated with activities or processes. When one considers that a particle's mass is equivalent to a certain amount of energy, one must realize that the particle can no longer be seen as a static object. The particle must be reconceived as part of a dynamic pattern; a process involving energy which then manifests itself as the particle's mass.[32] The terms 'energy' and 'dynamic' imply there is no such thing as absolute stability in matter; there must always be change so that energy can convert from one form to another. Further, Einstein's formula shows a direct proportionality between mass and energy; as one increases so too must the other.

Now take a step further and consider Max Planck's ground breaking finding that proved light was always associated with a specific unit of energy (i.e. a quantum). Planck's Constant, as it became known in physics, equates light with a unit of energy; so light is therefore also equal to a specific amount of energy.

Utilizing the mathematical transitive property, that is, if a = b and b = c, then a = c, one would have to conclude that matter is actually just a mass of stabilized light, where mass = energy = light.[33] Again, the implication of this finding in quantum physics seems to have more application to the philosophical and religious fields than the hard science field from which it originated, and will be further discussed later in this work.

The Conundrum of Consciousness:

Though perhaps counterintuitive, consciousness cannot be easily sidelined from scientific examination. Doctors have found a person's state of mind can have significant effects on their body's ability to heal itself.[34] While that anecdotal observation has not provided enough solid evidence to cause every doctor to prescribe meditation as a form of medicine, quantum physicists have found definitively that at the sub-atomic level, the act of observation actually affects the reality being observed.[35] This fact became known as the Heisenberg Uncertainty Principle: one cannot observe a phenomenon without changing or affecting it.[36]

Some physicists have wondered whether the universe in some strange sense might be brought into being by the participation of those consciousnesses that have chosen to participate.[37] The term 'participator' then has become an incontrovertible new concept given by quantum mechanics. It strikes down the idea of passive observation, given by classical theory, and shows that the vital act is the act of participation. In this way, there can no longer be a scientist who stands safely behind a thick glass wall and watches what happens in an isolated manner from the observed experiment without influencing the outcome simply by observing it. Quantum mechanics insists such isolation cannot occur.[38] Nobel Prize-winning physicist Wolfgang Pauli described that from within one's inner center our psyche seems to move outward, experiencing, influencing, and even creating the physical world through the act of participation.[39]

Thus physicists have found themselves, through the study of quantum mechanics, to be in the unanticipated field of the study of the structure of consciousness.[40] Christian de Quincey likened this phenomenon to being in the odd position of having to confront daily the indisputable fact of one's own consciousness, and yet having no way of being able to explain it.[41] What is consciousness and where does it come from? That is a philosophical question that dates back thousands of years. We can conclude consciousness is not composed of matter. But we have only assumed thus far that matter does not possess consciousness.[42] We must still ask, 'From whence then does consciousness originate?'

Greek philosopher Descartes was famous for his ability to doubt any given theory or philosophy. He could doubt what people said. He could doubt the validity of what his eyes showed him of the world. He could doubt himself; his own thoughts and feelings. He could even doubt that he was present in a physical body. But the one thing that he could not doubt was the fact that he was doubting. This revealed his one and only certainty: he was thinking. Descartes thus concluded if he was thinking, he had to be a conscious, experiencing being. As he put it in Latin, *Cogito, ergo sum*: I think, therefore I am.[43]

This was and is the paradox of consciousness. Its existence is quite undeniable, and yet it remains totally inexplicable. For the materialist meta-paradigm, consciousness is a monumental anomaly.[44]

Religious people may claim God is the creator and the source of all creation. But physicists might say the same of consciousness.

Philosophically, the implications of quantum mechanics are mind blowing. Not only does quantum mechanics insist that we influence our reality, but also, at least to some degree, we actually create our reality. Because quantum mechanics tells us that we can know either the momentum of a particle or its position, but not both, we are forced to choose which of these two properties we will want to determine. Metaphysically, this is very close to saying that we will create those specific properties because we have chosen to measure them. In other words, it is possible that we can create something at a specific position, like a particle, for example, simply because we were intent on determining some *thing* existed at that position.[45]

Returning to our earlier discussion of conscious' interpretation of the physical world, it can even be argued that our entire physical world – everything we can see, hear, taste, smell, and touch; as well as our private, inner world – every thought, feeling, fantasy, intimation, hope, and fear – is a form that consciousness has taken on for our benefit. Thus, consciousness becomes both the source and creator of everything we know.[46]

Consider the concept of correlation. Things are not correlated in nature; they simply are. Correlation then is a concept that humans use to describe connections between objects or events that we perceive. For example, there is no concept or word, 'correlation,' except as is created by people. This is because only people use words and concepts, and 'correlation' is a concept. Likewise, particles are also correlations. If people weren't here to construct concepts, none would exist. In other words, without people, or more specifically without experiencing consciousness, there wouldn't be any particles![47]

This train of thought could be likened to the idea of multiple possible outcomes, or wave functions, of a photon and all realities connected to it – the detector/measuring system, and the "observing"/participating technician, etc. When one intends to follow and measure the path of an electron, the possible outcome of the wave function is unknown until a perception is made and mathematically, the wave function collapses. The scientist thus realizes where the electron hit the detector plate once he determined he wanted to make a measurement, but in the absence of that intention, the electron could have seemingly struck anywhere or indeed, nowhere. The wave function collapsed because a perception was made as intended by consciousness. Looking outward from the photon to the detector to the technician to the supervisor, we could continue until we include the entire universe. But who is looking at the universe, or alternately, how is the universe being actualized?

To find the answer to this question, we must come full circle. All indications are that we are actualizing our universe. Since we are part of the universe, the universe must be self-actualizing. This train of thought compares closely with many aspects of Buddhism. This idea could well become one of the more important contributions of quantum physics to future models of consciousness.[48]

Geoffrey Chew noted one important aspect of quantum theory, known as the hadron bootstrap conjecture, is the logical conclusion that the existence of consciousness, along with all other aspects of nature, is necessary for self-consistency of the whole.[49] In other words, consciousness (i.e. the light) creates matter, and without which nothing could exist. Consciousness can thus also transform matter and make matter what it wills.

Quantum Field Theory:

With this last statement, it should come as no surprise that some quantum physicists would take the next step and consider the idea that physical reality is essentially non-substantial, but rather a momentary manifestation generated by some underlying energy or influence. This idea is the basis of a branch of quantum physics, known as quantum field theory. Theories, of course, are unproven ideas that tend to have some measure of support, whether mathematically or experimentally, but may not have been definitively proven or accepted by the scientific community at large. Quantum field theory contends underlying and interacting fields, similar to an electro-magnetic field, permeate all of reality, and the fields' interactions seem particle-like because fields interact both instantaneously and in very minute points of space.[50]

This idea originated from the realization that photons are also electromagnetic waves. Since those waves are also vibrating fields, quantum physicists concluded the photons must be manifestations of electromagnetic fields. Hence they coined the idea of a 'quantum field,' or a field that can take on the form of particles, i.e. 'quanta.' This was an entirely new concept that has since been extended to describe all subatomic particles and their interactions with one another, where each type of particle corresponded with a different field. Within these quantum field theories, the classical contrasts between solid particles and the space surrounding them is overcome. A quantum field is seen as *the* fundamental physical entity on which physical reality is formed; a continuous medium that is present everywhere throughout space. Particles, then, become merely local condensations of the quantum field; concentrations of energy that can come and go, losing their individual character and dissolving into the underlying field in an instant.[51]

As noted, there is significant evidence for field theory including a realization that Isaac Newton's concept of the void of space was false. Quantum physicists determined particles were constantly being spontaneously created and annihilated in vacuums without any nucleons or other interacting particles having originally been present.[52] According to field theory, such should be expected to occur forever, without end, because the fields permeate all of reality – regardless of the presence of matter or a seeming void.

Another laboratory observation provides a similar oddity for field theory to consider. When an electron passes through a photographic plate, a visible 'track' seemingly marks its track through space. This track, under close examination, is actually a series of dots. Each dot is actually a grain of silver formed by the electron's interaction with atoms in the photographic plate. When the track is closely examined under a microscope, it may look something like this:

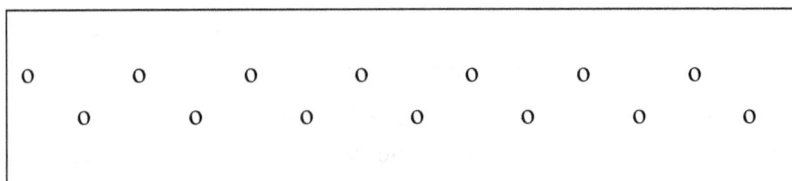

```
O      O      O      O      O      O      O
   O      O      O      O      O      O      O
```

Because the scientist expected to see the track of the movement of an electron through the photographic plate, the scientist may assume the bubbles correspond with one and the same electron. However, this assumption would be a mistake. Quantum physics tells us the same thing Buddhists have been saying for more than two millennia: Connections between the dots are a product of our imaginations and are not really there. In rigorous terms, proving the moving object to be a singular particle with an independent existence is an un-provable assumption.[53] Quantum field theory might suggest instead that each of the bubbles was an independent manifestation of interacting fields that just happened to correspond with an *anticipated* track of a sub-atomic particle that had been expected by an observer, the scientist, to occur at a certain place and time.

Field theory provides a further basis for at least two other mind-blowing developments in quantum mechanics: super-luminal connections and Bell's theorem.

Super-luminal connections:

Super-luminal connections, known as the Einstein-Podolsky-Rosen effect, have been hypothesized and mathematically proven through the realization that two sub-atomic particles may be instantaneously connected such that their rotational spin on an axis will always match their pair.[54] Consider if the particles were placed into two separate boxes, and then an outside influence such as an electromagnetic field were applied to one box to change the spin of that box's particle. The particle in the other box has been experimentally proven to change immediately in response to the stimulus applied to the paired particle, despite their physical separation. Now take that idea a step further and remove one box to an impossibly far distance. When the experiment is repeated, the *instantaneous* response of the particle at the farther box still occurs and thus proves that a connection between two particles has occurred faster than the speed of light. Light has a specific speed, taking a certain amount of time to move between two fixed points, but the Einstein-Podolsky-Rosen effect is instantaneous, regardless of distance.

This discovery in quantum physics implies telepathy or other super-luminal connections that provide for the instantaneous transfer of information may not only exist, but are indeed a part of everyday life.[55] As we shall see in the next section, Bell's theorem proves that for quantum theory to work, it requires connections that appear to resemble telepathic communications.[56]

The concept of Oneness:

The pioneers of quantum physics observed a strange 'connectedness' among quantum phenomena during their experiments in the early twentieth century.[57] Then in 1964, J. S. Bell, a physicist at the Switzerland-based European Organization for Nuclear Research (CERN) zeroed in on this strange connectedness, creating a new mathematical proof, known as Bell's theorem. Bell's theorem proved that if the statistical predictions of quantum theory were correct, then some of our commonsense ideas about the world were profoundly mistaken: at a deep and fundamental level, the 'separate parts' of the universe were connected in an intimate and immediate way.[58] Bell's theorem states there is no such thing as 'separate parts.' In other words, everything in the universe is connected in an intimate and immediate way that was previously claimed only by mystics and other scientifically-objectionable persons.[59]

Bell's work found that either the statistical predictions of quantum theory or the principle of local causes (i.e. cause and effect) was false. It did not say which one was false, but only that both of them could not be true. Physicists Stapp, Clauser, and Friedman, confirmed that the statistical predictions of quantum theory were indeed correct. The startling conclusion was inescapable: The principle of local causes must be false! However, if the principle of local causes was false, and hence, the world was not the way it appeared to be, then one must wonder what is the 'true nature' of our world?[60] Physicist David Bohm concluded when there was no separate parts in our world, i.e. locality failed, and so the idea that events were autonomous happenings must be an illusion.[61]

Instead, parts must be seen to have immediate, unbreakable connections, in which their dynamic relationships depend on the state of the system as a whole. Thus, one is led to a new notion of unbroken wholeness throughout the entire universe. This denies the classical idea of the world being analyzable by its 'separate,' independently existent parts.[62]

Bell's theorem may be the most important single work in the history of physics, and has direct applicability to the connection between the hard science of quantum physics and the philosophical science of spirituality.[63]

When one achieves the enlightened state, a common description of the spiritual experience is that of an all-pervading Unity. The concept of separation between entities no longer applies: We are all *One* and everything is but a manifestation of that Unity. The Source of that manifestation seems beyond description and is at the heart of the experience itself.[64] The Source is simply That Which Is, or perhaps more accurately, All That Is. Everything is thus a manifestation of All That Is.

Conclusion:

The material and ramifications of this section have been very deep, and I have contrived to condense tomes-worth of hard, mathematical information into a few pages of very brief overviews. Indeed the reader may find it beneficial to read this section twice over or even thrice, both before and after the rest of the book's material, to grasp the metaphysical implications inherent therein. The ideas exhibited by quantum theory – once understood – should shock the uninitiated.[65]

An important take-away from this chapter would be to realize there is a lot more to life and the nature of reality than most of us learn in school, from our parents, or even from most organized religions. I would therefore ask you to consider what has been discussed in this chapter, and to keep an open mind about what will be discussed in the coming chapters in this book. I will eventually seek to bring some level of conformity between what will be discussed and what has been discussed so that some of the more fanciful-seeming topics might be brought back around to some semblance of plausibility or scientific basis. By seeking to find the hidden truth therein, we may finally come to know the true nature of reality.

Chapter Three

Near-Death Experiences

Introduction

The topic of near-death experiences (NDE) is an appropriate first step into a discussion on metaphysics because it has been a highly studied field of interest to doctors, psychologists and scientists of all sorts, and therefore has a wide field of respectable research backing the phenomenon. NDEs as a category have certain characteristics that are observed by all who have a near-death experience regardless of their prior religious backgrounds or beliefs, including atheists who had no prior belief in an afterlife before their experience. NDEs are also quite common. In 1980 (published in '82), a Gallup Poll found approximately 8 million American adults had experienced an NDE, accounting for nearly one person in twenty, or five percent of the adult population.[66] Surveys in Australia and Germany suggested as high as 15% of a population might have had NDEs.[67] According to the Near-Death Experience Research Foundation (NDERF), an estimated 774 NDEs occur every day, many of which are reported to and publicly available through the NDERF website.[68]

Dozens of studies have been conducted on NDEs, including such topics as what comprises an NDE, what attributes people have when they experience an NDE, and what proof there is to support the validity of an NDE.

NDEs stand apart in the field of metaphysics because, if true, NDEs would prove that the human body (or mental conscious) has a soul that survives bodily death. People who have seemingly died from common ailments such as heart attacks and accidents are routinely brought back to life through the marvel of modern medicine. Following resuscitation, many report the most fantastic stories of an experience when they seemingly exited their bodies after the medical event. Again, an interesting aspect about NDEs is that the experiences tend to have a set of commonalities across cultural and religious boundaries, thus lending some credence to the value of anecdotal reporting.

Can an NDE be considered just a dream or the hallucination of a dying mind, becoming overactive as its neurons fire their last bursts? In short, no. Doctors and scientists have proven in many cases the mind of 'dead' persons who subsequently came back to life and reported NDEs had no EEG activity that might account for a vivid imagination.[69] Further troubling to that idea is the story of Dr. George Grigorievich Rodonaia, a Soviet dissident who was killed, but returned to life after *three days*. For obvious reasons, his account is particularly compelling within the field of NDEs. His story is compiled here from multiple sources.

Dr. George Rodonaia

Before immigrating to the United States from the Soviet Union in 1989, Dr. George Rodonaia worked as a research psychiatrist at the University of Moscow. Dr. Rodonaia underwent one of the most extended cases of a clinical near-death experience ever recorded.

From his work assisting in the publication of *IBERIA*, an underground freedom newspaper in the former Soviet Union,

Rodonaia became known as a vocal dissident and was dubiously honored by allegedly being placed on the KGB's hit list.

In 1974, at the age of eighteen, life became complicated for Rodonaia when he was invited to pursue advanced research at Yale University in the US. Rodonaia was thrilled at the thought of studying at Yale and living in the United States, but since he did not have a wife or family members in the Soviet Union that might discourage him from seeking asylum in the US, the Soviet government would not allow him to leave their country. By 1976, however, Rodonaia was married and had a son, and the Soviet government grudgingly agreed to allow him to study in the United States.

However, on the day of his scheduled departure for the United States, the KGB allegedly tried to kill him. While waiting for a taxicab on a sidewalk in Tbilisi (now modern day Republic of Georgia) he saw a car jump the curb, drive onto the sidewalk, avoid a few trees, and head directly towards him. In an instant, Rodonaia was hit head-on at a high rate of speed and flew about ten meters, landing facedown, when the car ran over him again a second time, seemingly to ensure he was actually killed. Rodonaia suffered broken ribs, torn muscles, and mangled feet among a slew of massive and critical internal injuries.

Devoid of any signs of life, Rodonaia was shortly pronounced dead at the scene and was deposited in a Tbilisi morgue for three days. Morgues in Tbilisi are not like those in the United States. There, bodies are quick-frozen immediately and kept in that state for three days before an autopsy is performed or the body is otherwise dispensed. Rodonaia's body was stone cold **dead and frozen for three days** as it laid in the morgue in Tbilisi, Georgia, USSR.

To Rodonaia's sense of self, however, there was no loss of consciousness. He experienced one of the most extensive and convincing near-death experiences ever recorded if based on no further input than the fact he was clinically dead and his body was frozen in a morgue for three days during which his near-death experience occurred. It is therefore worth considering Rodonia's NDE as he related it, in summary.[70]

The first thing Rodonia could recall about his NDE was that he discovered himself in a realm of total darkness. He had no physical pain, and was still aware of his existence as 'George,' but he did not understand where he was or why. The darkness that surrounded him was utter and complete darkness – the greatest darkness he could ever imagine; darker than dark, blacker than black. The darkness seemed to press upon him as a physical entity and the experience terrified him. He was shocked to find that he still existed, and realized that he should be dead following the car crash, but his current state confused him. The one thought that kept rolling through his mind was: How can I be conscious when I know I am not? The conundrum troubled him.

Slowly he got a grip on himself and began to think about what had just happened to him in order to try to figure out what was going on. The exercise, however, resulted in no beneficial conclusions. He could not understand why he was in the darkness and could not figure what he should do to rectify the situation. And then he remembered Descartes' famous line, *Cogito, ergo sum*: "I think, therefore I am." The realization relieved him of a huge burden for it was then he knew for certain he was still 'alive,' although inexplicably located in a very different dimension of reality. Interestingly he pondered if he continued to exist that should be just cause for a positive outlook on the situation. He would be happy merely with the comfort that he continued to exist.

Expanding that thought, he wondered what could be positive in darkness. The answer was immediate and obvious: light would be a positive turn of course. Immediately, with that thought of light, there was light and Rodonia was in the light. The light was bright white, shiny and strong; exceptionally bright. At first the brilliance of the light was almost painful and he could not look at it directly. However, little by little he began to relax. Within the light, he realized that he felt warm and comforted, and all of a sudden everything seemed okay. Any concern he previously had for his body melted away, because it was clear to him at that point that he did not need his body anymore. The body was suddenly seen as a limitation of one's true self.

Once Rodonia was in the light, he gained the impression that the sequence of events merged together as if time as he had known it had suddenly come to a halt; past, present, and future were inexplicably fused together in a timeless unity.

Dr. Rodonia recalled experiencing a life-review process, during which he saw his life from beginning to end, complete and in perfect detail but the entire sequence was relived in an instant though perfect in every detail. He participated once again in the real life dramas of his 'past' life, almost like they were holographic images in which he was immersed. During the review he did not experience any sense of guilt or remorse for things he had done, and neither did he feel concern about his faults or joy about his achievements. Rather, his life had simply been an experience for what it was and he was content with that. He accepted his past life for the experience of what it was.

Throughout this entire period, the light radiated a sense of peace and joy to Rodonia, and he was happy to be in the light. Suddenly, he understood what the light meant and what it was. He learned that all the physical rules of human life were nothing when compared to the unified reality of the light. He also came to see impressions of darkness were just another aspect of the infinity that is the light. He realized this reality was everywhere: The light was everywhere. The light was an integral part not only of Earthly life but also of the infinite life. Because of the light, everything was not only connected, everything was also 'One.' Rodonia felt a perfect connection to and wholeness within the light; a sense that all was right with himself and the universe. All was as it was meant to be.

After three days in the morgue, Rodonaia's body was removed from the freezer vault and wheeled to an autopsy room. A team of doctors then commenced splitting apart his lower torso. As the blade cut through flesh, Dr. Rononaia amazingly and spontaneously came back to life, felt the pain of the incision and opened his eyes. One doctor, thinking this a mere reflex, closed Rodonaia's eyes, but Rodonaia promptly opened his eyes again. Again the doctor closed them and once more Rodonaia's eyes popped open, only this time the doctor jumped backward – and screamed.

Rononaia's body was cold from being dead and frozen in a morgue for three days and he began to shiver. The team of doctors immediately stopped the autopsy and took Rodonaia to the hospital, where he remained in intensive and rehabilitative care for the following nine months, most of which were spent under a respirator.

Another notable feature of Rodonaia's NDE – and this is common to many – is that he was radically transformed by the experience. Prior to his near-death experience, Dr. Rodonaia worked as a neuro-pathologist. He was also an avowed atheist. Yet after the experience, he devoted himself to the study of the psychology of religion and eventually obtained a second Ph.D. in that subject. He became an ordained priest in the Eastern Orthodox Church, and also served as an associate pastor at a Methodist Church in Nederland, Texas, until he passed away in 2004.

NDE Traits

Near-Death Experiences were seemingly made famous through the extensive work and publishing of Dr. Raymond A. Moody who published his famous treatise *Life after Life: The investigation of a phenomenon; survival of bodily death* in 1975. Dr. Moody found that there were at least nine, and as many as 15 typical traits of Near-Death Experiences.[71]

Despite many striking similarities among various NDE accounts, no two accounts are ever identical. Further, the order in which a separated conscious experiences the various stages or traits of a near-death experience may vary and are not stuck to a hard-and-fast model. Moody found there was no one element of the composite experience that every single person reported. However, a few of the elements of near-death experiences come fairly close to being universal experiences.[72] Extremely few persons experience all of the common NDE traits, and even persons who have had more than one NDE in their lifetime may experience different traits in each of the subsequent NDEs; again, no two NDEs are ever exactly the same.

Moody hypothesized the number of traits experienced and the depth of the near-death experience itself may be connected to the manner in which death occurred and the amount of time a person was considered clinically deceased. Generally, persons who experienced death for longer periods of time had more developed experiences, including more traits of the common NDE model, than did those persons who were merely on the verge of death, or were quickly resuscitated.[73]

Following Moody's groundbreaking work in the field, NDEs have been widely studied by doctors, scientists, and many others, thus adding to the template model of common NDE traits. Given the fact that no two NDEs are ever the same, people experience individual traits within their NDE, and no one experiences every *possible* trait that has ever been reported in the NDE literature. Thus, there is no one standard clinical NDE model of the 9 - 15 accepted NDE traits. Therefore, a composite model of NDE traits is presented herein of example traits I found to be common throughout much of the NDE literature.

Composite Model Near-Death Experience Traits include:

1) **A Sense of Being Dead.** This may include seeing one's 'dead' physical body, remembering the event that caused one's death, or simply realizing their consciousness was no longer in a physical body or physical state of reality.

2) **Peace, Calm and Painlessness.** The process of physical death often includes abrupt physical pain so the sudden absence of that pain may come as a striking reality where feelings of peace, calm and painlessness suddenly fill one's reality and focused attention with their prior expectation for continued physical pain.

3) **Out-of-Body Experience.** A consciousness that leaves a physical body may still have occasion to witness physical reality for a brief time in the region near where the body remains. This experience can add much for "proving" the validity of NDEs, especially when a person is resuscitated and is able to describe physical events, persons or items for which they should not have otherwise been aware during the time they were "dead."

4) **Tunnel Experience.** Many NDErs describe being sucked into a dark tunnel shortly after exiting their physical body, and then sense their movement towards a bright light at the end of the tunnel.

5) **Rising Rapidly into the Heavens/Light Phenomenon.** Once the consciousness has left the physical body it is rarely allowed to remain long in or near the physical realm. In the absence of a tunnel experience, the consciousness will likely feel that it is rapidly ascending above the Earth and into "the Heavens" where it soon enters "the Light." NDErs describe everything in Heaven as being composed of light: plants, buildings, people, etc. Differences between entities as well as perceived levels of heaven tend to be based on the frequency of one's light and the concentration of conscious energy therein.

6) **Seeing People of Light.** Once in the light, the recently deceased consciousness may see other people in the light. Descriptions of these people attest to them being comprised entirely of light. Oftentimes those people are deceased loved ones and friends who are greeting them upon entry into the light. Sometimes spirit guides will assist a recently deceased consciousness to find the tunnel/light, and encourage them to move towards and enter the light.

7) **Experiencing a Supreme Being of Light.** A Supreme Being of Light is often described as an entity far above – wiser; more loving and powerful – one's normal friends and family members gathered to greet the recently departed upon entry into the light. The Supreme Being of Light is always reported to emanate love and make the newly deceased consciousness feel welcome and secure. The Supreme Being of Light may lead a life review, and is often attributed as the force that insists on the spirit's return to the physical body.

8) **A Life Review.** A life review is always described as having occurred in a manner outside of the normal concepts of time. A

person's entire life events are witnessed *in toto* while a guide or the Supreme Being of Light discusses each of the events with an attitude of querying what knowledge was gained or what benefit was attained by the experience as a consequence of a person's actions. Further, life events are re-experienced as if the soul was living them again, but not only from a first-person perspective but also from the perspective of everyone touched by the event. If one caused pain, that pain is thus experienced from the other person's perspective. The NDEr thus understands the emotional and wider ranging impact of their humanly actions on Earth.

Amazingly, NDErs report there is no external judgment or condemnation in this life review process. Any judgments of right/wrong for any individual action is applied only by one's own self during the life review. The guide or Supreme Being of Light often acts as intermediary so that one does not place too much negative self judgment on the actions conducted during life, but rather encourages the soul to learn from the experience; a tacit imploration to improve and make better decisions upon one's return to physical life.

9) **Altered Concepts of Space and Time.** Space and time seem to function differently than when one is in the physical body; i.e. linearly in a forward direction. Generally, time in the nonphysical realm is described as being an infinite state of Now with no past, present, or future differentiation.[74]

Spatial relations are likewise different in that travel across seemingly infinite space can be instantaneous, and yet there are sometimes impressions that even space itself does not exist when there is only a "Unity." The latter concept is extremely hard for a human to consider as having any range of validity, but in a nonphysical reality where nothing exists but consciousness, and consciousness creates the reality it desires to experience, space and spatial separation or distances are theoretical constructs that only exist in one's imagination for the benefit of the consciousness and the experience(s) consciousness desires to create for itself.

10) **Complete Knowledge of Reality.** NDErs often describe their experience in the nonphysical realm as being more real than reality.[75] Senses tend to be heightened, and experiences are not only instantaneous but completely transparent and fully understood. It is as if a veil of amnesia was suddenly lifted from the consciousness and the spirit suddenly understands the meaning and purpose of life. The fact that one can experience a high level of consciousness while physically unconscious or clinically dead is medically inexplicable. Further, the NDEr understands their connection to everything around them, and a seeming flood of information about life and the nature of the universe suddenly becomes available and completely clear to them. Thoughts become clear and incredibly rapid, and communications between the soul and other entities is instantaneous via a form of telepathy.[76]

11) **Being One with Reality.** NDErs may experience infinite connections with everyone and everything around them, and that experience often has a very tangible effect on their behaviors upon return to the physical world of the living. This is especially so when coupled with the effects of learning the tangible impacts and consequences of their own actions on others, and having experienced self-judgment of those actions during the life review. As such, returning NDErs may feel one of the most important commandments for a fulfilling life on Earth is to love – everyone and everything around them – and to be nonjudgmental of others' actions.

12) **Reluctance to Return.** The experience of heaven is euphoria. NDErs uniformly characterize their experiences as ineffable, i.e. inexpressible.[77] It is hardly surprising that once a near-death experience must be concluded, the consciousness is reluctant to leave and must be forcibly returned to the body even though the spirit may plead or resist the need to return. Upon return, one's conscious self is often described as feeling a need to shrink or somehow squeeze to fit back into the physical body. The physical body is also characterized as a restrictive coat of heavy/dense energy; quite a shocking change from being a free-floating, light-based energy form.

13) **Disappointment at Being Revived.** There can be unpleasant feelings, including loneliness and depression, even anger or tears at the realization they are now back in their physical bodies and no longer in the utopia experienced on the other side.[78]

There are many more potential traits not included here because: not every trait is universally perceived; not every person is equally impacted by the trait, limiting its spontaneous recall; and lacking foreknowledge of the potential trait, an interviewer might not specifically query every possible trait's presence within the near-death experience.

For example, one experiencer related there was a problem trying to express what had happened during the NDE. The human vocabulary is based on words needed to describe three-dimensional experiences but life in the NDE was distinctly multidimensional. As such, the reporter did not have an adequate vocabulary or means to relate the experience.[79]

Returning to the near-death experience related by Rodonaia, despite the fact that he had an exceptional NDE that lasted three days in human, physical terms, even he did not experience all of the so-called common NDE traits listed above. This simply reinforces Moody's conclusion that everyone's NDE is unique to his or her own circumstances. The absence of any NDE trait does not deflect from the potential validity of their experience. Further no NDE trait could be required to occur for researchers to positively identify whether or not an NDE occurred.

I would suggest descriptive experiences of NDEs should be both compared to the template model for potential conformity as well as anecdotal correlations, if any, sought when conducting analysis of the probability of the validity of any near-death experience. This idea seems to correspond to a reporting structure also followed by the Near-Death Experience Research Foundation (www.nderf.org), which posts and summarily analyzes NDE reports from respondents all across the globe.

Logical and Medical Support of NDE Traits

Dr. Jeffrey Long and journalist Paul Perry collaborated on one of the most important works in the NDE research field, *Evidence of the Afterlife.* According to Dr. Mario Beauregard, Neuroscientist at the University of Montreal, Canada, Long's work on NDEs provides compelling evidence that mind and consciousness cannot be reduced to merely overactive brain activity at the moment of death. Thus pointing to a need to reconsider the possibility consciousness could plausibly survive bodily death. Further, using the treasure trove of data from first-hand accounts of NDEs available from the NDERF website, Long found that medical evidence fails to explain these reports, eventually concluding there was only one plausible explanation – that people survive bodily death and have traveled to another dimension during their NDE. The following are some of the arguments that would support a conclusion that the human's consciousness does not expire after death:

1. **Consistent Traits.** Elemental traits in NDEs are generally consistent in all age groups, religions and ethnicities around the world. They are also irrespective of gender, social class, education level or marital status. This fact refutes the possibility that NDEs have any relation to dreams or hallucinations, which are never universally congruent.[80]

NDEs from non-Western countries are also incredibly similar to those that occur to people in Western countries.[81] That is, NDE traits may be similar, but their interpretations may allow for cultural and religious differences. Christians may experience the 'Supreme Being of Light' to be Jesus while Muslims might interpret the being to be Mohammad, and Spiritualists to consider the being a high-level spirit guide.

Within these cultural filters, there is no right or wrong perception. That which is presented to the departed conscious is that which the consciousness is ready and prepared to experience, and so it makes sense that a Christian might believe the loving, Supreme Being of Light is Jesus. The belief and interpretation of the experience is neither right nor wrong; it is simply culturally appropriate according to their preconceived expectations. There will be more on this topic later in the book that will help the reader understand why this experience is culturally appropriate while fulfilling the conundrum of being neither right nor wrong.

2. **Realistic Out-of-Body Experiences.** Out-of-body experiences (OBEs) are one of the most common elements of NDEs. What NDErs report seeing and hearing of physical, Earthly events in the out-of-body state is almost always realistic. When the NDEr or others later seek to verify what the NDEr observed or heard during the OBE, the OBE observations are generally confirmed as accurate. Even if the OBE observations during the NDE included events that occurred far from the physical body's

location on Earth, and thus far from any possible sensory awareness of the NDEr, the out-of-body observations are still almost always confirmed as accurate. This fact alone rules out the possibility that near-death experiences are related to any known brain functioning or sensory awareness. This also refutes the possibility that NDEs are unrealistic fragments of memory from the brain.[82]

3. **Heightened Senses.** Not only are heightened senses reported by most who have experienced NDEs, but also normal or supernormal (panoramic) vision has occurred in those with significantly impaired vision, or even legal blindness. Several people who have been totally blind since birth have reported highly visual near-death experiences, which shall be further covered later in this chapter. In many cases, adventitiously blind NDErs have described medical equipment being used on their 'deceased' bodies that was not even invented before they became blind and thus could not have been imagined or otherwise described accurately if the items were not somehow observed visually during the out-of-body state as a result of the NDE. This is medically inexplicable.[83]

4. **Consciousness During Anesthesia.** Many NDEs occur while under general anesthesia – at a time when any conscious experience should be impossible. While some skeptics claim that these NDEs may be the result of too little anesthesia, this ignores the fact that some NDEs result from anesthesia overdose. Additionally, the description of an NDE differs greatly from that of one who experiences anesthetic awareness. The content of NDEs that occur under general anesthesia is essentially indistinguishable from NDEs that did not occur under general anesthesia. This is

strong evidence that NDEs are occurring independently of the functioning of the physical brain.[84]

5. **Perfect Playback.** Life reviews in near-death experiences include real events that previously took place in the lives of those having the experience; even if the events were forgotten or happened before they were old enough to remember.[85] While such memories can be dredged from the subconscious through such means as hypnosis – thus showing those memories are accessible – this does not explain how one having an NDE could somehow experience the emotions, feelings and effects of their actions on persons around them, as is always reported of those experiencing a life review during an NDE.

6. **Family Reunions.** During an NDE, personalities encountered are virtually always deceased, and are usually spouses, relatives and/or friends of the person having the experience – sometimes they are even relatives who died before the NDEr was even born. Were the NDE only a product of memory fragments, they would almost certainly include far more living people, including those with whom they had more recently interacted and thus were a more prominent part of their nearer-term life experiences.[86]

7. **Children's Experiences.** The near-death experiences of children, including very young children who are too young to have developed concepts of death, religion, or near-death experiences, are essentially identical to those of adults. This refutes the possibility that preexisting beliefs or cultural conditioning produces the content of NDEs.[87]

8. **Aftereffects.** It is common for people to experience major life changes after having NDEs.[88] These aftereffects are often powerful, lasting, and life enhancing. The changes also generally follow a consistent pattern, as the NDErs themselves almost always believe that NDEs are, in a word, real.[89] Aftereffects of NDEs will be considered further later in this chapter.

Descriptive Comparison of NDE Traits

Given the interest in NDEs in the research field, it is not surprising that a number of comparative surveys are available to statistically consider the frequency by which NDErs experience many of the traits identified by Moody, *et al.* Not every poll measured every trait, so there are comparative discrepancies by placing the various surveys side-by-side. However, it is interesting to note statistical averages between them in order to gain, potentially, a better view on the prevalence of polled NDE traits.

NDE Trait Survey #:

NDE Trait	1.	2.	3.	4.	5.
Out-of-Body Experience	26%	70.9%	37%	66%	67%
Accurate vision	23%				48%
Audible sounds	17%				33%
Feelings of peace/ calm	32%	74.5%	60%	70%	95%
Light phenomena	14%	56.4%	16%	62%	38%
Life review	32%				19%
In another world	32%	34.5%	10%	18%	
Encountering other beings	23%				57%
Tunnel experience	9%	38.2%	23%	32%	38%

Survey footnotes:
1. Gallup, George, Jr. and Proctor, W. (1982). *Adventures in Immortality: A Look Beyond the Threshold of Death.* New York, NY: McGraw-Hill.
2. Lindley, J. H., Bryan, S. and Conley, B. (1981). Near-Death Experiences in Pacific Northwest American Population: the Evergreen Study, Anabiosis: *The Journal of Near-Death Studies.*
3. Ring, Kenneth. (1980). *Life at Death.* New York: Coward, McCann & Geoghegan.
4. Green, Timothy and Friedman, Penelope. (1983). Near-death experiences in a Southern. California population, Anabiosis: *The Journal of Near-Death Studies.*
5. Ring, Kenneth and Cooper, Sharon. (2008). *Mindsight: Near-Death and Out-of-Body Experiences in the Blind,* 2nd ed. New York: iUniverse.

Near-Death Experiences of the Blind

Near-Death Experiences of the congenitally or adventitiously blind are particularly important to the scientific study of the field of near-death experiences. The blinds' descriptions of experiences, especially visual experiences during an NDE, lend particular credence to the validity of the near-death experience phenomenon. For example, persons born blind do not experience visual dreams because they have no concept of light or visual images.[90] Further, children who lose their sight before age seven also do not generally retain visual imagery in their dreams.[91] Dreams of the blind, even the adventitiously blind, thus tend to emphasize their other physical senses for which they can readily relate: hearing, touch, taste, and smell.[92] When they suddenly experience sight during an NDE, including colors, light, and visual impressions of their surroundings, it is often the first such experience of their lives and is thus particularly remarkable to them and inexplicable to medical researchers.

What follows are two very brief summaries of anecdotal accounts of NDEs for two separate blind experiencers originally reported by Dr. Kenneth Ring in his groundbreaking book, *Mindsight*. The accounts may serve as scene setters for the validity of near-death experiences of the blind.

Vicki Umipeg experienced two separate NDEs, approximately a decade apart. She was born blind, and as such could not even understand or comprehend a description of, or the nature of light. During her first NDE, she found herself out of her body and able to see her surroundings for the first time in her life. During both NDEs, she perceived her own non-physical body/soul to have a distinct form, which seemed as if it were made of light.[93]

Vicki experienced multiple standard NDE traits; the most personally surprising of which was crystal clear visual perception.

Vicki experienced her death and an out-of-body experience, including witnessing her deceased body. Shortly thereafter, Vicki felt pulled into a tunnel and when she emerged she was in a place of incredible light.[94] Vicki noted the brightness of the light was not unpleasant. Rather it was incredibly warm, beautiful and intense.[95]

Vicki described the light was more than what humans typically consider light to be: The light could be seen as well as felt. Additionally, the light conveyed information and feelings: words, music, and energy, but mostly, love. Further, the light came from everywhere, so love was everywhere. It seemed as if love came from the 'grass' – also constructed of light – and love came from the 'birds,' and every other conceivable location and entity within the light realm.[96]

Brad Barrows had many similar descriptions of the light from his near-death experience. Brad Barrows was also blind from birth, but he was able to see for the first time during his NDE. He described the light of heaven as seemingly all-encompassing: The light seemed to comprise everything. The grass and trees were somehow made of light, and everything was both bright and colorful, and yet translucent. Buildings were also made of light. They even gave off light, and yet light could penetrate everything as well. There was no shade under the trees but neither was there need for shade.[97]

As previously noted, everyone has a different experience during an NDE, possibly because their attention is drawn towards that which is most amazing to them during the unusual experience. For Brad Barrows, this was the feeling of peace he experienced during the NDE. He felt heaven was so unbelievably peaceful it would be impossible to describe the peace, calm and tranquility he found in the light.[98]

Reports of Vision in NDEs and OBEs in the Blind

Of course, not everyone who is blind and experiences a near-death experience or out-of-body experience (not associated with death) reports being able to see during their experience. There are many reasons that could account for this discrepancy.

First, Ring noted it was not clear whether the respondents blind from birth, who claimed not to have seen, were actually unable to see or whether they simply failed to recognize what seeing was.[99] For people who have never known what it means to see they have become so accustomed to living without the aid of sight that they do not feel encumbered without the ability. By extension, moving about freely as a 'free-spirit,' with clarity of senses may thus seem to them that their other senses, and possibly even the concept of total knowledge, have made up for what they presume to be a continuation of their lack of sight.

Second, some reports of the near-death experience note that sight, communication, and other physical concepts do not operate with a large degree of equivalence in the spirit world. Sight, for example, is often described not as sight, but as total awareness, including awareness of one's surroundings. They are in a state of 'all-knowing' though this phenomenon is not necessarily via direct visual perception. Further, other NDE accounts provide that the human body's concept of sight in an almost 180-degree field-of-view is exceeded in the non-physical realm to perfect, panoramic 360-degree and even spherical vision. This has significant overlap with the concept of total awareness, and thus is not necessarily surprising that some blind NDErs do not realize they are seeing because the awareness they are experiencing in the out-of-body state matches no concept of physical sight familiar to humans.

One of the blind men interviewed by Ring was perplexed by the concept of sight during his NDE because he did not know what the researchers meant by the word, 'seeing.'[100]   This reaction matches closely to the second point, provided above.

Not all cases can be explained, however. One blind woman reported not having visual perception in her NDE but did claim visual perception during multiple out-of-body experiences not otherwise associated with death.[101]

Ring's study of NDEs and OBEs in the blind included 14 participants who were blind from birth, 11 who were adventitiously blind (became blind due to disease or traumatic event), and 6 who were legally blind; that is eyesight so poor or impaired as to have no effective ability to see.[102]

The following chart provides those participants' responses for whether they did or did not experience sight during their near-death- and/or out-of-body experiences.

Experience	Ability to see during the experience		
	Yes	Not Sure	No
NDE	15	3	3
OBE	9	1	0

It is rather easy to account for the blind persons who were not sure about whether or not they experienced sight in the non-physical state, as previously discussed in items one and two, above. For the three people who experienced no sight in their NDE, one could be reminded of the experience of Rodonaia in our first example at the beginning of this chapter.

Upon first realizing he was dead and no longer in his physical body, Rodonaia felt surround by absolute darkness. This did not change until he asserted to himself that he should be in and experience light or order to be happy. The simple act of asserting clarity of thought concerning light created the experience he intended; a theme that is repeated elsewhere in this book, and throughout the literature concerning near-death experiences, out-of-body experiences, and the period of life between life.

Thus, the three blind NDErs did not experience light almost assuredly because they did not realize they were living without any crucial sensory input for which they were accustomed. Without a perceived need, there was no reason to seek the light, ask for light, or even consider a need for light. And thus they experienced sensory input that was closer to their preconceived notions of what was right and not necessarily what was possible or available to them. (Of interest: Some literature of life between life experiences note that spirit guides will eventually intervene on behalf of these previously blind souls to help them find the light and realize their full capabilities at sensory perception while in the spirit realm.)

In general, Ring noted blind people report experiences that conform to the prototype NDE model developed and outlined by Moody, which again adds further validity to the research results concerning near-death experiences.[103]

Scientific and Anecdotal Support

Certainly there are opponents to the validity of the near-death experience. English parapsychologist Susan Blackmore is a chief proponent of the retrospective reconstruction hypothesis, which contends that from a combination of prior experiences or expectations, overheard conversations or other sensory cues, plus information gleaned afterward or even simply by lucky guesses, it might be possible for an NDEr to imaginatively reconstruct a pictorial representation of events that occurred during an NDE.[104]

However, this idea has no support among those who actually experience an NDE, and is limited in its inability to account for instances where unusual objects can be described by those who are both unconscious and physically handicapped, whether deaf, blind, or otherwise, thus limiting opportunities to obtain such second-hand information. The retrospective reconstruction hypothesis is also unable to account for the clarity and universal commonality of the otherworldly segment descriptions common to NDEs.[105]

Verifiable out-of-body experiences that occur during an NDE lend some credence to the validity of the near-death experience. These are often descriptions of the resuscitation process or identifying physical items present in the room where the resuscitation process occurred. There is generally no explanation that could satisfactorily explain an NDErs' knowledge of these observations made while they were unconscious or "dead" except that a person's consciousness was somehow out of his or her body at the time.

People whose bodies have recently expired and are in the process of being resuscitated may find themselves in the out-of-body state and from a vantage point in the near proximity of the resuscitation process that affords them the ability to observe, and later describe the equipment, procedures, surroundings, and personnel working on their physical body. If the person being resuscitated has the added physical trait of being deaf, blind, or even dead then his/her claim of witnessing, seeing or hearing things that would have been impossible from the physical body's own vantage point tends to add particular credibility to his/her first-hand account.[106]

These types of incidents where a person is out of his/her body during a near-death experience and can then observe events or gather information that can be verified by others upon the NDErs' return to a conscious state are known as veridical near-death experiences. Thankfully, the research case histories of NDEs are full of such accounts. The following are just a few example cases of veridical NDE evidence:

A Report from a Dutch Nurse

A Dutch nurse reported a 44-year-old cyanotic, comatose man was delivered to the coronary care unit by ambulance one evening. When the staff tried to intubate the man they initially had difficulties because he used dentures. A nurse removed the patient's upper dentures and placed them on a nearby crash cart. A week later that same nurse met the patient again during routine rounds to distribute medication. The moment the patient saw the nurse he exclaimed to those with him that she knew where his dentures were. The nurse was surprised by this declaration so the patient explained he remembered being brought into the hospital and watching the staff perform CPR to resuscitate him. The patient continued that the nurse removed his dentures from his mouth during this process and put them on a cart, described as having many bottles on top and a sliding drawer underneath. The nurse was intrigued by this story and inquired further, quickly learning the man claimed also to have observed himself from above, and saw his own body lying on the bed where the staff were working to revive it. The patient was even able to describe correctly and in detail the room in which he had been resuscitated as well as provide descriptions of those persons who had been present. The patient added the experience was impressive and caused him to no longer fear death.[107]

Maria's Shoe

In 1977, a migrant worker, Maria, was taken to Harborview Hospital in Seattle, WA, in an unconscious state, having suffered a cardiac arrest. A social worker visited her the following day in her hospital room, at which point Maria described leaving her body and floating above the hospital. Desperate to prove that she was not delusional, Maria described seeing a worn, dark-blue tennis shoe on the ledge outside a window on the far side of the hospital. Not believing Maria but wanting to help, the social worker went room to room, checking the ledges from each by pressing her face against the sealed windows. The social worker eventually found a shoe that perfectly matched the details Maria had related. The vantage point on the ledge was such that it would have been impossible for Maria to have seen the shoe either from ground level outside the hospital, or from where she had been at any point in time while inside the hospital.[108]

NDERF

Out of the more than 2,500 self-reported NDEs on the NDERF website, there are more than a dozen reports that include remarkable verification of OBE observations, or visual observations made by blind persons during the NDE event. Each of the reports represents anecdotal evidence of the validity of the NDE due to verification of observations made while in the out-of-body state.

A typical example from NDERF is "George C.", NDERF case 2624, who posted his near-death experience to the NDERF website on 2 March 2011.[109] George suffered a heart attack and a series of heart failures during which a stream of nurses and doctors worked on him while he was unconscious, lying flat on his back with his physical eyes closed. After recovering in the ICU, George described his experience to a doctor and a nurse who both verified the persons present by description. The events George described witnessing were also from a vantage point above the heads of the doctors and nurses working on his unconscious body, providing him a view of events his body could not have otherwise seen.

Pattern of Aftereffects of NDEs

Further evidencing the unique power of NDEs is the transformative properties of the experience on people who return from the brink of death. The transformative property of the experience is nearly universal, attesting to the intense influence the experiences carry over to the person's continuing life in the physical world.[110] Aftereffects cannot be faked. They affect not only the NDEr, but by connection everyone in the experiencer's life as well.

Around eighty percent of the people who have had NDEs noted that their lives were forever changed by what had happened to them. NDErs do not return with just a renewed zest for life and a more spiritual outlook. They also tend to experience specific, often severe psychological and physiological differences on a dramatic scale, and these changes are enduring, generally affecting the NDEr for the remainder of their life. Further, this was true whether the near-death experience occurred as a child or adult.[111]

Whether their NDE was beautiful or terrifying, NDErs commonly report the experience was unlike a dream, more real than real; clearly the most powerful event in their lives.[112] The aftereffects are one testament to the validity of the experience given the wide-ranging occurrence of these aftereffects across cultures and age groups, and – again – the fact that these aftereffects cannot be faked.

Major Characteristics of Psychological Changes:

Experiencers may struggle to find words to describe their NDE, but insist they now know something new about reality; that there is more to reality than what is here in the physical world. As such, most are deeply changed in their attitudes toward life, work, religion, and relationships.[113]

In several studies, nearly all near-death experiencers reported a strong decrease or even complete loss of fear of death as a result of their NDEs.[114] They had experienced what happens after death on 'the other side,' and they now knew their conscious self would not end with physical death.[115] Many experiencers also noted there was not a single moment of loss of consciousness at the point of bodily expiration; their spirit simply moved from a physical to nonphysical state, but their personality, awareness, and consciousness all remained intact and fully alert at all times.

At least 98% of surveyed NDErs came to believe that there is life after death following their experiences.[116] From their experience, over 80% of NDErs also learned that life has a meaning or purpose and that revelation directly affected the way they conducted their lives ever after on Earth.[117] The average NDEr also came to regard him/herself as an immortal soul who currently resides in a physical form so that lessons could be learned while he/she experienced life on Earth.[118] After the NDE they knew they were not just their body, and they no longer needed to identify their self with their human body. Their body came to be viewed simply a vessel that allowed them to complete their work in this life to gain important life lessons for specific purposes that had been arranged prior to this incarnation. Indeed, many go on after their near-death experience to embrace the theory of reincarnation. Eventually, the returning NDEr will assimilate these experiences and lessons into their physical life, and consider their present life and body to be important and special again.

During the NDE, experiencers are usually struck by the cosmic importance placed on love of neighbor; finding that we are all connected – indeed that everything in the universe is connected – and because of these experiences, learn the most important thing in life is to love everyone around them unconditionally and without judgment.[119] As such, NDErs come to love and accept others without the usual attachments and conditions that society expects. Instead of judging, criticizing, and condemning, they perceive themselves as equally and fully loving of each and all, openly generous, and excited about the potential and wonder of each person they see. Their desire is to fulfill a prime directive during the NDE to be a conduit of universal love.[120]

Confused family members tend to regard this sudden change in behavior as oddly threatening, as if their loved one had become aloof, unresponsive, even uncaring and unloving to them in particular. A sad paradox from this experience is that to love one's enemies unconditionally may seem cold and callous towards the feelings of one's closest friends and family, especially when they have suffered injury at the hands of others. In this case the NDEr seemingly fails to perform a duty expected of society, which is to protect, lash out, or connect emotionally with the victim's injury or sense of injustice. Spouses may mistake this unconditional way of expressing joy and affection -- i.e. heart-centered rather than person-centered -- towards persons other than themselves as flirtatious disloyalty. Divorce often results.[121] In one study, 65% of NDErs' marriages resulted in divorce as opposed to about 50% in the general population.[122] Major changes in values, careers, and religious views also contributed to stress in a returning NDEr's relationships.[123]

Near-death experiences almost always lead to spiritual curiosity. People who are not overtly religious before an NDE report that they both believe in God and have an appreciation for spiritualism after their experience. However, they also tend to abandon religious doctrine that is followed solely for the sake of doctrine.[124] NDErs come to realize through their experience that religion is not a matter of one 'right' religious group or belief

65

versus all other 'wrong' groups or beliefs. People who experience an NDE often come out of it saying that 'religion' basically concerns one's ability to love others – not doctrines or religious denominations.[125]

Experiencers generally have a newfound respect for the attainment of knowledge and learning. They may leave successful businesses and employment in the spontaneous pursuit of new knowledge or life direction. NDErs also feel more responsible for the direction they take in their lives. They are also sensitive to how their actions affect and impact others both immediately and long-term.[126] Hard-driving achievers and materialists can transform into easy-going philosophers; but, by the same token, those more relaxed or uncommitted before can become energetic movers and shakers, determined to make a difference in the world. Although initially bewildered, families can be so impressed by what they witness that they, too, change, making the experience a shared event.[127]

NDErs often experience problems reentering and readjusting to the mundane 'real' world. As previously noted, they often have marital difficulties because the spouse feels that he/she is now married to a different person who is much changed following the NDE experience.[128] Most NDErs also develop a sense of timelessness. They tend to 'flow' with the day's events, and display a more heightened awareness of the present moment, claiming an importance of being 'in the now.' Making future preparations can seem irrelevant to them. Others often label this behavior 'spaciness.' NDErs refer to their episode as if it were a type of divider separating their 'former' life from the present.[129]

An estimated 89% of NDErs report an increase in intuition, psychic phenomena, or healing abilities following their unique experience, and psychic displays can become commonplace.[130] This behavior may not only be worrisome to relatives and friends it can be frightening to them as well. A person's religious beliefs (pre- or post-NDE) do not seem to alter or prevent this amplification of psychic faculties and stimuli. Yet, NDErs willing to learn how to control and refine these abilities tend to consider them to be beneficial.[131]

Major Characteristics of Physiological Changes:

While psychological changes affect the NDErs' relationships with others, their post-NDE physiological changes affect their relationship with their own body, which generally forces them to accept major lifestyle changes or suffer massive ill effects, including allergic reactions, nausea, and chronic illness. These physical differences eventually lead NDErs to alter their approach to health and healing, employment, finances, and lifestyle issues. Many say that it is almost as if they have to relearn how to use their own body and brain.[132]

NDErs may experience unusual sensitivity to light and sound, which can be a serious issue and may well necessitate some lifestyle changes. While most NDErs must limit sunshine exposure, others may feel that they can't get enough. Almost all NDErs though have similar difficulties with loud or discordant sounds. Many report they can no longer tolerate hard rock music. Instead, the vast majority report a preference for classical, melodic-style music, and/or natural sounds, and many become passionate about the potential for using music to heal.[133]

Most NDErs must change their diet and health practices to accommodate their physiological changes. NDErs generally exhibit accelerated metabolic and substance absorption rates, along with a decreased tolerance of pharmaceuticals and chemically treated products and food. They often report an imperative command received during their NDE to return to the land, interpreted as a need to eat organic food and utilize homeopathic and alternative medical procedures. Failure to follow this injunction may lead to increased allergies or food sensitivities, and nausea if one does not accept his/her body's newfound preference for more organic vegetables and grains, and less of meat.[134]

Other physiological changes include substantially more or less energy, lower blood pressure, electrical sensitivity, and altered thought processing.[135] Interestingly, most of the physiological effects can be physically measured, and are quite noticeable to both the NDEr and the people with whom they routinely interacted before and after the NDE. Not all people who experience an NDE feel comfortable discussing the experience with others, and many take years to fully assimilate and understand their NDE.[136] However, whether the experience is discussed or even understood, these aftereffects are an immediate component of the NDErs' lives for which they will have to deal for the rest of their lives.

Comparison to Findings from Quantum Physics

Some components of the composite NDE model have obvious similarities to some of the scientific findings of quantum physics, as discussed in the previous chapter. In particular, this includes the Light Phenomenon, Being One with Reality, and Altered Concepts of Time and Space.

Light Phenomenon.

In the last chapter we discussed some of the implications of Einstein's famous equation, $E=mc^2$. Einstein's equation shows a direct proportionality between mass and energy; as one increases so too must the other. We also discussed Max Planck's finding, known as Planck's Constant, which equated each photon of light with a specific amount of energy. Thus, we return to the conclusion reached through the mathematical transitive property that all matter is simply a mass of stablized light.[137]

This scientific conclusion matches very well with anecdotal observations made by millions of NDErs during their brief sojourns into heaven. Everything the NDErs observe while in the other dimension is seemingly made of light. Indeed the substance of the universe – of all that is seen and unseen – is reportedly comprised of light. They learn that atoms and matter in the physical realm, described as the lowest level, is merely dense light, stabilized at a very low frequency.

A unique extension of the Light Phenomenon observed by NDErs is that the Light itself is Conscious. Put another way, the Light is the Consciousness of the universe, and the Consciousness is the Light. Even more so, the NDErs experience that all of the light of the universe – i.e. all of the Consciousness – is connected and really one-and-the-same Entity. This leads in well with the next NDE trait, Being One with Reality.

Being One with Reality.

J. S. Bell, et. al. proved mathematically that everything in the universe is connected at the subatomic level. A simple extension of this mathematical theorem, known as Bell's theorem, is that everything in the universe is simply a part, an extension, or manifestation of that One Entity. This idea corresponds well with the knowledge gained by NDErs during their near-death experience. NDErs report a literal connection to everything around them, and learn there is a reason why humans are implored to learn to love one another, and to love their neighbor as their self: their neighbor literally is their self – simply a different manifestation of the Unity – of All That Is.

This leads to an interesting conundrum. Human consciousness, through the psychological ego, experiences life as an independent entity, not as part of a collective consciousness.[138] And yet humanity is expected to trust in this assertion as fact, as part of their evolutionary – and educational – process in life. It should come as no surprise then that this knowledge is difficult to conceive or implement, and the effects of its assimilation lead to the drastic NDE aftereffects described in this chapter. Humans cannot normally live by this spiritual commandment without drastically changing in ways that stand out at odds with society and loved ones in their life. This is not to say that the challenge is impossible, but merely at odds with current society and thusly not an easy task to undertake.

A related phenomenon to The Unity of All Things is the concept of superluminal thought; an idea supported again by both science and input from NDErs. As previously discussed, the Einstein-Podolsky-Rosen effect proved that connections can occur instantaneously between two entities regardless of the distance separating them.

This can be more easily understood, perhaps, if one considers the Space-Time and/or Unity results as valid and thus there is no actual distance separating any two entities because either space/distance is an illusion, or the seemingly illusory separation between two objects is actually a continuity within the Unity, since there is no void within All That Is. All That Is comprises everything in the universe, both seen and unseen, so by definition there is no place that could exist outside of All That Is. Therefore, it is a smaller leap to consider communication within the self to be instantaneous, so if the self is considered to be part of All That Is, then that which the self communicates with is also a part of the same Entity.

Within the NDE literature further support can be found for the concept of instantaneous communication because all NDErs who experienced communication with other entities in the out-of-body state noted that such was conducted via telepathy where mental images served in the absence of vocal communication and was passed instantaneously directly into one's mind.[139]

Altered Concepts of Space and Time.

This is another area that is very difficult for humans to accept as valid, but has both been proven mathematically through the efforts of many renowned physicists and experienced as truth by NDErs. The difficulty in acceptance is that humans live in a three-dimensional world and the altered concept of time and space insists on a four-dimensional reality, Space-Time, where past, present and future all meet in a singularity, *Now*.

These two NDE traits coalesce within the life review. In regards to the altered concept of space and time, NDErs report the life review is instantaneous despite the fact that every intimate detail of a person's life is reviewed *in toto* to help the soul gain a deeper level of understanding of the events from his or her life. Imagine reliving an entire lifetime in an instant without losing any of the detail or emotions, on top of engaging in an academic discussion of each life event to determine the lessons learned therein! That is the implication of the Life Review.

In regards to being one-with-reality, life reviews are remarkable in that the consciousness experiences full, omniscient knowledge of the consequences and repercussions of their actions on others in that life. They not only relive life events from a first-person perspective, but also feel and understand how their actions affected others from their alternate point of view.[140] Researchers Ring and Cooper noted that the emphasis in the life review was generally focused on feelings and emotions, as well as how one's motives played into their actions.[141] Anger and self-defense is quite justifiable, for example, but deliberate cruelty would be frowned upon.

This idea corresponds well with the previous imperative to love one's neighbors as one's self. If the most important commandment of life is to love others unconditionally then it stands to reason that a life review would be most rewarding when one's effects on others had been loving, helpful, and positive. Still, as previously seen, the aftereffects of NDEs are not always positive on the NDErs' own marital relationships given their higher precedence of divorce. Thus, one might conclude the viability of the commandment to love one's neighbors as oneself, without also causing undue pain to one's family and friends in the process, can only be accomplished when society as a whole advances to a point where such unconditional love can be understood without damaging intimate interpersonal relationships.

Chapter Four

Out-of-Body Experiences

Introduction

An out-of-body experience (OBE) is one where people feel their mind, their awareness, their perceiving, thinking consciousness is separated from their physical body at a location in perceptual space other than their body's head and brain, and yet they still perceive events with a vivid and real sensory perception characteristic. Further, during an OBE there is no clouding of consciousness or perception as would occur during a dream state, but rather perception is considered to be near perfect and distinct; sometimes even described as more conscious or more aware than during normal waking conscious.[142] During an OBE, the ego may see its physical body from a separate vantage point, or realize that it is observing events from a location other than would be possible from the body's physical position.

The term "out-of-body experience" was coined by C. T. Tart in 1960 to avoid alternative names that were present in the literature at the time, and implied a negative judgmental connotation concerning some nonexistent knowledge of etiology of the experience; for example, such terms as astral projection, astral travel, ESP projection, doubling, etc.[143]

To a person experiencing an OBE, the experience is real – beyond a dream or hallucination – and, again, may be described as more real than waking reality. In an OBE, an individual is totally conscious, as we would typically define the state. Much of a person's physical sensory perception is also replicated. He can see, hear, and touch, though the senses of smell and taste are generally muted or nonexistent. The person's perspective will be from a position outside of their physical body, either near or distant. If near the body, it will usually be from a vantage point that would be impossible to observe from within the physical body, such as floating against the ceiling. The starkest difference is the extreme reality of the OBE that sets it apart from dreams.[144]

An OBE can be a life-changing event because it can affect a person's perceptions of reality both through the effects of the experience as well as experiences or knowledge gained during the OBE.[145]

Most OBEs are once-in-a-lifetime events, usually triggered by accidents, illnesses, stress, or other physically and psychologically traumatic events that take a human to the brink of death. Many OBEs may occur during sleep, or more commonly during the hypnogogic state: the natural transition point between full wakefulness and sleep.[146] The hypnogogic state is often associated with a state of increased susceptibility to inspiration, occurring at a point of complete relaxation as the consciousness slips through the threshold between conscious awareness and the dream state.[147] Many contend the hypnogogic state is more susceptible to spiritual encounters, experiences, and inspiration because the ego is quieted as it slips into sleep, allowing the subconscious to commune more directly as a bridge between the super-conscious and the ego-based waking-conscious.

More rarely, OBEs may be experienced through conscious, deliberate efforts.[148] Many training programs and some technological inventions have been designed in the hopes of being able to increase a person's chances at successfully achieving a deliberate attempt to enter the out-of-body state. The pretext of these training programs and technological inventions is often to help the person achieve the hypnogogic state while maintaining a heightened state of awareness. Robert Monroe labeled this state as mind awake/ body asleep.[149]

A 1954 study by H. Hart found 27% of his survey respondents had experienced an OBE in their lifetime.[150] Celia Green's 1968 study similarly found 34% of her survey respondents had experienced an OBE.[151] J. Palmer and M. Dennis' 1975 study found as many as 25% of their survey respondents had experienced an OBE, with experiential data highly dependent on the age of the survey respondent where younger persons were more likely to respond in the affirmative.[152] Buhlman's book, The Secret of the Soul, described his own out-of-body experiences as well as those of more than 16,000 other survey respondents from around the world.[153] From the wide body of available data, OBE experiences will be described throughout this chapter.

The inevitable conclusion of these findings is that OBEs are natural experiences that have been experienced and recorded since the beginning of historical records.[154] Some OBE researchers even contend that every night all humans separate from their bodies during sleep to learn, experience, and recharge energetically and spiritually.[155] However, the nature of the sleeping state of consciousness almost always prevents one from remembering this everyday experience.

Hospice caretakers have long known that those approaching death may begin to have spontaneous OBEs, or deathbed visions as a natural prelude to their 'permanent' transition of consciousness from the physical to the spiritual.[156] Some on the cusp of death may experience an OBE quite like a near-death experience, and many have provided a statement or description of their vision of the afterlife. Daniel Webster noted on his deathbed, "I still live…pretty." Momentarily emerging from a coma at the end of his life, Thomas A. Edison stated definitively, "It's very beautiful over there." Similarly, King Louis XVII provided during his final moments of life, "I suffer much less. The music is so beautiful… Listen, listen. In the midst of all those voices I recognize my mother's!"[157]

Out-of-Body Experience Description and Common Traits

Providing definitive proof of OBEs is not an easy matter, and indeed there is more support for the validity of NDEs than OBEs. However, the sheer number of OBEs tends to normalize the experience, thus lending it some weight as a credible body of anecdotal evidence. Unfortunately, an out-of-body experience does not necessarily correspond with an ability to relate accurately events or descriptions of seemingly observed locations in the physical world in the time period of Here-Now. Still, this negative proof neither supports nor detracts from the perceived reality of the out-of-body experience for those who have had an OBE.[158]

Robert Monroe described aptly the difficulties of proving the validity of the OBE, though he himself experienced thousands of OBEs in his lifetime. He noted most knowledge about OBEs stems from reports of once-in-a-lifetime experiences, which places the possible extent of that knowledge at a serious disadvantage. First, most people cannot reproduce an OBE at will, which limits the ability to study OBEs under precise laboratory conditions. Second, when a person suddenly experiences a brief OBE, the thrill of being in a novel environment quite different from his/her normal experience does not help him/her serve as a reliable or deliberate observer. That person will typically be too excited and too busy just trying to cope with the strangeness of the experience.[159]

In the out-of-body state, time, by the standards of the physical world, may seem to be non-existent, or simply cannot correlate with events that occurred in the physical world while the consciousness was incorporeal. The human awareness may perceive a sequence of events; a past and a future, but no cyclical separation. Both continue to exist co-terminously with *Now*.[160]

I once interviewed a person who experienced a spiritually induced OBE during an intense prayer session. The interviewee was holding hands and praying with a disturbed young woman who was having difficulties in life due to drugs and negative influences from her peer group, and they intensely sought intervention through prayer to help the young woman. The interviewee described feeling a jolt of electricity that seemingly knocked both of them physically unconscious though the interviewee's sense of awareness seemed to suddenly be above and separated from the physical body. The interviewee could see the body while in this state of awareness, but there was no positive correlation with any other physical item that had been in the room where they had been praying. For example, the young woman's physical body was unseen, and the only remarkable item was an intense blue-white light shining in the distance.

The interviewee described the experience in the out-of-body state: Time seemed not to exist. All of the past, present, and future was resident in one moment, the "Here-Now." The interviewee felt as if all the knowledge of the universe was accessible and life suddenly made perfect sense. Unfortunately, this knowledge was not brought back once the veil of amnesia returned upon regaining consciousness; merely the impression of having had access to that knowledge for a brief period of time, and how wondrous it had been. Humanity's purpose was clearly understood for that brief moment, as well as an enduring feeling of connection with all reality as if we were all part of "One" entity.

While in the out-of-body state, the interviewee could see with perfect 360-degree panoramic vision. However, though the interviewee did not detect any other conscious presences in the out-of-body state, an intensely bright bluish-white light was observed that seemed to captivate one's attention. There was no telling how much time elapsed because one moment felt equivalent to an eternity. The interviewee described the experience as more real than life, and quite unlike a dream – one could sense, think, feel, and experience with perfect mental acuity; a feat no dream could rival.

Once back in the physical state, the interviewee learned 20 minutes had lapsed and the church group had found the praying pair lying unconscious on the floor so they called an ambulance. The girl shortly returned to consciousness just before the interviewee, and she described a similar, though even more intense spiritual experience bordering on a near-death experience with a life review and engagement with "beings of light." The girl cried from joy of the experience and remorse at her past life habits, and thanked the interviewee for helping to cause that experience through their prayer. She noted the experience had affected her deeply and she intended to change her life permanently for the better.

Dr. Twemlow's study of OBEs found that many experiencers shared similar traits with the interviewee's case, above. Comparing common traits of OBEs with their precedence, Twemlow found: [161]

Common OBE Traits	% Occurrence
More real than a dream	94%
Environment same as physical body	62%
Saw physical body from distance	51%
Passed through objects	50%
Felt vibrations in body preceding event	38%
Heard noises in early stages of separation	37%
Aware of presence of nonphysical beings	37%
Change in sense of time	33%
Saw brilliant white light	30%
Tunnel experience	26%
Felt attached to the physical body	21%
Able to sense touching physical objects	18%
360-degree panoramic vision	4%

Twemlow similarly found people generally felt calm and reassured during their OBE, mimicking descriptive experiences of people who reported near-death experiences. Comparing common emotions during OBEs with their precedence, Twemlow found:[162]

Common OBE Feelings	% Occurrence
Sense of calm, peace, quiet	72%
Freedom	68%
Sense of life purpose	63%
Joy	55%
No special feelings	36%
Sense of power	29%

Similarities to the Near-Death Experience

Reported experiences between NDEs and OBEs share many similarities. Monroe opined the difference might lie only in the perception of the events and situations encountered.[163] Moody's assessment that the depth of experience during an NDE was likely attributed to the manner of death and amount of time a person was clinically dead, could almost certainly carry over to the depth of experience within an OBE as well.[164] Out-of-body experiences that last seconds or a few minutes are probably unlikely to proceed beyond momentary visual impressions of observing one's body from a vantage point other than normal, as typified by the interviewee's out-of-body experience, above.

Indeed, traumatically induced OBEs may share the closest approximations to the NDE simply because they may be preludes to an actual near-death experience, albeit the experiencer did not actually die. Traumatically induced OBEs may occur during violent accidents, physical attacks – such as rape or physical altercations –severe illness, highly painful experiences, stress, or sleep deprivation.[165] The scientific- and descriptive-literature are full of accounts of these traumatically induced out-of-body experiences.

Military fighter pilots and astronauts may experience induced out-of-body experiences if they are rendered unconscious during flight due to excessive G-forces, known as G-LOC (Loss of consciousness). NASA conducted experiments on US military pilots, utilizing a powerful centrifuge to render the pilots unconscious from excessive G-forces. Each of the experimental subjects reported he had passed out and then described a detailed out-of-body state of awareness during the time he was otherwise physically unconscious.[166]

American author Ernest Hemingway described his own traumatically induced OBE after being injured in combat as a member of the Ambulance Corps in World War I. Injured, he tried to breathe but could not and suddenly felt himself rush bodily out of his injured physical form. The process was swift, and he suddenly realized he was dead. He realized as well the concept that one's experience ended at death was in error. He floated around the WWI battlefield for a time, but suddenly felt an impossible tug pull his spirit back into his body. Inexplicably, his body breathed and he had been instantaneously called back to the pain of mortal wounds.[167]

Buhlman described the story of Sam P. of Maryland who related his own traumatically induced OBE. When Sam was about twelve he had an OBE that occurred when he was being severely beaten by a gang. When the pain seemed unbearable, Sam suddenly found himself floating outside his body from a vantage point that allowed him to observe his body being beaten. From this external vantage point, Sam realized he no longer experienced pain, and realized as well that at that point he had no sense of fear about what would happen to him or his body. At that point, he felt an overpowering sense of peace. When the gang eventually lost interest and stopped beating Sam's body, he was shortly pulled back into his body and the pain immediately returned.[168]

For those experiencers who have been able to purposely recreate the out-of-body experience a number of times, and potentially extend the experience through conscious effort, they have been able to achieve experiences incredibly similar to those of extended near-death experiences. Robert Monroe was one such gifted OBE traveler who documented hundreds of his own OBEs, most achieved through conscious effort, including attempts to validate the experience under laboratory conditions.

During some of his longer OBEs, he intentionally journeyed to an area of the spiritual world one might liken to a description of Heaven and an encounter with the Creator. He described his experience as thus (paraphrased from the original): You are Home; you are aware of the Source of the entire span of your experience and of your true nature, as well as the vastness beyond your ability to perceive and/or imagine; the Father, the Creator of all that is or was. You are one of His countless creations. How or why, you do not know. You are one with and integrated as a part of the whole. At our core, there are no differences in sex; everyone is both male and female, positive and negative.[169] Each of the three times Monroe visited this locale in the spirit world he did not return voluntarily but was forcibly guided back. After each experience, he suffered intense nostalgia, loneliness, and homesickness for days. Back in his physical body, he felt as an alien among strangers in a land where things were not right when compared to his 'real home' with the Creator.[170]

Such in-depth out-of-body experiences are exceptionally rare, but the experiences show similarities to near-death experiences, which may help normalize the anecdotal experiences in the concept of their validity, especially for our discussion herein.

NDE-Like Transformative Qualities

Similar to NDEs, out-of-body experiences often have life-changing transformative qualities. An OBE is usually one of the most profound experiences of a person's life, and therefore may radically alter a person's beliefs about the nature of reality and their own relationship with the world around them. Monroe summarized this type of transformation as the difference from no longer simply *believing* in survival after death to *knowing* one will survive death.[171] Because the person will have directly experienced continued waking conscious without need of a physical body the person is assured of his/her continued survival after bodily death.

Twemlow quantified these post-OBE transformative qualities through his study of the experience. He found the following precedence of common aftereffects and transformative qualities of OBEs:[172]

Transformative Qualities of OBEs	% Occurrence
Became interested in psychic issues	85%
Felt their life had changed	60%
Felt a spiritual experience from the OBE	55%
Felt they possessed psychic abilities	43%
Felt confused following the OBE	27%
Kept the experience secret	25%

Longer term impacts of OBEs	% Occurrence
Wanted to experience an OBE again	89%
Developed a greater awareness of reality	86%
Felt the experience had a lasting benefit	78%
Changed belief in life after death	66%
Felt the OBE was the greatest thing that had ever happened in their life	43%

The qualitative character of the aftereffects of OBEs is very similar to those of NDEs, as listed in the previous chapter. Buhlman's study of more than 16,000 respondents found persons who experience an OBE will likely develop:[173]

- An increased respect for life
- An increased spiritual connection

-Reduced feelings of hostility and violence
-An increased interest in the search for knowledge and wisdom
-An increased self-respect and sense of responsibility
-Personal verification of immortality
-Expanded awareness of our interconnection with others

The point of the above descriptions of the nature of the out-of-body experience and its aftereffects on the human conscious has been to normalize the experience so that the reader may consider a temporary incorporeal state of experience to be a legitimate, if unique aspect of the human experience. If one accepts the validity of the out-of-body experience, then there are many lessons learned from the experience that can be applied to the discussion presented in this book concerning the nature of reality.

Comparison to quantum physics: Energy Principles

Arguably, the most important lessons learned from the collective body of OBE literature are the principles of energy, which define the 'rules' by which reality is created and experienced, both in the incorporeal and physical states of reality. In order to understand this conjecture, energy principles must first be considered from the incorporeal state, and then comparisons can then be drawn to the physical state.

Robert Monroe's decades of experience in out-of-body research determined the power of thought, i.e. the focus of one's intentions, provided the energy inputs required to accomplish any perceived need or desire while in the out-of-body state.[174] He noted one only had to think movement, and the thought became a fact.[175] If one intends or expects – perhaps subconsciously – his surroundings to appear as the physical environment in which his physical body is still resident, then that is what he will perceive.

This explains why experiences in the out-of-body state may not correspond exactly with the physical realm: they are totally separate locations and any perceived similarity is a falsehood imposed by one's own expectations that a similarity needs to exist. In other words, our thoughts intending the area around our dissociated spirit to appear as the physical realm near our body creates a visual impression of the same.

If one believes he has died and has a preconceived notion of heaven and hell, and feels (even subconsciously) he was sinful during that life and thereby deserving of a harsh judgment, then his experience in the astral realm will likely not be pleasant.[176] Conversely, if one projects feelings of love, or asserts that they deserve only pleasant experiences, then their experience in the astral realm will match their preconceived notions of the experience.[177] In the out-of-body state, like attracts like, or in other words, one's thought projects and expectations becomes one's perceived reality.[178]

Buhlman summarized these findings as the laws of Basic Energy Mechanics:[179]

Basic Energy Mechanics

1. The nonphysical universe is progressively less dense in substance and increasingly thought-responsive as we explore further toward the spiritual source of energy.

2. Our thoughts are a form of creative energy and have a natural tendency to interact with and affect the nonphysical environments we encounter. The farther within the multidimensional universe we explore the more rapid and pronounced this thought reaction becomes; i.e. we think change and change happens ever faster.

3. Our thoughts, both conscious and subconscious, will influence the nonphysical energy that we observe. The degree of influence we experience is in direct proportion to the intensity of our thoughts and the density of our surroundings.

It is important to understand that the unseen, incorporeal world that surrounds us has direct applicability to our experiences in physical reality. Thus the direction of our thoughts in everyday life can affect our physical reality and experiences. Following the lessons of quantum physics, this can be attributed to the fact that all matter, form, and substance is derived from energy that originates from the unseen dimensions of the universe. Pure consciousness is highly thought-responsive and takes shape first in incorporeal form. As we direct our focus and attention towards an intended outcome, we help that conscious idea attain permanency of form in the physical world. In the same way, we can manipulate and change outcomes in the physical realm through deliberate, focused intention, though solidified energy transforms more slowly to meet our intentions than would occur in the spirit world.[180] Significant patience may therefore be necessary to observe changes in the physical world as a result of focused thought-intentions.

This idea supplements our other findings in quantum physics. If consciousness is the base of all reality, both seen and unseen, and the light of the Creator is both conscious and a part of everything in existence, then the conclusion of Physicist David Bohm must be valid; i.e. That all matter is but frozen light.[181] Therefore, an intense effort at directed, conscious thought concerning our desired intentions should have the capability to mold consciousness' experiences within physical reality. Indeed, Magnus concluded the physical realm can respond to one's thoughts and intentions though the slow speed at which changes may occur in physical reality might not always seem directly attributable to one's own efforts.[182]

This idea carries forward as well into subconscious thoughts and societal norms/groupthink. One does not have to realize his thoughts have impact in order for it to be so. Indeed, the very idea may seem ludicrous, but many would contend it is time for humanity to realize the power of positive and progressive thinking so that the human species may move forward peaceably.[183] Further, the more people who think the same way, the greater the chances for the focus of their attention to actually occur. Still, proving this contention is as likely as being able to 'prove a negative.' Some efforts and progress towards this proof have been conducted utilizing random number generators and then monitoring those generators for anomalies during mass societal events, such as the attacks that occurred on September 11th, 2001. However, a further examination of this effort and its merits and potential successes will not be discussed here.

Returning to Buhlman's findings, we find important lessons as well in some basic energy principles:[184]

Basic Energy Principles

1. Everything seen and unseen is a form of energy; that energy is derived of consciousness.

2. Focused thought (i.e. directed consciousness) possesses the innate ability to influence, restructure, and ultimately mold energy, matter, outcomes, and the experiences that consciousness will perceive.

3. The less dense the energy structure or environment, the faster the pace at which the restructuring may occur. Changes in the physical realm take time to occur.

4. The effectiveness and speed by which consciousness restructures an energy-based environment is determined by the intensity of the thought impacting the environment and the density of the energy-environment being acting upon.

These energy principles are important because humans inherently possess the ability to shape and mold their individual reality. However, we must first recognize this ability in order to consciously take advantage of it to shape our perceived reality as desired. The process of energy restructuring occurs much faster in the non-physical state where the environment is extremely thought-responsive, but one should not become discouraged if desired changes in the physical realm take time.[185]

If one were to contend life is but an educational process in the long continuum of eternity then life in the physical world would be an ideal training ground to learn to control one's thoughts and focused energy by trial and error through a series of successive lives, overcoming energy-controlling issues such as negative emotions, psychological issues, fear, jealousy, trust issues, pride, etc., in an effort to prepare one's higher self for elevated planes of consciousness where energy is immediately responsive to one's thoughts.[186]

Robert Monroe learned through his decades of OBE experience and experimental results that physical inputs can help focus one's conscious awareness to aid in this lifetime learning process. Pain or pleasure will turn attention to the event causing the experience, and the experience is effectively stored in memory because of that attention. Further, if emotion is involved, the storage process will be enhanced even further.[187] Physical experience thus deepens the energy-manipulation learning process. For an experiencing human consciousness, the depth and effectiveness of learning life-based experiences is in direct proportion to the intensity of the experience. This concept is quite difficult to grasp and insufficiently covered here, but will be considered again from a different perspective later in this book.

Other Lessons Learned

There are many other lessons learned from the body of literature on OBE research, though they are less definitive than the discussion on thought-based energy manipulation, above. Still, as a body of work many of these lessons support well the conclusions reached in other researched fields within this book, and therefore deserve mention as supplementary evidence.

OBE travelers have concluded from their personal experiences that the soul is the core of human consciousness. Buhlman argued the soul exists beyond the human concepts of space and time; thereby, humanly concepts of shape, form, and substance cannot apply.[188] The soul might be more aptly described as 'conscious light' that uses various forms of energy, including the physical form of the human body, for its means of expression, communication, growth, evolution, and exploration in order to achieve the lessons and life experiences that it desires (not all of which will be pleasant – *purposely!*).

Similar to conclusions reached by NDE researchers and experiencers, OBE travelers have also concluded consciousness is not lost at death. The conscious soul merely sheds the physical shell it had worn to complete the purposes of its life lessons, and then returns to its permanent soul form. Buhlman opined that death was a grand illusion: At death our consciousness simply transitioned from one dimension to another to continue its evolutionary process.[189]   Monroe agreed in that human consciousness is inherently nonphysical, and as such is not time-space dependent.[190]   Human consciousness thus is not lost or destroyed at the moment of death; it merely changes form from physical to nonphysical and continues to exist, think, and *be* as it was while still in the physical.

This assertion would seem to agree with the First Law of Thermodynamics: Energy can be neither created nor destroyed, but can only change from one form to another. If one accepts that the soul is simply a form of dynamic energy, then it stands to reason that the energy form of the human soul cannot be destroyed, lost, or even reduced at the moment of physical death – it must continue to exist in some form, somewhere.

Monroe's experiences in the OBE state convinced him the dynamic form of energy that comprises the human soul is also resident in all carbon-based organic life on Earth. That essence enters the human body at some point prior to birth and then departs again at death, presumably more educated from the experience. However, the difference between the energy resident in humans vice other, less advanced life forms was only the degree of complexity of the organization of that energy-consciousness.[191]

Monroe continued his finding by citing human consciousness is but a manifestation of that dynamic, organized energy originating from the Creator. As an energy form, human consciousness may be likened to a vibrational pattern – multi-layered and of many interacting and resonating frequencies – that responds to and acts upon like-patterns from other external sources. This vibrating energy field, while seemingly distinct, is actually part of a whole that expands throughout the entire universe, comprising the entirety of existence: i.e. the entirety of that energy form is all One Unity.[192] Buhlman took this assertion a step farther by concluding the physical universe itself is conscious; albeit at a level that cannot be understood by the human mind.[193]

Adding to this idea while returning to our earlier discussion on energy, if we accept that the universe is conscious and we are part of that consciousness that comprises All That Is, then it stands to reason we have within our collective conscious the means to create our own perceived reality by the way we direct and focus our thoughts. Buhlman felt we were the producers, directors, and actors that created the play of our own lives.[194] Within the physical experience we thus learn of our creative abilities and personal responsibility.

So if we can theoretically be in charge of our lives, why can we not halt 'bad' things from happening in our lives? This important query will be continued later in this book, but let us recall a discussion already mentioned in this chapter in that one of the important purposes of life is to experience life lessons and the manipulation of energy, through which physical inputs and emotions play an important role in those lessons' effectiveness. Hypothetically speaking, what good would an experience be for imparting lessons if there were never hardships? How could one understand what is good if there were no 'bad' by which it could be compared? How could one understand love and happiness without pain and loneliness as a comparison? Further, though this may seem to be a harsh statement, what is 'bad' to one person is simply a perspective; it is not an absolute. We will see later in this book how 'bad' scenarios may actually be important life lessons for which the soul specifically sought to experience in this life to help it progress as a learning entity.

Of course it would do no good if the soul realized it would experience a specific bad occurrence at a specific location, date, and time in the future, or the event would not have the emotional effect required to impart the important life lesson; thus, potentially wasting the opportunity to learn a sought-after lesson in this life. Therefore, the acceptance of human life requires the immortal soul-consciousness to abide by certain rules inherent to physical reality. For example, the concept that space and time truly does exist is reportedly one such rule. Without this particular agreement, it would be impossible to have a primary human conscious experience in physical life on Earth.

The soul must further agree that consciousness expressed as a human has certain characteristics and limitations. Monroe termed this as a blanking, sublimation, or veil of amnesia that blocks the conscious' ability to recall previous experiences, i.e. those before the current human life, as a part of the process.[195] This is to assure there will be minimal interference in the performance of a human life's decision-making processes caused by input from previous life patterns, actions, and experiences, or disruptive influence from the ever-present Over Soul.

To the human consciousness, life may purposely seem to be both lonely and all that there is, with no hope of life after death or reincarnation, simply as a means to force the consciousness to focus exclusively on solving the tasks and trials that will be set before it. After all, one who does not fear death may approach life-or-death decisions quite differently than one who wants to hold onto the life experience as long as possible for fear of a permanent end with humanly death.

Finally, the OBE travelers' experiences provide an insight to a trivial point of curiosity that may interest some readers; i.e. the form of one's consciousness outside of the human body. Buhlman answered simply the soul possesses no inherent shape or form.[196] Monroe was a little more descriptive. He described the nonphysical body as being similar to gelatin when it was removed from the 'mold' of one's body. The consciousness will remember its human form and be nearly identical. However, the longer one remained separated from their body, the weaker that memory, connection and dependence would become. Distance also seemed to be a factor. The farther one moved away from Earth/the physical realm, the memory, or perhaps more accurately the need for the memory of the previous human shape, seemed to become less distinct. Eventually, unless specifically intended to remain in human shape, one's consciousness may appear as a ball, teardrop, small cloud, or blob of glowing light-energy.[197]

Researchers later in this book will add to this point of curiosity utilizing vantage points gained from different means of insight, though in general agree with both of these OBE travelers' observations.

Conclusion

Evidence gained from the out-of-body experience tends to suggest that human consciousness purposely incarnates in a physical life experience because of what it is – an intense learning process; a school of a very unusual sort. Respected OBE traveler Robert Monroe concluded that one singular experience in physical life could not possibly be enough to experience *all* that life has to offer.[198]   Indeed, for a complete human experience, a soul-consciousness would need to incarnate as both male and female, rich and poor, talented and handicapped, black and white, etc. so as to be able to have a first-hand account of the vast richness of human life's abundant experiences on Earth.

Indeed it would seem our discussion of the nature of reality and meaning of life has only just begun because the more snippets we glean about what lies beneath the surface of human existence, the more we realize we simply could not previously conceive of

the truth as humans trapped within the physical limitations of that
existence.

Chapter Five

Reincarnation

Introduction

A belief in reincarnation is common amongst Eastern religions and cultures, but many Western religions also have historical traditions and sects that incorporated reincarnation in their canon. Mainstream Islam, for example, does not accept the precept of reincarnation but certain Shiite sects do; pointing towards passages in the Koran that imply the validity of reincarnation such as the Koran's Sura 71:17-18, "And Allah hath caused you to spring forth; from the Earth like a plant; Hereafter will He turn you back into it; again, and will bring you forth anew."

Judaism also has minority sects that believe in reincarnation, such as Kabala. The Zohar, a central text of Kabala from the mystic tradition of Judaism provides,

The souls must reenter the absolute whence they have emerged. But to accomplish this end they must develop all the perfections, the germ of which is planted in them; and if they have not fulfilled this condition during one life, they must commence another, a third, and so forth, until they have acquired the condition, which fits them for reunion with God.

Ancient Judaism, dating before the first century AD, had a much wider acceptance of reincarnation, which influenced early Christians to accept that the cycle of rebirth could only be transcended by following the teachings and inspiration of Jesus of Nazareth.

Judaism's Torah and Christianity's Old Testament asserted Elijah would reappear before the coming of the Messiah. In the Christian Gospel according to Matthew, chapter 11, Jesus identified John the Baptist as being Elijah reborn. Thus, Jesus asserted the passage from the Jewish holy book had been fulfilled through Elijah's rebirth as John. Failure to accept the validity of Elijah having been reborn as John would also undermine the claim Jesus was the Messiah, thus showing both early Christians and Jews – since Jesus was a Jew – believed in reincarnation.

Indeed a belief in reincarnation continued in the theology of Christianity for centuries. One of the most prolific writers about Christian theology, the Catholic Priest Origen, who lived around 200 AD, was an ardent proponent of reincarnation. Origen could not believe a just and loving God could create humans and then summarily condemn them to eternal damnation if they had not lived righteously. Origen believed in the precept of universal salvation, and reincarnation as the primary tool for humans to work through spiritual evolutionary issues from one life to the next. In *De Principiis*, Origen's major work and the first systematic theology of Christianity, he wrote, "Every soul...comes into this world strengthened by the victories or weakened by the defeats of its previous life. Its place in this world as a vessel appointed to honor or dishonor, is determined by its previous merits or demerits. Its work in this world determines its place in the world which is to follow this."

However, believers in reincarnation stood as impediments to the Catholic Church's absolute authority. Those early Christians who believed in reincarnation were neither induced by promises of heavenly bliss nor intimidated by threats of hellfire in the afterlife. By inference, they did not need ordained Catholic priests to administer sacramental rites such as Confession and the forgiveness of sins in order to 'earn' eternal rewards in the hereafter. Their spiritual self-reliance was anathema to Catholic leaders, as their subservience could not be guaranteed.[199]

In 553 AD, Roman Emperor Justinian called the Fifth Ecumenical Council to rectify early Christian Church teachings into a single, universally accepted theology. Fifteen teachings were thereby declared anathema and heresy, including the concept of the preexistence of souls and reincarnation. However, belief in reincarnation did not merely die because of Justinian's Council. Rather, the belief had to be forcibly rooted out and purged, as was accomplished through the Inquisition's use of organized torture and state-sanctioned terror. Through such, the Inquisition sought to frighten people into following approved Catholic orthodoxy as non-conformers were systematically tortured and killed by the hundreds of thousands in order to achieve this state- and church-sanctioned goal. Still, it took another three hundred years before the Inquisition almost successfully rooted out the connection to and belief in reincarnation from Christianity, the primary Western religion, and Western culture by extension.

Since then, reincarnation has survived only on the fringes of Western society; a concept understood but generally discarded from plausible acceptance in Western scientific, cultural, and religious bodies. However, evidence for reincarnation is continually being experienced and expressed throughout the world, which has caused some scientists to reevaluate and explore the validity of this body of evidence. Examples include spontaneous past-life recall, as well as biological connections between successive lives, reported cases of xenoglossy (speaking foreign languages for which one has no prior experience), and hypnotic past-life recall. The evidence has attracted a growing cadre of scientists with medical and advanced research degrees, including amongst many others, Ernest Pecci, M.D.; Chet Snow, Ph.D.; Ian Stevenson, M.D.; Helen Wambach, Ph.D.; Brian Weiss, M.D.; and Roger Woolger, Ph.D.

These scientists and many others have sought to find evidence to support or terminally disprove the concept of reincarnation. One might even consider all that would be required to prove reincarnation existed would be to find a single case of definitive evidence. This mimics Dr. William James' famous observation one does not need to show that no crows are black to defeat the law that all crows are black; rather it is enough to merely find one crow that was not.[200]

The late Dr. Ian Stevenson, former professor of psychiatry and director of the Division of Personality Studies at the Health Sciences Center, University of Virginia, was one of the premier scientists in this regard. Stevenson researched children worldwide who had and talked about spontaneously recalled past lives. During his career, Stevenson assembled more than 2,600 case studies, many of which were published in exhaustive tomes that included in-depth discussions of his research methodologies to aid academic peer reviews of his research and conclusions.

One of Stevenson's harshest critics was ironically, himself. Despite spending an entire career focused on researching a phenomenon that continually pointed towards the validity of reincarnation, Stevenson never accepted the precept of reincarnation, but rather allowed that some of his case studies seemed to indicate the evidence was merely suggestive of reincarnation. Stevenson claimed some type of flaw existed in every case he had ever investigated, which prevented him from being willing to declare any of the work over his entire career could *prove* reincarnation. However, he did admit the body of evidence was growing in quantity and quality over time, thus increasing the plausibility of the concept of reincarnation.[201]

I would suggest Dr. Stevenson was overly humble at the quality and implications of his work and findings. Indeed, much of his casework is widely quoted by many authors on the subject of reincarnation and many cases in this genre seem stronger than merely suggestive. However, only a tiny fraction of those cases could be considered in the limited space provided herein.

Case Studies of Spontaneous Past-Life Recall

Stevenson felt it was particularly appropriate to research children in regards to spontaneous past-life recall because children were too young to have acquired any preconceived notions of the validity of reincarnation, or substantive information about a deceased person who had lived in another location for which their memories might correlate. Additionally, the occurrence of delusions and psychotic conditions in children is rare thus virtually eliminating the possibility of hysterical dissociation or split personality disorder on the child's part.[202] Also, in many cases in which a child in Western Society remembered living a previous life the family often found such claims to be a baffling and unwelcome event that was not condoned by their Christian-based culture. Thereby, a child's verbal recollections were often met with active dissuasion, reprimand, and even scolding by parents who did not wish to take the child's statements seriously, or have neighbors, friends or other family members know about and potentially ostracize the family because of the child's culturally unacceptable claims.[203]

Stevenson found if a child was going to speak about memories from a spontaneously recalled past life, the child nearly always began doing so between the ages of two and four. In most cases that Stevenson researched, the child continued to talk about the previous life until somewhere between ages five and eight, at which time the memories gradually began to fade and the child began to focus on his/her current life instead of the past life.[204] Many times, these children would recall the manner in which the previous personality had died, particularly if the death had occurred following violent circumstances.[205] This memory in particular could aid Stevenson's research to identify the previous personality, and then verify the manner and circumstances of death and other aspects of the recalled personality's life against the child's proclaimed memories.

In the next section, we will explore some of Stevenson's research in which the manner and circumstances of death impacted the newly born personality through the location and appearance of unique birthmarks and birth defects that eerily corresponded with wounds received at or near the time of death by the previous personality. More frequently, however, the child could recall a number of proper names, places and other specific details from the deceased person's life that were then researched by Stevenson's team to determine not only the correlation of those statements but also how obscure such information was; the objective being to determine how plausible it was for the child to have acquired the information through normal means.[206] In those cases where the information recalled was specific, accurate and truly obscure, little could account for how the child might have acquired such information or memories from a previous life other than through the concept of reincarnation.

Though Stevenson researched and assembled thousands of case files on instances of spontaneous past-life recall, he never obtained enough information to convince himself, definitively, of the validity of reincarnation despite the fact he could not account for how such memories, emotions, and other phenomenon he researched might have occurred. Hemendra Banerjee, an "extracerebral memory" investigator similar to Dr. Stevenson but without the medical credentials, noted he was personally convinced of an investigated case's validity when he witnessed spontaneous *emotional* recognition.[207] Spontaneous emotional recognition occurred when a child claiming to be reborn visited an area or people meaningful to the previous life and then expressed an intense emotional reaction in their presence.

The following are a few of the thousands of cases Stevenson, Hemendra Banerjee, and others have investigated that highlight this unique body of evidence.

The case of Jagdish Chandra of India[208]

Jagdish Chandra was born in Uttar Pradesh, northern India, in 1923. When Jagdish was three years old, he began speaking of a previous life he had lived in Benares, another Indian state. Intrigued by these stories, which were culturally acceptable to most people in India, Jagdish's father began keeping written notes on the boy's memories. Jagdish claimed his 'real' father was named Babuji Pandey, had two sons and a deceased wife, and had owned an automobile, a rarity for Indians at that time. Jagdish further described his mother and some family relatives, and provided explicit details of his former home, including the location of a safe hidden in a wall in an underground room at their residence.

Jagdish Chandra's present father located Babuji Pandey and took Jagdish to Benares to meet him. Babuji Pandry tested Jagdish's proclaimed memories by asking the boy to direct them to his former home as they walked through the maze-like streets of Benares. Jagdish did so despite having never been there in his current lifetime. Jagdish also recognized some relatives he had known in his previous life, and displayed a detailed knowledge of the religious and dietary customs of his former family.

Stevenson noted these recalled memories were from a very young child who lived far from the location of the recalled past life and in a separate caste so that his current family, neighbors and associates would also have had no natural exposure to information about the previous life. Most of Jagdish's claims proved true upon investigation, and the child also exhibited behavioral traits appropriate for the previous life. As with all of Stevenson's cases, however, the professor was reluctant to claim sufficient evidence was present to serve as definitive proof Jadgish was Babuji's deceased child reincarnated.

The case of Kumkum Verma of India[209]

Kumkum Verma also began speaking about a past life in India at age three. Kumkum recalled living as 'Sunnary' in a neighboring town. She also recalled being married to a man in the blacksmith caste, having a son named Misri Lal, a grandson named Gouri Shankar, and two daughters-in-law; one of whom had caused her death by poisoning her food. Kumkum described Sunnary's home as having a pond near the house and an iron safe hidden inside for which she kept secured by harboring a pet cobra near the safe. Interestingly, Kumkum also exhibited no fear of snakes as a child and had once even stroked a cobra that had fallen from a tree near her. Kumkum further described an orchard of mango trees near Sunnary's home and stated Sunnary's father had lived in the town of Bajitpur.

Kumkum's aunt carefully recorded Kumkum's memories as Sunnary though her parents dismissed the stories for some time. Kumkum repeatedly asked to return to Sunnary's home in Urbu

Bazar but her parents refused. At age four, a friend of Kumkum's father had occasion to follow up on the story's details and located Sunnary's son, Misri Lal, in the city of Urdu Bazar, as well as Sunnary's grandson, Gouri Shankar. Misri confirmed most of the claims made by Kumkum about his mother's life, including her death following a sudden, unidentified illness, though at the time he had suspected his mother had been poisoned. Unfortunately, relatives had dissuaded him from performing an autopsy so there was no confirmation concerning Kumkum's claim Sunnary had died of poisoning. Much of the other confirmed information, however, was obscure, personal information, that would only have been known by immediate family members so there was no logical explanation for how a three-year old in another town, who had never had contact with their family, could have known such information.

The case of Corliss Chotkin of Alaska[210]

Before he died in 1946, Victor Vincent, a Tlingit Eskimo in Alaska told his niece, Corliss Chotkin, he would be reborn. Victor asserted Corliss would recognize him because the baby with Victor's reborn soul would have the same two scars Victor possessed: one on his back and one at the base of his nose. Eighteen months after Victor's death, Mrs. Chotkin had a baby with two birthmarks that matched the scars Victor Vincent had borne. Because birthmarks are generally not inherited, the presence of two identical birthmarks at identical locations is of some note.[211] As the child grew older he spontaneously recognized people and places known previously to Victor Vincent, and he told his parents of incidents in Victor's life that the child would not have otherwise known or heard. The child also displayed personality traits and mechanical skills previously exhibited by Victor Vincent. At one point as a small child, he asked his mother if she did not recognize him, and then asserted he was the re-born spirit of Victor Vincent.

The case of Shanti Devi of India[(212)]

Shanti Devi was born in Delhi, India, in 1926 and began describing memories at age four of her previous life as 'Lugdi,' a woman who had lived in Mathura, a town some 80 miles away. Lugdi had died the year before Devi was born of complications during childbirth. Devi's memories of the birthing process seemed quite unnatural for a child of such a young age to conceive, and caused her parents to take particular attention of further descriptions of Lugdi's recalled life. For example, Devi also described various benign aspects of Lugdi's life, commenting on her home, garden, husband, children, food, etc. By the time Devi was eight, people were taking her story seriously.

Upon request, Devi provided the name and address of Lugdi's husband and an inquiry found the man did indeed live where Devi had claimed and his previous wife, Lugdi had died in 1925, a few days after the birth of their son. When they met, Devi's recollections of her previous life as Lugdi and the emotional reaction she had with meeting Lugdi's son, only one year older than Devi, his reborn mother, convinced all present Devi was Lugdi reincarnated. When Devi later visited Mathura, she directed the driver to Lugdi's home, pointed out several landmarks on the way, recognized and identified Lugdi's parents and other members of her family, and described how Lugdi had hidden 150 rupees under the floor of the home. Lugdi's husband admitted he had found the hidden rupees and removed them after Lugdi's death. Altogether, Devi made at least 24 correct statements about Lugdi's life and apparently gave no incorrect information. Quite uniquely in this case, Devi retained her memories of Lugdi's life and maintained a personal conviction she had lived this past life throughout her own life. Devi died at age 61 in 1987.

The case of Romy Crees of the USA[213]

"Extracerebral memory" investigator, Hemendra Banerjee, investigated more than 1,100 spontaneous past-life recall cases in his career, including the case of Romy Crees, a toddler in Des Moines, IA, born in 1977, who claimed she was Joe Williams, a husband of Sheila Williams and father of three. Romy described in graphic detail her death as Joe via motorcycle accident and exhibited a phobia of motorcycles. Dr. Stevenson found that phobias almost always corresponded with the manner of death in the previous life, and might occur in about one-third of the case studies.[214] If the phobia were to manifest, such would occur before the child had begun to speak and would tend to diminish as the child grew older.

Romy recalled attending school as Joe in Charles City, a small city approximately 140 miles from Des Moines. Romy asserted Joe had lived in a red brick house, and provided descriptions of Joe's mother, including the fact that she had leg pains, had burned her hand following a fire caused by Joe, and liked blue flowers.

When Banerjee and Romy visited Joe Williams' seventy six-year old mother the woman disavowed knowing anyone in Des Moines and was quite disbelieving of the little girl's story until the girl correctly identified everyone in a family portrait taken in December 1974. Joe Williams and his wife had died in a motorcycle accident in 1975, and his last present to his mother had been a bouquet of blue posies. Joe's mother also confirmed she had leg pains, had burned her hand from a fire caused by Joe, and many other details Romy had provided, which convinced her personally that Romy was not lying about being her deceased son, Joe.

The case of Mahavir Singh of India[(215)]

Mahavir Singh (pseudonym) was born in 1982 in the Agra district of Uttar Pradesh, India. At age two, Mahavir told his mother he had seen the son of his brother, Pathi Ram, from his previous life as 'Khem Raj,' passing by outside. Mahavir later expounded he personally had five children and a wife; an odd assertion for a toddler to make. But Mahavir made many other statements about *his* family, business and financial situation, and dying near the Ganges River.

Though unrelated, living in separate communities and castes, and previously unfamiliar with the other family, Pathi Ram eventually heard of the story of the boy who claimed to be his brother and came to investigate. Pathi Ram revealed he had a brother, Khem Raj, who did have five children and had indeed died near the Ganges. Mahavir further recognized the businessman, Teja, who had owed Khem money. Mahavir made at least 15 other statements about Khem's family that were confirmed to be true by Pathi Ram, which convinced Pathi that Mahavir was Pathi's brother, Khem, reincarnated.

The case of Dilukshi Nissanka of Sri Lanka[(216)]

Professor Erlendur Haraldsson of the University of Iceland investigated the case of Dilukshi Geevanie Nissanka who was born in Sri Lanka in 1984. At less than two years of age, Diluksi started talking and began describing a previous life she had lived near Dambulla, some 80 miles from her own village. She made about 30 statements concerning this previous life including the circumstances of her 'death.' By age five, Dilukshi had finally impressed upon her family the need to check the validity of her facts and visit the area where she had remembered living previously.

Dilukshi led her family to her former home at Dambulla, some four miles from the town proper. Dilukshi's definitive statements of her previous life as Shiromi and her emotional reaction at recognizing former family members and objects in the family's home caused her former family to recognize her as Shiromi, their former daughter who had died from drowning. Professor Haraldsson concluded at least 12 of Dilukshi's statements about Shiromi's life were proven while some others may have been near hits or near misses with variances attributed to the inexact quality of language translation or changes to area scenery that may have occurred over time, thus hindering the process of proving statements referring to historical descriptions that could no longer be confirmed.

Biological Indications of Reincarnation

Amongst the more than 2,600 case studies Dr. Ian Stevenson researched of spontaneous past-life recall were at least 225 case studies of possible correlations between a child's birthmarks or birth defects with the child's memories of past-life events of physical trauma. Stevenson's book, *Where Reincarnation and Biology Intersect*, summarized 112 of those cases. The birthmarks in these cases were not similar to normal moles – areas of increased pigmentation, or 'nevi' in medical terminology. Instead, they were usually hairless areas comprising a mass of puckered, scar-like tissue, generally raised above or depressed below the surrounding tissues. Some were even bleeding or oozing as open wounds when the baby was born.[217] Stevenson was particularly interested in the potential correlation between these types of birthmarks or birth defects because they might be able to provide an objective type of evidence to prove the validity of reincarnation.[218]

Birth defects, for example, may be caused by genetic disorders, toxic chemicals ingested during pregnancy, uterine conditions, and/or certain infectious diseases. However, a large number of birth defects still have an unknown cause, ranging in frequency from 43% to 70% of all birth defects that cannot be otherwise explained.[219] Thus, birthmarks and birth defects that correspond with the location for which a child specifically recalls being critically wounded in a past life might be able to suggest a deceased personality either influenced or was associated with the later-born baby. This could potentially help researchers understand why, at least in some cases, people may exhibit unique birth defects at certain locations.[220]

Typical of the evidence Stevenson collected in this regard were more than two hundred birthmarks on children who claimed to have been killed by bullets or bladed weapons that pierced the corresponding parts of their bodies in the recalled, previous life. Of particular import were seventeen such cases, in which Stevenson was able to review the medical documents, such as hospital records or autopsy reports, which established the past-life individual had indeed died in the manner recalled by the child, and the mortal wounds corresponded with the location, size and shape of the birthmarks or birth defects of the child being studied.[221]

The following are a few extremely brief summaries of the more than two hundred cases Stevenson investigated that highlight this particularly important body of evidence.

The case of Tali Sowaid of Lebanon[(222)]

Tali Sowaid was born in the tiny village of Btebyat in the mountains east of Beirut, Lebanon, in August 1965. Tali had prominent, circular-shaped birthmarks with increased pigmentation on each cheek on his face. Soon after Tali began to speak as a young toddler, he started referring to a life he had lived as a man in the nearby village of Btechney, approximately four kilometers from Btebyat. Tali further described his death as having occurred while he was drinking a cup of coffee before leaving for work: A man had stealthily approached him from behind and shot him in the face at point-blank range. Tali's description of his 'death' corresponded exactly with the murder of Said Abul-Hisn, who had lived in Btechney, though there was no normal way to account for how the child Tali might have known so many intimate details of Said's life or the circumstances of his death. The assailant had indeed approached Said stealthily from behind and shot him in the face at close range. The bullet had entered Said's face at one cheek and exited at the other, traversing his tongue on the way. Tali also had notable difficulty articulating words properly, including 'S' sounds, which require the tongue to be elevated. One could extrapolate this may have been a residual effect of Said's injury to his tongue where the bullet had passed through it.

In addition to his normal investigation of the child and circumstances surrounding the possible validity of the spontaneously recalled past life, Stevenson was also able to study Said's medical records and autopsy report. He found the birthmark on Tali's left cheek, which was the smaller of the two, corresponded to the wound of entry on Said's left cheek, and the larger birthmark on Tali's right cheek corresponded to the wound of exit on Said's right cheek, as would be expected of gunshot wounds.

The case of Nasruddin Shah of India[(223)]

Nasruddin Shah was born in a Muslim family in a small village in Uttar Pradesh, India, in April 1962. Nasruddin's father was a poor day laborer. Nasruddin had several birthmarks, the most prominent of which was a lens-shaped birthmark on his left chest. When Nasruddin began to speak as a small child, he described a former life he recalled living and even seemed to have difficulties differentiating between his current and seemingly recalled past life. Nasruddin claimed definitively he was a Thakur, the second highest-ranking caste of Hindus in India. He also asserted he lived in Phargana, a nearby village. Nasruddin stated his name was actually Hardev Baksh Singh, and recalled experiencing death when a spear was thrust through the ribs on the left side of his chest during a fight over cattle. Nasruddin's statements, including those above and many others, corresponded exactly with the life of a man called Hardev Baksh Singh, a Thakur landowner in Phargana, India. Hardev had indeed become involved in a quarrel over some cattle. The fight soon became violent, and his adversary drove a spear through Hardev's left upper chest, killing him. The autopsy report provided Stevenson confirmation of the correlation between Nasruddin's birthmark and the location of the fatal spear wound in Hardev Baksh Singh.

Further remarkable in this case was Nasruddin's Thakur-like behavior. Even though Nasruddin was born and raised as a Muslim, he always considered himself to be Hindu. He also thought of himself as one of particular distinction, as might be expected of one in the high-ranking Thakur-caste. For example, Nasruddin refused to participate in menial labor activities, such as collecting cow dung for fuel, which most village boys in India undertook to support their families without question. He also resisted acceptance of the Islamic religion, and would not say Islamic prayers or go to the mosque with his family.

The case of Necip Unlutaskiran[224]

Necip Unlutaskiran was born in Adana, Turkey in 1951. As a young child, Necip Unlutaskiran claimed his real name was actually Necip Budak, and he stated he lived in the city of Mersin, about 80 kilometers from Adana. Necip recalled his death from his previous life being attributed to stabbing, and each of his prominent birthmarks corresponded with locations he recalled being stabbed in his former life. Necip also recalled leaving children behind in his former life and begged his mother to take him to see them.

Necip's grandfather eventually took the boy to Mersin where Necip accurately identified several members of Necip Budak's family. They further confirmed the accuracy of Necip's statements about the life of Necip Budak. Necip Budak had been repeatedly stabbed with a knife and died of his wounds at a hospital where the wounds were noted in an autopsy report. Stevenson compared the autopsy report with Necip's birthmarks and remarked of his findings that Necip's case exceeded all other spontaneous past-life recall cases where biological indications of reincarnation were present and for which supporting medical documentation was available to study and make comparisons between the wounds of the deceased and the birthmarks of the living.

Further remarkable in this case was Necip's admission his previous personality had stabbed his wife in the leg, leaving her with a scar. Necip Budak's widow admitted the truth of this statement and provided visual confirmation to some of Stevenson's escorting females in a private backroom during their investigation.

The case of Hanumant Saxena of India[225]

Hanumant Saxena was born in Uttar Pradesh, India, in 1955. Hanumant was born with a large birthmark on the lower part of his chest near the midline. The birthmark was irregular in shape and included a pattern of several similar birthmarks situated close to one another. When Hanumant was about three years old, he began talking about a past life he had recalled living in which his name was Maha Ram. Hanumant recalled being shot in the chest as Maha Ram, and pointed to the location on his chest where his birthmarks were prominently located.

Stevenson and his team of researchers discovered Maha Ram was born and lived in the same village as Hanumant, and had lived from approximately 1905 to 28 September 1954, when he was fatally shot in the chest by a shotgun at close range. The autopsy report showed nearly exact correspondence between Hanumant's birthmarks and the shotgun pellet-wounds that had killed Maha Ram.

Hanumant Saxena made further statements that proved to be correct about the life of Maha Ram, and when he visited Maha Ram's home, he recognized family, friends and places that had been familiar to Maha Ram. Hanumant continued talking about his previous life as Maha Ram until he was approximately six years old; however, he also liked visiting Maha Ram's house and mother, who still lived there, and continued doing so until he was ten years old.

The case of Dellal Beyaz of Turkey[226]

Dellal Beyaz was born in Samandag, Turkey, in July 1970. Dellal had a substantial birthmark on the crown of her head that oozed for days after her birth like an unhealed wound. As a young girl, Dellal described having lived a previous life in Kavash, about 30 kilometers from Samandag. Dellal recalled her death in that life as having occurred while she was hanging clothes out to dry along a clothesline on the roof of her house, when she stepped backwards and fell through a hole in the roof.

Dellal's statements closely matched the life and death of a woman named Zehide Kose who had died as described by Dellal. Zehide fell through an unprotected stairwell while hanging out clothes, landed on her head on the concrete floor below, and died of her wounds. Dr. Stevenson confirmed the fatal injury and location through a review of Zehide's medical records, which corresponded closely with Dellal's birthmark and location.

The case of Mehment Karaytu of Turkey[227]

Mehmet Karaytu was born in the village of Kavakli, near Adana, Turkey, in 1931. Mehmet was born with a triangular-shaped birthmark located on his lower back. At age three, Mehmet began describing a previous life he had lived as 'Haydar Karadol.' A friend had killed Haydar after an altercation attributed to alcohol consumption. Haydar's friend stabbed Haydar in the lower back with a kitchen knife. The shape of Mehmet's birthmark corresponded with the triangular profile such a knife wound would cause, and the location of Mehmet's birthmark corresponded with that of Haydar's fatal wound.

The case of Ma Win Tar of Burma[228]

In 1962, Ma Win Tar who was born in Burma with severe defects of both hands. Several of Ma's fingers were missing while others were only loosely attached to her hands at birth and had to be amputated. In addition to these birth defects, there were also

113

three depressions around her left wrist, which appeared as though a rope had been tightly wound around her arm. At less than two years of age, Ma started talking and shortly began describing a previous life as a Japanese soldier assigned to Burma. As she grew older she insisted she was Japanese, not Burmese, and complained that Burmese food was too spicy. Ma also exhibited mannerisms that were appropriate for Japanese but highly inappropriate for Burmese, such as slapping. Ma's spontaneous memories of her previous life as a Japanese soldier included being captured by Burmese villagers, tied to a tree and burned alive. One might associate the seeming rope marks on Ma's wrists as a birth defect attributable to being tied to a tree at the point of death in her last life; however, Ma's recollections of the Japanese soldier's manner of death did not necessarily account for the birth defects on both of her hands.

The case of Maung Aung Htoo of Burma[(229)]

Maung Aung Htoo was born with deformed hands and feet in Burma shortly after World War II. Maung began speaking of his past life as a Japanese soldier at age three, and displayed mannerisms, preferences, and characteristics typical of Japanese people vice Burmese, such as food preferences, high work ethic, and insensitivity to pain. Maung recalled his death as a Japanese soldier; claiming mutinous soldiers in his own unit had tied him to a tree and chopped off his fingers and toes.

The case of Maung Hla Hsaung of Burma[(230)]

Maung Hla Hsaung was also born with deformed hands and feet in Burma following World War II. When Maung first began speaking, he did so in an unknown strange language, as reported by his Burmese parents, though later he began to speak Burmese. When Maung was almost three years old he started describing a former life he recalled living in Japan, and he frequently asked to be allowed to return to Japan. Maung also displayed mannerisms, preferences, and characteristics that were typical of Japanese but not so for Burmese, such as a preference for long trousers instead of the Burmese Longyi, a preference for sweet vice spicy foods, insensitivity to pain, a tendency to be cruel, and role playing as a soldier – an oddity for his family and culture.

Hypnotic Past-Life Therapy

Hypnotic states are normal, everyday states of consciousness, typified by concentrating on one sensory input, such as a hypno-therapist's instructions, to the exclusion of other sensory inputs. Examples of everyday hypnotic states of mind include daydreaming and even watching television. During these periods our attention is concentrated or transfixed on one item specifically and thereby our awareness is turned inwards; the same as occurs during hypnosis. Being a normal experience, hypnosis is not dangerous and indeed is often used for therapeutic purposes. Hypno-therapists noted therapeutic effects could be realized by seemingly regressing people to recall memories of earlier times in their life where they had experienced a trauma. Thereby, in a safe, benign environment, under the guidance of a therapist, a subject could again face troubling issues, usually from their point of origin, and often achieve satisfactory resolutions and overcome issues, phobias, and other concerns that may have plagued them for years.

Using conventional hypnosis to regress clients back into childhood to work on long-term issues, many hypno-therapists in the 1960s (and earlier) experimentally stumbled upon what appeared to be memories of their clients' past lives. During a past-life regression, a subject only needs to be in the lightest, alpha brain-wave-state of altered awareness, the same as a normal hypnosis session. This can be achieved through a light hypnosis induction, which normally takes 10 to 15 minutes, although meditation or other personal techniques of inwardly focusing one's thoughts on past-life memories can also be used to similar effect.[231] Whether or not the memories recalled during these sessions were legitimate, clients often achieved amazing therapeutic effects from these past life recall sessions, which further encouraged hypno-therapists to incorporate the procedure into their regular program. Indeed some researchers found that some of their clients who had failed to respond to conventional treatment therapies lasting many years time often made dramatic improvements following only a few sessions of past-life therapy.[232] From these successes, pioneering therapists, many of whom had medical credentials, began assembling a large case file from which to begin drawing conclusions regarding the possible validity of past-life recall through hypnosis.

The late Dr. Helen Wambach noted of the unique character of past life hypnotherapy sessions, clients experiencing a past life during hypnosis tended to experience deeper and more intense levels of emotion than mere visual imagery.[233] For many hypnotic subjects the emotional level of the experience imparted more meaning to them than the intellectual component. These experiences seemed to be more real than mere dreams; they were intense and, at least for the client, had meaning. This meaning may be expressed through emotive statements, crying or tears, and subjects under hypnosis tended to have an increased feeling of certainty about the accuracy of their reporting; thus, when they reported they experienced death by drowning, for example, they re-experienced the death and its unique pain as if for real.[234]

However, after re-experiencing the death event under hypnosis, most patients were able to overcome their fear of drowning, for example, seemingly because they were able to recall from whence the fear had originated and the mere act of doing so had allowed the fear to resolve itself.

In contrast to spontaneous past-life recall, during past-life hypnotic regression clients may show striking changes of speech, behavior, mood, and emotion. They may claim a convincing sense of vividness and proclaim certainty as they express memories of being in other locations and periods of history. They may speak with foreign accents or even foreign languages, or alternately, be able to write a foreign, previously unknown script. They will assert they have different names and identities, and may even claim to belong to the opposite sex. Most often, they display a trove of information that is surprisingly appropriate for the personalities they claim to be.[235]

After helping hundreds or even thousands of patients to experience a past-life during a hypnotherapy session, many hypnotherapists have wondered whether there was any truth or validity to the hypnosis-induced 'recall' of these past lives. Indeed, many stories would seem plausible for reasons that shall be further discussed shortly. Of note, hypnosis allows a subject to experience enhanced recall (i.e. hypermnesia) perhaps through their focused effort of concentration and the power of suggestion while in the hypnotic state. However, researchers have found this enhanced recall increases both the client's level of certainty of accuracy in their reporting as well as the amount of information provided, but does *not* necessarily increase the accuracy of provided information: an increased precedence of accurate recall is generally counterweighted by an increased number of errors as well.[236] Thus, hypnosis is not a truth serum so past life accounts obtained during hypnotic regression should not be accepted at face value, or as 100 percent accurate.

Still, there have been many hypnotic past-life regression sessions that have produced unique information, which has proven both impossibly accurate and completely obscure such that it would have been impossible for the client to know the provided information via any normal means.[237] A number of these cases have been independently investigated to ensure no fraud was involved and the information was indeed both obscure and accurate. Of past-life hypnotherapy cases, hypno-therapist Joe Keeton, who has conducted hundreds of past-life regressions, believes that only about two in every hundred regressions may not be the product of imagination and fantasy, and thereby deserve special consideration.[238] Special note will be applied to a few of those well-documented cases, below.

However, as a genre of information to consider, here are a few more reasons to take the idea and genre of past-life hypnotic recall seriously:

1) Few people are aware of Dr. Raymond Moody's groundbreaking research on near-death experiences so it should be expected that a good number of hypnotherapy clients would also be unaware of the NDE phenomenon. When clients are hypnotically regressed back to a previous life and then taken through their death and departure scene again, the descriptions of those clients' experiences at death match, on par with, the reported statements of people who have experienced an NDE.[239] For those persons without prior knowledge of NDEs, this limits the normal opportunities a person under hypnosis would be able to recall a piece of information acquired via normal means – such as reading, television, hearing a similar account from others, etc. – and then projecting it as their own recalled experience. One must wonder

then, how a person would acquire this information unless he/she was actually recalling, through the aid of hypnosis, what had occurred to him/her immediately following death in a past life. Significantly more will be discussed on this topic in the next chapter.

2) As will be noted in a later section in this chapter, pure fantasy has little part to play in hypnotic past-life recall. Subjects under hypnosis do not tend to recall past lives as kings or other famous persons. Indeed most lives are boring, unglamorous lives, typified of the lowest class of society; i.e. the highest percentage of the population throughout the history of mankind. Wambach studied this phenomenon, and reported on the statistical significance of past-life recall as being preferential to investigating the merits of any singular case. In particular, she was troubled by the idea one could plausibly fantasize under hypnosis about being born and dying as an infant or young child. Surely a more reasonable fantasy should include riches and fame. However, Wambach knew the incidence of infant mortality approached 50 percent in both primitive societies and during past centuries before modern medicine increased the odds of survival for both children and childbearing mothers. Therefore, statistics insisted if past-life recall under hypnosis had any basis in fact, people must indeed recall instances of living as a child who died before the age of five, which was indeed born out in her research.[240]

3) Additionally, the subject of xenoglossy will also be discussed later in this chapter. Briefly, xenoglossy refers to an ability to speak a foreign language, usually while under hypnosis during a past-life recall session, for which the person has had no prior exposure. This is a powerful level of evidence that may lend special credence to the phenomenon of past-life recall under

hypnosis, though the incidence rate is exceptionally low. Still, in the words of William James, these 'white crows' need not be numerous; they merely need to exist to lend exceptional validity to the idea of reincarnation.

4) Finally, there is the repetitive and 'common-sensical' character of past-life reviews that emotes its own influence on the reader and researcher. In 1950, English psychologist Dr. Alexander Cannon, who had used hypnotic past life regression on more than 1,300 clients in his practice, admitted that for years the theory of reincarnation had been an anathema to him, and resultantly he tried his best to disprove the idea at every opportunity. He even argued with his clients while they were under hypnosis in an attempt to make them admit they were speaking nonsense about their recalled experience. Over the years, however, he eventually realized these stories remained consistent no matter the client's personal or religious beliefs on the topic prior to the hypnosis experience, and after investigating more than a thousand cases of past-life recall, he admitted to himself there must be such a thing as reincarnation.[241]

Case Studies of Hypnotically-Recalled Past Lives

The case of Laurel Dilman of the USA[242]

Past-life psychotherapist Dr. Linda Tarazi conducted exhaustive research on one of the so-called 'white crows,' hypnotically regressed client Laurel Dilman (pseudonym). Dilman volunteered as a member of a group to be the subject of eight past life sessions between June 1977 and January 1978, during which she recalled a former life as Antonia Michaela Maria Ruiz de Prado, born November 1555 on the island of Hispaniola as the daughter of a Spanish officer, Antonio and his German wife, Erika. During these initial sessions, Dilman, an American who did not speak Spanish and had never visited Spain, provided significant and highly specific information about this past life memory, which upon initial review by Tarazi proved entirely true.

Seeking to gain better fidelity of the possible validity of this hypnotically recalled past life, Tarazi convinced Dilman to undergo a further 36 past life regression sessions between June 1981 and March 1983. The purpose of those later sessions was to seek even more, highly specific details that could help prove or disprove whether this past life memory was based on fact or fantasy. With Dilman's memories of these facts in hand, Tarazi embarked on an exhaustive search for errors and inconsistencies in Laurel's memory that involved hundreds of hours of research in two dozen libraries and universities, as well as consultations with historians, archivists and university professors who specialized in Spanish history for that period, and even a personal visit to Cuenca, Spain, where Tarazi was able to examine the town's archives and historical Spanish Inquisition records.

Based on this research, Tarazi verified more than 100 facts from Antonia's story, many of which were quite obscure. Tarazi concluded at least 50 of Dilman's reported facts concerning the life of Antonio could have been easily discernible through consultations with history books or encyclopedias. Another 30 facts, however, were only discovered with significant difficulty in rare books found in specialized research libraries. Further, over a dozen facts were only published in Spanish, and a few facts were not even published at all, but could be confirmed from the Municipal and Diocesan Archive records in Cuenca, Spain. Of the more than one hundred reported facts of Antonia's life, none proved to be false!

Some examples of Dilman's reported facts from the life of Antonia included:

- The date of the first publication of the Edict of Faith on the Island of Hispaniola;
- Spanish laws for shipping to the Indies;
- Types and details of ships used in the Mediterranean and the Atlantic during the time period of Antonia's life;
- Dates and contents of the Spanish Indexes of prohibited books and how those indexes differed from the Roman Index;
- Names of priests executed in England between 1581 and 1582, and their method of execution.

Of significant interest, two of the facts were initially not supported by archival authorities in Spain, but upon further research eventually proved to be correct. The first was the location of the tribunal of the Inquisition in Cuenca, Spain. Dilman described it as a castle standing above the city of Cuenca. However, the government tourist office in Cuenca provided a photograph of the Inquisition's building that differed from Laurel's description. However, Tarazi found an obscure history book on Cuenca, published only in Spanish, which revealed the Inquisition had moved to the castle in Cuenca in December 1583, five months before Antonia's arrival in Cuenca, which fit her description exactly. The second was a reference to a college at Cuenca for which no reference was seemingly available to confirm. After much difficulty, however, Tarazi found a century-old reference, again only in Spanish, which quoted yet other obscure Spanish sources from the Sixteenth century that described a college that was founded in Cuenca in the mid-Sixteenth century.

A third oddity that stood out from the history books was that although there were normally three Inquisitors at a tribunal,

Dilman had mentioned only two having been present. Tarazi found the Episcopal archives in Cuenca noted during the period 1584-1588 – the entire period Antonia lived in Cuenca – there had indeed been only two Inquisitors at Cuenca. Tarazi concluded that considering the number of sources and their sheer obscurity combined with the inherent difficulty of extracting the pertinent information from those sources, it seemed improbable that Dilman could have acquired all of the information through some duplicitous means. When the fact that some of these sources were in a foreign language Dilman could not speak and only located in a foreign country where Dilman had never traveled, then the chances dropped to the realm of impossibility.[243]

The case of G.M. of Australia[244]

Past-life psychotherapist Peter Ramster conducted exhaustive research on another one of those 'white crows,' hypnotically regressed client "G. M.," an Australian woman who had never traveled outside of Australia. Under hypnosis, G. M. recalled living as Rose Duncan, a young woman who was born in Somerset, England, in 1765 and died of pneumonia in 1782. Under hypnosis, G. M. provided many facts that could be checked concerning Rose's life and her recalled historical period in England, including descriptions of the area, buildings, towns and villages, daily life and clothing, and certain verifiable personalities in 18th century England. After researching as many of these facts as possible in research libraries in Australia and some other resources that were available via phone call, such as historians and archivists, Ramster conducted a fact-finding mission to England, accompanied by G.M. and Dr. Basil Cottle of Bristol University, UK. As with the case of Antonia, Rose Duncan's case produced facts that proved to be both amazingly obscure and accurate.

Ramster found that some of the villages that G. M. recalled no longer even existed, but could be confirmed on older maps of England. Other details of G.M.'s hypnotically recalled life were confirmed in England in museums, historical libraries, and in the unpublished parish records of Somerset, England.

For example, G. M. had repeatedly referred to a "tallet" from her previous life, a word not referenced in any modern dictionaries. However, in the library of Taunton, Somerset, England, a dictionary of obsolete, West Country English words noted the word was used specifically during the time period and location of Rose's life and meant a room under a roof, such as a loft. The word was no longer used, and indeed had never been used anywhere except in the West Country of England. This information showed G. M. had used the otherwise unknown word correctly while under hypnosis and referring to Rose's recalled life.

G. M. made frequent mention of a particular abbey near Rose's home in England and its surroundings. The abbey was described as surrounded by marshy ground, and even G. M.'s descriptions that were no longer evident later proved true, including certain prominent paving stones, pyramids and hills and other features that were used by historical Druids. For those items that were no longer present for verification, Ramster found pertinent evidence in a historical manuscript on the subject, printed in England around 1794.

Further, G. M.'s description of the clothes worn by the Druids that frequented the area between 1775-1780, and the way they filed up a nearby hill in a spiral line was confirmed by Geoffrey Ashe, a local historian, though the mere fact Druids had assembled in the local area of Glastonbury had been unknown to the university historian from Bristol, England.

G.M. also described an establishment known as The Pilgrim's Inn, situated near a humpbacked-shape hill she had called Wearyall Hill. Ramster eventually found an inn of equivalent description that was now known as "The George and Pilgrim," and ascertained it had been known as The Pilgrim's Inn in the 18th century.

While visiting the location described as Rose Duncan's former home, G.M. pointed to the spot where she claimed five houses used to stand, one of which had sold cider. An area homeowner confirmed five houses had stood on the site but were torn down 25 years prior, including one that had been a cider house some 150 years prior. Subsequent to this discussion, Ramster consulted an 18th century survey map of the area and found five houses were indeed annotated at the location G. M. had identified.

Finally, G.M. also recalled a neighbor of Rose Duncan's who had stolen some paving stones from the local abbey and then used them as flooring material in his cottage. G.M. located the neighbor's cottage, which had since been turned into a chicken shed. During an inspection of the chicken shed, Ramster found hidden beneath a thick layer of dirt and bird droppings stones that matched those at the abbey. Under hypnosis in Australia prior to their trip, G.M. had even described and drawn the stone mason's markings for the stolen, blue-gray abbey stones, which were indeed found in the chicken coop located on the other side of the Earth from G.M.'s home. The markings were described as three vertical lines on the top left hand corner and a large spiral on the right hand side of the stones. Again, personal inspection had proved G. M.'s hypnotic recollection of Rose's memories were accurate. Ramster concluded that G.M.'s ability to find a specific stone, previously drawn months prior in Sydney, found in a location and country she had never visited was a feat far beyond the element of chance.[245]

The case of Doris Williams of the USA[246]

Past life Therapist D. Scott Rogo uncovered at least six cases through past life regression that exhibited enough unique proof to justify a belief in reincarnation, including the case of Doris Williams who had a life-long fear of deep water, ocean travel and small boats.

Under hypnotic regression, Doris recalled a former life she had lived as Stephen Weart Blackwell, a clerk with the Brown Shipping Co. located at 167 West State Street in Trenton, New Jersey. Doris recalled Stephan had wanted to go to medical school but his mother had denied the request, forcing him into his current line of work, which involved frequent trips to England for business. During one fateful trip, Doris recalled Stephan was a 43-year old passenger on the Titanic on its maiden voyage, and she recalled the events that occurred in Stephan's memory on April 14, 1912, the night the Titanic hit an iceberg and subsequently sank. Doris provided in great detail the clothes Stephan had worn, the exact place where he had stood on the deck of the Titanic as passengers waited for lifeboats, and the sounds he had heard, including hysterical crying and oddly complacent music as the ship went down.

Most of the details Doris provided were later verified by Rogo's investigation. As might be expected, some of the details were relatively common knowledge. Further, the presence of a certain Stephen Blackwell on the Titanic could have been discerned by anyone with access to a library since it was found in Walter Lord's bestseller, *A Night to Remember*. However, other details Doris provided were quite obscure. For instance, Stephan Blackwell's employment was only listed in a half-century old US Senate investigative report on the Titanic's sinking, which confirmed he had indeed been employed by a Brown Shipley Company, once located at the address Doris had recalled.

The case of Jenny Cockell of the USA[247]

Jenny Cockell was born in 1953, and while still a child began spontaneously recalling a previous life she had lived as 'Mary' in the small village of Malahide near Dublin, Ireland, from about 1898 until the 1930s. In 1987, Jenny began seeing a past-life hypnotic therapist who helped her explore these memories of living as Mary over a series of sessions. Jenny thereby recalled the location and physical description of the small cottage Mary had lived in, as well as the names of her husband and four children. In 1989, Jenny took a trip to Malahide, Ireland, and found the location where Mary's cottage had been and soon found neighbors who recalled the woman, Mary Sutton, who had lived in the cottage and died during childbirth in 1932. One of Mary's children, who Jenny was able to meet during this trip, was convinced Jenny was his mother reincarnated because of memories Jenny described of his life as a child that he felt no one could have known except for his own mother.

Xenoglossy[248]

The term xenoglossy was originally coined by Charles Richet and means an occurrence of speaking a language without having prior knowledge of that language. There are two subcategories of xenoglossy, including recitative and responsive xenoglossy. As with the more familiar term, speaking in tongues, recitative xenoglossy involves the use of spontaneous phrases or passages of a language but an inability to understand what has been said or understand questions in the foreign language to be able to respond with answers in the same language. Responsive xenoglossy refers to the more important subcategory that will be considered here, which is an ability to converse intelligently in the otherwise unknown foreign language, and implies an understanding between the subject and questioner during the period of responsiveness.

Because native fluency and command of a language requires practice, repetition, and generally some period of immersion, an authentic case of responsive xenoglossy would provide important evidence of the survival of human consciousness after death and the transmittal of that consciousness into a new life as a logical means to explain how such command of an otherwise unknown foreign language could have been passed from one life to another.[249]

Past life researchers rarely obtain even cursory evidence of xenoglossy, however. The late Dr. Wambach noted only a very small percentage of people are able to respond well enough to hypnotism to write or speak in a foreign language from one of their past lives.[250] Dr. Paul Cunningham further discerned subjects under hypnosis have a slower rate of speech, use fewer words and have longer periods of latency than comparable subjects in the normal waking state, which may further explain the complaints many naysayers propose concerning xenoglossy; i.e. even if a person speaks in an unknown language, he/she tends to use few words, and may have a slow, disjointed pattern of speech.[251] This phenomenon is noted in many of the cases studies, below, and is used as a common example by naysayers as to why the few hypnotically induced xenoglossy cases that have been published do not seem overly credible. Therefore I will reserve judgment at this point and allow the reader to come to his/her own conclusion as to the validity of this piece of evidence in its applicability for reincarnation.

Case Studies of Xenoglossy

The case of Uttara Huddar of India[252]

Uttara Huddar was born in Nagpu, India in 1941. Between 1974-1979, a split-based female personality that called herself Sharada Chattopadhaya, spontaneously manifested and took over Uttara's body for periods between two and forty-three days at a time.

When Sharada first manifested, she did not realize she had died and returned in another person's body. She also did not recognize Uttara's family and friends, and provided details of the names and places in Bengal with which she had been familiar as Sharada.

Uttara, who spoke only Marathi, suddenly spoke fluent Bengali with a native accent during the periods that Sharada assumed control of Uttara's body. Stevenson and his team of investigators found that Sharada's Bengali was free of all English-loan words and had more Sanskrit words than did modern Bengali. Bengali of that description would typify the language, as it existed between the 18th and 19th centuries. Sharada was also unfamiliar with electrical appliances, gas stoves, fountain pens, or modern vehicles, which had all been developed after the industrial revolution, signifying Sharada likely lived between 1810-1830.

Stevenson lent this case of xenoglossy extra credibility as a possible case of reincarnation because if Uttara had fraudulently learned Bengali, then she would have acquired a modern version of Bengali and not the language as it had existed 150 years prior.

The case of Jensen Jacoby of the USA[253]

Jensen Jacoby was a male personality manifested by a 37-year old American housewife under hypnosis during eight sessions conducted between 1955-56. Jensen spoke Swedish, which the American housewife could not. Indeed she had never even been exposed to the Swedish language. Stevenson's investigation concluded there was no mundane way to explain the woman's ability to speak and respond in the unfamiliar foreign language while hypnotized and speaking as Jensen. Jensen would generally respond in English to English-initiated questions and in Swedish to Swedish- initiated questions.

A transcript of these sessions showed Jensen used approximately 60 Swedish words in conversation before Swedish-speaking interlocutors introduced the words, and about 100 Swedish words altogether. While Jensen's Swedish grammar was not perfectly fluent, the pronunciation was judged by some authorities to have displayed a native Swedish accent. This seems important because in order to adopt a perfect accent, one must be exposed to the language for an extended period of immersion, generally from a very young age. Stevenson added in order to converse in a language one must practice it, which also implied the Jensen personality had used Swedish during its prior lifetime. However, Stevenson was still hesitant to definitively connect Jensen's possible prior life to the American housewife's current life as a definitive case of reincarnation.

The case of Rosemary of England[254]

In 1931, Rosemary, a young girl from Blackpool, England, began to speak in an ancient Egyptian dialect. While speaking ancient Egyptian, she claimed to be the personality of Telika-

Ventiu, a Babylonian princess and Pharaoh Amenhotep III's wife, who had lived about 3,300 years prior. During more than a thousand language tests, the girl spoke about 5,000 phrases and short sentences in the old Egyptian language. They were recorded phonetically and the first 800 of them were later identified and translated by an Egyptologist. He claimed Rosemary's speech substantially and consistently conformed to what Egyptologists knew of the ancient Egyptian tongue, though the language itself had long since gone extinct. Three books on the Rosemary case have been published and two gramophone discs of the xenoglossy case were recorded.

The case of 'Gretchen' [(255)]

'Gretchen,' was a female personality manifested by an American housewife under hypnosis during multiple hypnotic sessions conducted between 1970-74. Gretchen spoke only German and used an estimated 206 German words in conversation before German-speaking interlocutors introduced the words. However, Stevenson found most of Gretchen's responses to posed questions were short utterances or affirmations to an interviewer's questions; basically a simple repetition, using the questioner's own words in declarative response format. Gretchen's German accent was also imperfect and some words were incorrect Anglicized versions of German words, such as "schicken" for chicken.

The case of the 'infant of Lubeck' [(256)]

While not a normal case of xenoglossy, Christian Friedrich Heinecken, known as the 'infant of Lubeck' reportedly talked within a few hours of his birth in 1721. The King of Denmark was intrigued by the young child's feats and had him brought to

Copenhagen for inspection in 1724. Shortly thereafter, the child fell ill and predicted his own death within the year. He died at age four.

An ability to speak at birth implies far more than mere genius talent, but rather a pre-existing ability to speak as the ability must have originated from somewhere. Such might be possible through the manifestation of a prior personality and that personality's itinerant language capability manifesting unduly early in the newly incarnated baby. A similar phenomenon was also suggested in the case of Maung Hla Hsaung, the child in Burma (previously described) who initially spoke in an unknown foreign language [implied Japanese] but later learned to speak Burmese.

Statistical Analysis of Hypnotically-Recalled Past Lives

Rather than choose a single past life subject to study in depth, and determine whether the revealed facts corresponded with the historical record, the late Dr. Helen Wambach chose to study a large group of hypnotically-regressed subjects and then examine various common phenomenon from their past life experiences, and compare the incidence of the group's reported phenomenon to known statistics from the historical periods in question.[257] As previously noted, Wambach did not trust subjects under hypnosis to produce minute details that would stand up to intense scrutiny, but felt there was unique validity in the emotions and, more importantly, the meta-data, or general impressions of her clients' and test subjects' experiences.

For example, even though 78 percent of her first group of hypnotically regressed subjects was female, the group as a whole recalled past lives with a sexual distribution that was roughly divided fifty-fifty between male and female. Indeed, throughout all of her study groups, Wambach found that regardless of the sex her clients had in their current lifetime, they split perfectly into 50.3 percent male and 49.7 percent female lives when regressed to their past lives.[258] This was almost exactly what the historical record would demand, regardless of the time period, and showed there was little influence by fantasy, which would have tended to provide past life memories of the same-sex as the subject recalling the life. Wambach felt this finding was the strongest objective evidence she had discovered during her extended experiment, and led her to conclude her subjects were actually tapping into some real knowledge of the past.[259]

In addition to sex distribution, Wambach also compared her subjects' recollections of their wealth/status, race, clothes, foot wear, food and eating utensils, money and supplies, population, and death experiences. In regards to the former, Wambach found less than ten percept of the population of past life recall subjects recalled a past life as a member of the upper class, whereas 59-77 percent tended to recall past lives as members of the lowest class. Wambach questioned if past life recall was merely fantasy, then why would a person choose to fantasize about such mundane and harsh lives? Wambach found of the average seven percent who remembered upper class past lives that these lives were not usually considered to be particularly pleasant experiences. The stressors and drama unique to the upper crust, political leaders, and wealthy were quite unpleasant memories for most, whereas some of the happiest lives were ironically lived by those of peasants and primitives.[260]

Five of Wambach's subjects described themselves wearing pants in the Caucasus Mountains around 2,000 BC, and having white skin and light colored hair; none of which they accepted as plausible according to their own view of history. However, Wambach's later research showed their subconscious had actually presented them with a more accurate picture of life in the Caucasus

Mountains around 2,000 BC than their conscious awareness would accept as valid. Wambach concluded that when our hypnotic experiences of the past life contrast with preconceived notions of the truth, and yet hold up under close scrutiny then we should reconsider the idea that past-life recall is only fantasy.[261]

The mode of death recalled by Wambach's subjects also matched closely with the expected mode of death for each of the time periods measured. As a median, 55-73 percent of recalled deaths were due to natural causes, 12-17 percent were due to accidents and 13-24 percent were due to violence, depending on the time period studied.[262]

The death experience Wambach's subjects recalled also matched closely with the template identified by Dr. Raymond Moody's research on the near-death experience. Wambach further concluded of this that the universality of the recalled death experience suggested that prior knowledge, such as through NDE research, could not account for the level of unanimity in reporting between all of her subjects. While some may have read Moody's books, certainly all had not and yet they *all* reported a uniform death experience similar to that found by NDE researchers.[263] Further, Wambach found to her surprise that her clients consistently reported that death had been the best part of the past-life hypnotic recall experience. Not only did her clients report the process of death was pleasant, but they realized an intense relief when their spirit was released from the body and gained complete freedom once again.[264] Her clients were no longer afraid of death, having experienced this phenomenon.

Conclusion

I find the philosophy of James Dillet Freeman to be exactly in line with my original concern about organized Western religion, and certainly applicable to the topic of reincarnation. Freeman's argument was thus,

> *Consider two children. One of them is born into a rich family, a happy family, a harmonious family. He's brought up in a secure world. He gets a good education. He marries. He has happy children of his own. He has good health all his life, or most of it, and at sixty, seventy, or eighty, he dies peacefully in bed. Another child is born ill, half-starved, maimed in body and mind. Maybe he lives for minutes – or maybe for hours or months or a few years. He's abused all that time, twisted in mind, taught to rob and kill – or maybe he's brought up in a savage world of civil war and trouble and is murdered in his youth. That one of these two turns out to be a moral, law-abiding citizen, and the other turns out to be a thief and a murderer cannot possibly provide a basis for eternal judgment.*[265]

Further still are words in some of the world's most influential religions that could only be interpreted as supporting the concept of reincarnation. Consider in the New Testament St Paul's letter to the Galatians 6:7, "Whatsoever a man soweth, that shall he also reap." Unless this warning is interpreted as fallible, then it proclaims strongly of the concept of rebirth because one life is plainly insufficient to prove this assertion correct, and indeed is equivalent to the Eastern Religious idea of karma.

The same could be noted of St. John's Revelation 13:10, "He that leadeth into captivity shall go into captivity; he that killeth with the sword must be killed with the sword." Given the fact that many soldiers have died quietly in their beds of old age, this statement would be robbed of any meaning if not for the possibility of future retribution in a subsequent life where one who had previously killed, with a sword or otherwise, could then be killed in a similar violent manner. The same argument could be extended to any other violent act humans commit against one another: rape, robbery, murder, or any such injustice; not everyone who rapes will be raped in their lifetime; not everyone who murders will be subsequently murdered. However, the possibility of subsequent lifetimes to experience the consequences of prior sins would certainly allow these passages in the Bible to bear out truthfully.

Still, such a cut-and-dry interpretation of karma should not be interpreted as an impossible and never-ending cycle of retribution for one's past sins. Dr. Michael Newton concluded from his thousands of hours of work studying pre- and post-life examinations of subjects through their inter-life period that the essential purpose of reincarnation was self-improvement.[266] Russian past life therapist Varvara Ivanova noted that specific difficulties would crop up continually in successive lifetimes until one learns how to overcome the adversities they are continually facing in life.[267] Thus, if one wants to rid oneself of the current difficulties they are facing, the surest answer is to face those difficulties head on and deal with them now in their current life, no matter how (temporarily) painful such a course of action may seem. If one hopes ever to break out of the cycle of reincarnation and having to face the same problems over and over, such action can only be accomplished in the present point of *Now*.[268]

Newton found that souls accept a compact with the Universe upon acceptance of a new life on Earth and as such they will not generally remember their previous lives on Earth, or even their true connection to their Oversoul and life in the spirit world. This is because learning from a blank slate is better and more meaningful than knowing in advance what could happen as a consequence of one's actions.[269] Similarly, if people were cognizant of their past deeds and mistakes, they might pay too much attention to the past rather than trying out new approaches to similar problem sets to apply to their current life. The new life must be taken seriously, as if it were one's only life, and thus considered by a human to be its only chance to experience all that is and solve those issues that it faces in the current life.

That certainly seems to be the most plausible explanation for the phenomenon of reincarnation to me. When a child spontaneously recalls a past life, invariably because of a traumatic and violent death, the recalled life is due to the emotional residue left with the spirit and carried over between lives. A 'veil of amnesia' is part-and-parcel of the so-called compact with the Universe, and usually prevents souls from recalling their previous lives, but is imperfect in these cases because of the power of the emotional residue from the traumatic death experience. The fact that emotional energy could also affect the next life through carried-over birthmarks and birth defects from prior wounds shows the power of that energy. In the cases of Japanese soldiers reborn as Burmese natives, one is given a unique insight into the workings of the Universe to see (limitedly) how a previous karmic debt might be, at least partially, repaid in the next successive life. In these cases Japanese soldiers who had abused Burmese natives during the course of their assignments in the country were given an opportunity to live as the natives they had abused in their prior life: the debt was related to but not exact in that they did not live as the Burmese natives they had abused during the same, overlapping time period.

Beyond emotion-induced cracks in the veil of amnesia, the process of hypnosis can focus conscious attention into its subconscious and even super-conscious states, providing a person unique access to their previous lives, even if those memories are imperfect recollections or possibly even amalgamations of multiple lives thus limiting the exacting nature of the recall process. Wambach found it was exceptionally rare to be able to recall foreign languages used in those lives well enough to use them in a responsive manner, but the mere fact that a few case studies existed showed that the phenomenon was possible.

To further rectify the findings of this chapter, consider Wambach's findings to be quite significant: impressions via meta-data and emotions are the most significant, readily accessible and relevant data sets that can normally be gained through research on clients' hypnotically-recalled past lives. While some data may indeed be accurate, perhaps eerily so, the process of hypnosis does not increase the accuracy of reporting so it should not be considered a truth serum for the current life, much less for past lives. Only a few exceptional specimens are able to tap into their subconscious deeply enough to be able to speak or write in a foreign language used in one of those previous lives, and likewise only an exceptional few could tap an unimpeded fountain of true facts from those past lives that could stand up to intense scrutiny. Therefore, it is less reliable to dispel an entire genre of potential evidence simply because every reported 'fact' from a previous life does not prove correct under exhaustive research. Rather, the meta-data from those lives should be explored for applicability and utility in research to determine whether the reported lives are plausible, or could aid scientific research on an issue.

It should not be surprising therefore, that spontaneous recall produces likewise fallible results and facts, perhaps even more so given the absence of directed consciousness as is achieved under hypnosis. Still, the genre of research provides its own unique support to the subject of reincarnation, and is likewise supported by the meta-data and emotions experienced and recalled by the children-subjects who experience spontaneous recall. Like hypnotic recall subjects, one hundred percent correlation between remembered facts and the ground truth is unnecessary for these cases to also have significant merit as already argued.

A take-away from this chapter might be that one should reconsider their former notions of prejudice against those who are not like themselves. Indeed, as authorities later in this book will note, the average soul has lived hundreds, if not thousands, of lives on Earth and likely has lived as every race, sex, nationality, religion, and other discriminator that has ever existed. Therefore hating one who appears different than oneself is akin to hating one's own self since we have all been like that person in another life, for whatever purpose our karmic debt or Over-soul had required at that time, or will in a future lifetime. Further, there is always the karmic concern that to hate another today for who they are may actually incur a karmic debt of living one's next life as the subject of one's current wrath in order to understand better the feeling of being discriminated against. Consider the genre of reincarnation research is full of stories of former Nazi soldiers being reincarnated to live their next life as Jews so that they could better understand the unique issues of the people they had previously mistreated. If one hates something intensely in this lifetime, the chance exists of having to live as the subject of that hate in a future life, perhaps to gain a better perspective of the issue as a developing and experiencing soul.

A final take-away should almost assuredly not only mimic Wambach's finding that death was pleasant, but that death was most certainly not an end, but rather a continuation of life with a subtle movement from one chapter to the next. Indeed, this knowledge in itself may provide the internal courage one might need to face one's challenges *Now* to make the hard decisions needed to overcome a present fear given the reality that death cannot hurt one's actual existence. Imagine what you could do, for example, if you could put aside fear. Assuredly, all of life's stressors come from some form of fear and the drive to avoid or overcome it: fear of death and fear of competition, for example, are primary among those. If you can put aside those fears, there may be no limit to what you can achieve in this or the next life. From this higher, soul-based perspective, the nagging fear of death can be put aside and replaced with an acceptance that life holds the opportunity for spiritual transformation.[270]

Chapter Six

Life Between Lives

Introduction:

We saw in the previous chapter that during normal regression hypnotherapy sessions, doctors and other therapists accidentally stumbled upon past-life stories from their clients; many of whom reported events that cannot be explained by normal logic, and have led many to believe such could be signs of evidence for the concept of reincarnation. Similarly, doctors and therapists using past-life regression as part of their normal therapies also seem to have accidentally stumbled upon the inter-life period between successive mortal incarnations. Through a combination of accidental discovery and trial-and-error, hypno-therapists eventually developed a reliable means by which they could access the deepest recesses of human memories where these 'soul memories' reside, and by tapping those memories have developed a rather unique picture of the spirit world.

Indeed, if one can follow the logic and data introduced in this chapter, most of the concepts developed elsewhere in this book will begin to show correlation and agreement. My own journey to answer the questions I posed to myself at the beginning of this book suddenly seemed on the verge of realization, for example, following my first exposure to inter-life research. Prior to finding this important source of research material the path had seemed non-existent, but afterwards areas I needed to examine for future research, or even return to for follow-up consideration, became immediately clear. The path had finally been laid bare before my eyes through the work of such pioneering researchers as Dr. Michael Newton, Dr. Shakuntala Modi, Dr. Joel Whitton, and Messrs. Ian Lawton and Andy Tomlinson. This is by no means an exhaustive list of researchers in this genre, merely a representation of the primary researchers who heavily influenced my early research.

In order to understand how these soul memories are available for human recall, consider a psychological representation of the mind with multi-tiers of consciousness, with each of the hidden inner layers more inaccessible than the last.[271] In this model, the primary, outer layer would be the waking conscious mind where everyday experiences are processed and the mind engages in critical, analytical thinking. The first inner layer would then be the subconscious, which stores human experiences throughout one's lifetime, and through which hypno-therapists try to tap via hypnosis to recall those memories that may no longer be readily accessible to the experiencing, thinking-level of waking consciousness. While the notion is debatable, it would seem most past-life memories would also be stored in the subconscious as they are more easily and readily accessible than the next, deepest layer of consciousness.

The deepest inner layer would then be the super-conscious, which houses one's true eternal identity and by extension the human's direct connection to the spirit world; i.e. its soul or perhaps more precisely its *soul-mind*. Like the subconscious, the super-conscious retains memories of its life in the spirit world between incarnations, and is also accessible through hypnosis, though as will be noted shortly, it is not usually readily or easily accessible in comparison to the subconscious. Similar to a veil of amnesia, the super-conscious is quite isolated from normal, waking conscious access but it may still be influencing human experiences from behind the scene, similar to the subconscious' ability to affect human behaviors without conscious awareness. If this is true, then our super-conscious may well be ensuring that we follow a pre-determined 'life plan.' This could mean ensuring we are put into positions that will force us to experience certain events or make conscious decisions to resolve anticipated or preplanned crisis events in an effort to – ideally – resolve karmic issues, or perhaps more accurately to experience and develop according to our soul's need; i.e. the life plan. More shall be discussed on these topics in this chapter and elsewhere.

Dr. Michael Newton argued convincingly the super-conscious houses the human's true identity, and postulated it may be more than a level. The super-conscious may be the seat of the soul itself given that the super-conscious mind has access not only to our soul memories but also has a higher level of perspective and is a deeper source of wisdom on which we are free to call for assistance and guidance.[272]

The super-conscious' recalled memories of experiences in the incorporeal, soul-state were accidentally discovered when hypno-therapists conducted past-life recall therapy sessions with persons who were especially susceptible to hypnotic induction. Like a Bell Curve, a small percentage of the population, about 15 percent, may be significantly more or less susceptible to hypnotic induction than the general population, which by definition has only a 'normal' level of susceptibility to hypnosis. Thus, when a client was able to reach an extraordinarily deep level of hypnosis after only a normal hypnotic induction and could then access their theta brain-wave-state – the deepest level of trance – these inter-life memories were accidentally experienced by the client and their often surprised therapists.

The early researchers noted these recalled inter-life memories were initially confusing to them because they did not realize their clients were recalling events that had happened at a time or location other than the past life the therapist had intended for recall. One minute the client may have been recalling events in a past-life, and the next moment the client was relating seemingly unrelated nonsensical memories, which the therapists later learned had occurred after 'death' and once no longer resident in the human body. These memories seemed implausible because the client might tell the therapist the person was now floating in a white field of light, and the therapist might not realize the client was no longer in their former body. Thus their client's statements did not seem to follow logically, and generally led to confusion in the early experimental period of this field. Eventually the researchers realized their client's disincarnated state, and through trial-and-error developed an understanding of the inter-life period, including a generalization of the soul's experiences in the spirit world between lives.

The researchers also improved their techniques to reliably help clients reach those deepest levels of hypnosis to access their super-conscious mind at will during an inter-life hypnosis session. Thankfully there is no significant hindrance that would prevent people from entering the theta state if they were susceptible to hypnosis and could enter the lowest alpha state. Anyone who can respond to a normal hypnosis session should therefore also be able to regress not only to a past life but also to the inter-life period.[273]

The key to reaching the deepest levels of hypnosis and experiencing an inter-life session is an extra long hypnosis session. The theta state is best achieved by an extended trance induction that may last up to 45 minutes, and includes stages of gradual deepening to slow one's brain waves and focus one's thoughts and attentions ever deeper in order to access those hidden memories. In the theta state, the conscious mind is inactive. Its reasoning centers and logic-filtering functions are highly disengaged and the super-conscious mind is able to access details available to their soul memories, and report those memories as literal observations. While subjects cannot consciously and purposely lie in this state, they may misinterpret memories or pictures seen in their mind's eye.

Newton found the surest way to fact-check his clients' reported memories of the inter-life period was to compare and cross examine clients' memories with those of others in order to assemble a reliable body of case work on this otherwise undeveloped research topic. With a baseline of expected inter-life experiences in hand from preliminary research, Newton concluded that any subject who left the hypnotic state and began constructing a deliberate fantasy would elicit responses quite inconsistent from other case reports.[274] His research efforts and development of the baseline inter-life experience – similar in some respects to Dr. Moody's groundbreaking work on the near-death experience – developed believable and consistent, though still anecdotal evidence, of the inter-life period, which will be highlighted briefly in this chapter.

Considerations of the Genre's Validity:

Other compelling anecdotal evidence should also be considered when one considers whether this unique research should be taken seriously. First, clients who have experienced an inter-life hypnotic session have themselves represented every one of the world's primary religions plus atheism prior to their first inter-life hypnotic session. And yet, despite their varying previous beliefs, they still reported information that conformed to a baseline already reported by all of the other inter-life clients regardless of prior religious belief. Their prior belief systems had no influence on the nature of their inter-life experience![275] This shows uncommonly uniform experiences of the inter-life period, making it easier to identify potential fraud, and further, to judge information received from other, less scientific methodologies, such as those that will be addressed in subsequent chapters, as to their potential validity.

It should also be noted that the inter-life research supplements well the findings previously presented in this book concerning Quantum Physics, Near-Death Experiences, Out-of-Body Experiences, and recalled memories from hypnotic past-life sessions, especially concerning peoples' memories immediately following a death experience. Of course the primary difference between the research concerning the inter-life period and those persons experiencing an NDE or past death experience through hypnotic recall is the client in an inter-life session is not just remembering experiences near the point of death, but rather the entire period of 'life' and experience after permanent physical death until well into the next incarnation, as experienced from an Over-soul's perspective.[276]

Another point of overlap between these genres is the common entry point to an inter-life session. Researchers have found it is generally easier for clients to enter the inter-life period from the point of death from a past-life while in a state of deep hypnosis.[277] From that point forward, the therapist and client may proceed chronologically or jump forward to a specific point within the inter-life experience to resolve or explore any specific issue(s).

There are also certain interesting points of agreement with physical and quantum principles discussed in Chapter 2 of this work. For example, Newton found his clients in deep trance who were experiencing reality during the inter-life period *consistently* described a cessation of the flow of time, as we know it in the waking world. While subjects experiencing a past-life by accessing their subconscious memories continued to experience a chronology of events that resembled the normal, forward course of time, subjects hypnotized into the super-conscious state experienced 'time' as one homogenous unit, comprising an amalgamation of the past, present, and future.[278] All time in the inter-life period was described as occurring *Now*.

That finding corresponds to Hermann Minkowski's mathematic explorations of the space-time continuum, previously discussed. While clients under deep hypnosis obviously reported through their human body in the present time, they had access to information across the *entire* space-time continuum, including what might happen in a possible future reality. However, they generally found it difficult to adequately explain unfamiliar topics such as those that were well outside their normal experiences of everyday, physical reality.

Also, Newton's clients consistently reported both the soul and all physical matter were comprised of energy, similar to an intelligent, 'conscious' light – points of similarity and overlap with principles also revealed by quantum physics. A concentration of this intelligent, conscious light energy, or in other words the 'Source' of the energy, is experienced and expressed by clients in an inter-life session as 'Love,' the 'Unity,' or 'All That Is.'

Clients consistently assert there is no evil energy but rather impurities that can be cleansed, fixed and reorganized such as if a knot were untangled allowing the energy to flow again unobstructed. Thus if people had committed atrocities during their last human life, they would not be judged evil and sent to hell for all eternity, but rather their energy would be fixed or reorganized to help prevent such atrocities from occurring again in a future life.

Newton's clients asserted from a position of authority as eternal souls, that energy cannot be destroyed; it can only be disassembled and reassembled using different combinations.[279] This assertion would also seem to agree with the First Law of Thermodynamics, which states energy can neither be created nor destroyed, but is only converted from one form to another through an intricate system that ensures the eternal conservation of energy.

Common Reporting on the Nature of the Spirit World:

<u>A description of souls:</u>

Descriptions of the human soul from reports Newton and others received from their clients exploring the inter-life period were amongst the most compelling in the genre of metaphysical research. In his first book, Journey of Souls, Newton described souls as appearing as a mass of energy or a ball of light that might have multiple colors seemingly indicating the energy's level of development, experience, wisdom, and special skills or interests. The youngest, most inexperienced souls would appear as pure, white balls of intelligent light energy while older, more experienced souls progressed through a spectrum of colors from yellow to orange/red, green, blue, and finally deep purple.

Despite their formless appearance, the soul energy can also morph the characteristics it displays at will or need, so as might be beneficial when greeting new arrivals in the spirit world. They may thus appear as projections of human forms those souls had worn in their former life, so as to be more recognizable to the newly arrived soul.[280]

As might be expected from the findings of the late Dr. Wambach, the soul itself was reported to be androgynous. Newton found that incarnating as both male and female is a mandatory step in human development, and thus the choice of sex in human life was not an unimportant factor influencing that development.[281] Still, because of their experiences during life as humans, incarnating souls resting in the spirit world may exhibit identity preferences and thus will purposely exhibit male or female forms or express those gender-based character traits while engaging with other souls.

Souls are literally particles of energy that originated from the Source of all energy: the Creator.[282] Of note, that energy is never actually separated from the Source, but rather is attached or connected to It, as all energy in the universe remains attached to the Source.[283] This finding would agree completely with the experimental and mathematical quantum theory findings developed by physicists Bell, Stapp, Clauser, Friedman and others, discussed in Chapter two.

Following this line of reasoning, it should therefore not be a surprise that all living things have souls. However, non-humans – animals, plants, insects, etc. – have very simple fragments of energy. Newton hypothesized intelligent energy may be arranged by a precedence of life: plants, insects, reptiles, and mammals – each in its own family of souls, and each experiencing life in the physical realm for creation's own purposes.[284] More importantly, Newton found all of his clients asserted the concept of moving 'up' or 'down' an evolutionary ladder from one form of existence to another, whether as a means of development or punishment, was simply an untrue concept.[285] The energy comprising grass, worms, or cows, for example, would always remain grass, worms, or cows, respectively. Souls inhabiting human bodies were not ascendants of primates, and neither would they be punished for misbehavior by moving back down an evolutionary chain of soul development. One can never move backwards when gaining experience. Development and growth always occurs with forward momentum.

Inter-life session clients asserted each soul is unique, and the intelligent, conscious light energy that comprises the soul might be partially described as vibrating waves much like electromagnetic light waves but without the preconceived limitations of what light and matter seem to entail on Earth.[(286)] Similar to fingerprints, each soul is also unique in the way its energy is comprised and vibrating. According to multiple reports, the frequency of the soul's wave energy changes over time as the soul develops experience from each of its successive lives. This experience is then further supplemented by training, work, and other 'life' experiences obtained in the spirit world. Together, these experience sets change the vibrational characteristics of the soul, which in turn changes the color and appearance of the soul as it matures and develops. Some reporting would also seem to indicate the energy may also strengthen, perhaps even grow denser or more concentrated, as the soul better develops its knowledge and ability at manipulating the energy field of the universe in order to achieve its purposes in assembling and manipulating the reality it wants to perceive.

All of the inter-life researchers found souls were able to impart the impression of semi-physical form on their surroundings in the light realm. This was attributed to consistent assertions by regressed clients that energy organization follows thought.[(287)] Many sources in this genre and the next noted one of the many purposes of life experiences on Earth was to help the soul learn how its actions, intentions, thoughts and decisions affected and manipulated energy in the physical realm where thoughts and intentions worked more slowly on the manipulation of physical matter (i.e. dense energy). The physical realm, therefore, was an effective training environment to prepare one's soul for the task of energy manipulation because in the spirit world, where thoughts are the key to energy manipulation, such energy manipulation occurs instantaneously. In video game parlance, physical incarnations might be equated to a beginner level to prepare oneself for permanent life in the higher realms of the spirit world, or the expert level.

Finally, it should be noted that part of a human's soul never leaves the spirit world when that soul incarnates.[288] A direct connection to the spirit world always remains intact through this split-based soul energy. The soul fragment left behind retains a higher level of knowledge of the soul's true life and existence as a soul, as well as its intended purposes for the human incarnation, and thus should more accurately be termed an 'Over-soul' because of its higher perspective on life's purposes and goals.

Clients visiting an inter-life session councilor find that through prayer, meditation, or other means of quiet reflection they can also receive intuition and inspiration from their Over-soul and spirit world that can give them clues on what they need to do in life, or simply answer a query on their purpose in life.[289] While an LBL session may be the most direct and fastest way to achieve this insight, the capability to reach out to the Over-soul is available to anyone who has the determination and patience to engage in daily meditation as a means of seeking these answers through their connection with their Over-soul.

Mechanically, meditation has similarities to deep hypnosis in that the brain is quieted, and thus brain wave activity is slowed. Hypno-therapists have found theta-level brain waves are more effective in communicating with the Over-soul, but one should recall that hypnosis is merely a tool, and indeed is a natural state of mind that theoretically anyone could reach of their own accord. A hypno-therapist merely acts as an interlocutor to help the client reach the state of mind necessary to realize their own goals, but the work is actually achieved at the individual level and thus can be similarly accomplished through one's own individual efforts.

Descriptions of "God" and Heaven:

The inter-life sessions have found 'heaven,' or the place where spirits reside, cannot be adequately defined or described by human words: It is a place where space and time ceases to exist, and yet descriptions of heaven continually use words implying space and time must have some sort of meaning.[290] For example, descriptions that heaven is boundless imply some form of space or dimension must exist if the description of it stretching forever is to make sense to the human mind. There are also many descriptions of clients remembering moving, or even being moved from one area of the spirit world to another, which again implies physical separation of one location from another; i.e. space.

Perhaps the most troubling point to rectify in the human mind is the concept of timelessness, which is not described as infinity, but rather a point where time ceases to exist and all that remains is the singular point of *Now*. Still, there are descriptions in the inter-life research that seem to imply that even within the *Now*, there is some form of constant evolution implying a change from one point of *Now* to another point of *Now*. For example, how can one soul be older, wiser, and more mature unless that soul had indeed existed for a longer period of time as a thinking, experiencing entity? That would imply the movement of time within the *Now*. (There is, however, agreement that *Now* never remains the same but is always in constant, dynamic flux.) Further is the description that after one human incarnation a soul returns to the spirit world to rest and contemplate its experiences from the last incarnation while also making plans for the next. Thereafter, the spirit returns to Earth for its next incarnation and human life experience; all of which imply the forward progression of events, or time, by our human definition.

I would propose as a means of rectifying these conflicting concepts of time, that there may indeed be multiple concepts of time. One concept of time describes the space-time continuum, which appears real and linear in the physical world but rather appears both changeable and illusory in the spirit world. Further, there is a separate concept for 'absolute' time in the spirit world, where the concept of *Now*-time reigns. There must be a forward progression of *Now*-time, but from the spirit world's perspective, they can see/experience the entire physical world's space-time continuum including our past, present, and probable future, thus providing an overlap with the quantum physics concept that all (physical world) time actually intersects at one point, *Now*.

At some point in absolute time, the Source of all energy and creation exploded in a flurry of development, creating All That Is, including the spiritual energy now comprising the human souls' existence.[291] Within absolute time one would have an impression that the physical world's entire space-time continuum was observable as existing within the present moment of *Now*, and was therefore capable of manipulation. Still, absolute time could not be manipulated, but rather is a dynamic infinity that forever changes in the ever present *Now*.

Newton's clients reported the most outstanding characteristic of the light realm was a realization that a powerful mental force directed everything according to a plan carried out in pure harmony. His clients noted this was possible because the spirit world was a place of pure thought.[292] Further, no one is a stranger in the spirit world. Because all are connected, there is a *Oneness* in the spirit world that eliminates feelings of hostility or suspicion.[293] As eternal souls that cannot be destroyed and never suffer from want or need, there is no competition, fear or anger issues in the spirit world as is common in the human experience on Earth. There is also a feeling of love that permeates the entire spirit world, and the Light of the Source is constantly described as a feeling of pure love that provides the underlying energy for all of existence. It should be no surprise then that the spirit world/heaven is often described as paradise.

Newton noted of his client's descriptions of 'God' that while they could feel the presence and influence of a supreme power directing the spirit world, they were uncomfortable with the terminology 'God' to describe this supreme power.[294] They characterized the word 'God' as having been misused by humans when trying to describe the Source of all creation. The word is too personalizing and makes the Source seem less than that which It is.[295] The word also conveys a human-ness on the Source, and though all humans are part of the Source, the Source is much more than merely human. The philosopher Baruch Spinoza (1632-1677) may have more aptly described the Source of Creation when he contemplated, "God is not *He* who is, but *That* which is."

One of the most amazing transitive properties of this description of the Source and the human soul is the reality that if all souls are part of, created by, and continually connected to the same divine essence generated by the Source of creation then all human souls continue to share in divine status with the Source.[296] This is an important difference from that presented by Western religions, which assert humans have fallen from divinity and must rectify their existence to return to God. Spiritual truth, however, learned through direct communion with one's own Over-soul, says that separation is nothing more than illusion.

Punishment:

If souls are divine, created by and connected to the Source, and indeed comprised of the same conscious light energy as the Source, then it is a small leap to understand there is no such thing as punishment in the afterlife.[297] Certainly, a life review, as will be discussed shortly, does occur and our actions are considered not only for their own merit, but also by how they affected others. However, there is no condemnation of souls' actions during their human life on Earth, and neither is there affirmation or congratulations for poor decisions; especially those that hurt or negatively impacted their fellow humans on Earth.

The concept of condemnation, punishment or eternal damnation is an ill-informed preconception and extension of Earthly conditions into concepts of the hereafter. There is no external judgment of right or wrong by others. However, souls, from their higher perspective once no longer associated with the human body, will judge themselves as to whether their own actions were right or wrong. Souls feel sad or disappointed for taking inappropriate actions during their own lives and will often seek to rectify wrongs, or in other words, personally experience the effects their conditions caused when they return to Earth in a future life. In this way, any punishment is both self-inflicted and delayed until their next physical incarnation. The concept of hell and punishment in the spirit world is simply a falsely conceived notion of the true nature of the home of the Source, which is pure love.

Now, it is true that souls may create their own surroundings in the spirit realm, and so humans who had intensely believed in the concept of eternal damnation from their religious beliefs established during their previous life on Earth may therefore temporarily experience events in the afterlife that conform to their expectations, desires and intentions. In this unfortunate case, a scene of hell in the afterlife may occur. The inter-life research, however, finds these experiences are purely temporary and are allowed solely to allow a conscious soul to assert its individual needs. Still, at some point, development must continue so those souls will be reminded of their divine nature and their direct connection to the Source.[298] Once the so-called 'damned' spirit remembers this truth, it accepts the fact it *should* be rejoined with the Source and once it seeks this conjunction it is immediately surrounded by light and love, and the hellish experience dissolves into the illusion that it truly was from the beginning.

Do not expect the Christian religion to appreciate this encouraging revelation of the afterlife. Any prospect that places the concept of salvation and eternal paradise back in the hands of the individual – without need of intervention through the efforts of the ordained clergy to administer sacraments on behalf of the Savior – and removing the negative enticement of eternal damnation for non-believers, is clearly counter to the Church's teachings and interests. Many Christians will likewise feel anger, ironically, because they tend to feel self-righteous and pleased that people who do not follow their personal beliefs of right and wrong will/should 'burn in hell.' How ironic it is that the followers of the most holy, loving and peaceful human to have ever been born, Jesus of Nazareth, who himself imported his followers not to judge one another but to love others as themselves, are personally upset at the potential of losing the ability to see others judged and sentenced to hell.

Maybe it is not a pleasant prospect, from a human perspective, to think those who have committed the worst atrocities in the history of the world will not be judged and sentenced to some form of punishment. However, humans do not think as timeless souls, from the perspective of the Creator, or understand the Creator's plan for creation. Because of that, judgment of right and wrong *should* be reserved. Those poor, possibly depraved souls who commit atrocities on Earth were likely either warped energy that needed adjustment in the afterlife, or were specifically serving some function for the development of creation for which humans from their current perspective could not possibly fathom.

Right and wrong are only applicable from the eyes of the beholder. As a species, however, if we treat others as we would want to be treated, following the words of Jesus, then we can do no wrong, and no karmic debt will be incurred in this life. The human soul is born of and comprised of a conscious light-energy that is described by those accessing their super-conscious as pure love. Thus expressions of love, including forgiveness of sins and suspension of judgment, are complete manifestations of that energy in a constructive and positive emotional form during life on Earth.

Death and Departure / NDE Similarities:

There are many elements of the death and departure sequence recalled during inter-life hypnotic recall sessions that share similarities to findings from the near-death and out-of-body experiences. Among these, some subjects report hearing a humming or buzzing sound as they exit their physical body at the moment of death.[299] Both NDErs and people who have had out-of-body experiences routinely provide similar reports. The point of uniqueness for those re-experiencing death while under hypnosis is that these sounds transform and become musical after the soul exits the tunnel experience and enters the spirit world. Also, both NDErs and persons hypnotically remembering a past death report floating out of their bodies at the point of death, and not being able to physically touch, influence, or move solid objects. Both groups are generally frustrated during attempts to communicate with their loved ones left behind, but are amazed they can hear/know the thoughts of the living. They almost always feel a pulling sensation away from the place where they died, and rather than fear their current circumstances, experience relaxation, peace, and curiosity about their new situation. Both groups also report a euphoric sense of freedom, and brightness around them. They will often journey to the spirit world by passing through a tunnel into the light, known as the tunnel effect.[300]

Inter-life researchers found souls may even leave their human bodies moments before imminent physical death when those bodies are in great pain or psychological trauma, such as might occur when mortally wounded or while plummeting to one's death.[301] There seems no further reason to inhabit a body through its final moments when death is imminent, and the soul may exit so as to limit the final moment of trauma.

Like Dr. Wambach's subjects, Newton's clients generally associated peace, freedom, and *relief* with the moment of death vice pain, trauma or fear; all of the three latter of which ironically were associated with birth as the soul entered the human baby and committed itself to a new and unknown challenge in a confining, limited human body that was then painfully birthed into a cold, relatively uncaring world.[302]

Inter-life researchers also found souls generally had little interest in their former bodies, including the body's ultimate disposition following death. This was not based on callousness or lack of care for the people left behind but rather an acknowledgement of the finality of death, excitement about returning to the light, and sudden understanding of the plan of creation, including a realization that those left behind were continuing an experiential journey they had indeed selected for themselves.[303] In other words, if the departed soul's premature death would cause the ones left behind pain and hardship, they had elected to live a life that would experience those feelings, and they must be allowed to continue with that intention as it was their own Over-soul's desire for that particular experience.

Upon arrival at the gateway of Heaven, Newton's research continues to agree with the near-death experience research. Friends, relatives, and soul mates that are among the dearly departed greet new arrivals to help provide assurance and love that all is well and the soul is back at home.[304] Spirit guides are usually also among the welcoming party and help acclimatize the soul to its current circumstances, and then escort it on its path of recovery in the spirit realm. Newly arrived spirits are impressed by a sense of harmony and order in the spirit world and quickly remember their true self, their Over-soul, which had been left behind in the spirit world, as well as their purpose for the recently ended life on Earth. The soul will not only want to review that life to begin learning the impact of its actions on that life plan, but will also want to rejoin with the soul-energy that had been left behind in the spirit world.

From that point forward, similarities with the near-death experience end because no returning human soul will have rejoined with the Over-soul energy that was left behind in the spirit world, though the NDEr may experience a life review. Interestingly, an NDEr may remember having experienced full recall of its life while in heaven, as well as its purpose for this life or more specifically its own life goals for the current incarnation. However, upon return to Earth the soul is only left with the memory of having remembered, but the actual details will once again be hidden behind a veil of amnesia. Similarly, the inter-life hypnotic session may also uncover the soul's life goals for its current incarnation.

Interestingly, however, sometimes this information continues to be specifically hidden from the client through intervention by the Over-soul or by spirit guides, especially if the client under hypnosis has not yet reached an important decision/experience point in the current life where that life plan will be fully tested. The Over-soul apparently does not want to cheat itself and deny it from the full experience that only a physical incarnation can provide. To cheat in the current life and fail to achieve a desired life experience would only force the soul to live yet another life in order to experience the desired life plan's goals; a waste of time and the gift of life that would be counter to the soul's own better intentions.

Finally, one should consider the implications this information provides about the nature of death and the loss of loved ones. Surviving the loss of a loved one is amongst life's hardest trials not only because of the loss of the love and companionship that person had provided, but also because of the human fear that death represents a permanent finality.[305] Even the most religious clergyman is still fearful of his own death because of the fear of the unknown: They profess faith, but faith is quite different than absolute knowledge.

Hypnotherapy sessions examining the inter-life period actually allow a person to return to any one of his/her many inter-life periods and not only re-experience the personal feeling of death but also obtain for him/herself a personal knowledge of what happens after death. This knowledge is so much more powerful and absolute than any that faith can provide. Therefore, I would encourage all readers to experience that knowledge for their selves to be able to make a more informed judgment on the validity of the material presented in this book. Universally, clients who have experienced an inter-life session like those who have experienced an NDE, are no longer afraid of death because they understand that death does not represent an end but rather a beautiful and perfect transition from this restrictive and painful life experience to pure freedom, peace, joy and love in the afterlife.

This knowledge is available to anyone through personal exploration, though is generally made easier with an inter-life hypno-therapist's assistance. However, neither myself nor any of the pioneers of LBL research hold a monopoly on the information presented in this chapter. If you question the validity of any point presented herein, then more so than any other chapter in this book, you can challenge the assertions and *experience* the truth for yourself. Indeed, I would encourage all readers to do so as this chapter helps tie together concepts already presented with those that will follow through the end of the book.

LBL Common Experiences:

Like Wambach's research to find common consensus on statistically relevant results within the past-life genre, inter-life researchers have found a common consensus among their thousands of clients in the general sequence of events during the inter-life period. In summary:

Arrival and Activities in the Spirit World:

After a soul is greeted by loved ones and spirit guides upon entry into the spirit world, it may be escorted to an area of healing where experienced specialist souls repair damaged or contaminated soul energy caused by trials and tribulations during the physical incarnation. If the soul requires rest from a particularly hard life, it may spend some time reflecting on its past life in private. Once ready, healed and rested, the soul will review its past life with a spirit guide, and may do so as well with a group of elder souls who had previously helped the soul choose the circumstances of its former life (and will again help it determine the best circumstances for its subsequent life in order to continue the developmental track suited to the soul's own individual needs). These reviews do not seek to condemn or judge the soul's actions, but rather to help the soul understand the impact of its decisions, to seek better alternatives to poor decisions and actions, and to provide encouragement so the soul will not give up hope on the long process of development which generally takes hundreds, if not thousands of lives to finally achieve its ultimate development objectives.

Once the life reviews are complete, the soul will reunite with its soul group; a small group of similarly developed souls that support each other's development and lessons. The group is supervised by at least one spirit guide of a higher developmental level who is generally in turn advised by yet other more developed and experienced spirit guides. The junior souls will attend various classes to study aspects of energy manipulation or other past lives to search for lessons learned, and many other subjects including specialty topics that may cater to a soul's future developmental interests, such as healing, teaching, and other intellectual and energy pursuits.

Life Planning:

At some point the soul will feel a compulsion to return to physical life so as to continue its development since lessons learned in the physical realm are more meaningful to the learning process than are simulated exercises in the spirit realm.[306] The soul will discuss its goals with its spirit guide(s), and later with the group of elders, and then will enter an area where it will be able to preview various life choices that could help meet its goals. Often these lives will represent easy, medium, and hard choices/solutions, and it is up to the soul to select the level of challenges it wishes to experience in the coming incarnation. Once the decision is made, it continues to discuss the life plan with its spirit guide, and will meet with other souls who will play important roles in the coming life, such as planned mates, parents, and close friends and family members, etc. Important decision points will be identified so the soul will not fail to recognize them when they occur. These may be known as triggers, and the soul is sure to review them numerous times so that its life purpose to achieve certain experiences will not be wasted.

It is important to note, however, the role of freewill once the human is presented with those planned decision points. The human can choose to make appropriate, even hard choices or it can make poor choices and will then need to live with those consequences. Many souls live through multiple lives working on the same difficult emotional issues such as jealousy, anger, trust, fear, pride, etc. Once those issues have been resolved appropriately the soul will be ready to move on to new issues and experiences though it may be tested with those old issues again on occasion to ensure the lessons were effectively learned. Generally, however, once a tough issue has been resolved adequately the soul can more quickly resolve those emotional issues when they return in future forms.

Dr. Joel Whitton found the average period between incarnations was historically 40-some years, though this period has been steadily diminishing over the past several centuries.[307] This may be attributable to population growth; more humans on Earth obviously require more souls to incarnate, or rather represent more opportunities for souls to experience human life and achieve their developmental goals. Dr. Ian Stevenson found in his research of children who spontaneously recalled past lives that the period between such lives may be as low as 18-months or less. The discrepancy is likely due to the fact that Stevenson's subjects were all killed by accidents or violence, possibly leaving the soul with a feeling of not achieving its life goals, disappointment due to premature termination of a planned life, and thus follow a compulsion to return and complete their planned life experience as soon as possible.

Newton discussed similar ideas in his works in that souls with unfinished business may feel compelled to return to life faster than those who lived long, full, and productive lives. Similarly, there are such things as 'filler' lives; i.e. lives that served no personal purpose of experiential development and thus there were limited lessons to be learned in the spirit world between incarnations. An example might be an infant's death, where it was the parents who needed particular experiential development such as experiencing the pain and loss of a young child.[308] The infant's soul may be reborn again quickly and then live a full life, such as the subsequent child of the same parents who lost the first baby. The infant's soul in this example provided a valuable service to the grieving parents in that the filler life served no purpose for its own development but rather was for the benefit of others – its parents.

Life Lessons/Studies:

Clients accessing their super-conscious tend to see their lives on Earth as resembling actors playing parts on a worldwide stage. The souls enter life with some pre-known scenes developed specifically so they can experience emotions and challenges that are ideal for their current level of development.[309] They may practice these scenes before entering life, but such practice does not predetermine the actions and decisions the soul will make once encountered for real on the 'stage' of life. Indeed, the veil of amnesia will prevent the waking conscious from recalling the manner in which the super-conscious had envisioned addressing these issues prior to the life's incarnation.

After the soul has concluded its life on Earth, it again studies each of these scenes and searches specifically for errors in judgment that can be studied and compared to alternate endings using new scripts with different choices to learn potential outcomes that could have resulted from each circumstance. This review process provides souls an objective means to learn better ways to solve issues experienced during life while encouraging creativity, original thinking and a desire to triumph over adversity by acquiring wisdom through human relationships. Similar to professional athletes, souls desire to improve their performance with each successive life.[310] Of course once they have perfected their performance on Earth, the need to incarnate will end and the soul will move onto new challenges in spirit/ethereal form. Inter-life researchers found this was the primary goal of souls who were still incarnating on Earth; i.e. to conclude their incarnations through continual improvement and perfection of their behaviors, attitudes, and actions towards their fellow man.

However, it may take hundreds, and more likely thousands of lives to learn all of the necessary lessons life has to offer. Consider any topic and it is evident that at a minimum two lives would be required to understand the issue fully. For example, in order to understand anger, one must both become angry and cause others to be angry, and that is only the surface of this one issue. There is also excessive anger as well as righteous anger, anger-management issues, anger counseling, and so many other aspects of anger that a soul could explore during life. Because of these polar opposites and the soul's need to explore the 'bad' side of any topic (from a human perspective) to understand better the 'good' side, it is clear the idea of karmic justice is a misnomer.

A soul that experiences the 'bad' side of an issue during one incarnation, such as committing violence, may indeed elect to suffer a similar pain or injustice and live as a victim in a future lifetime, but this is primarily to gain a better understanding of one's prior actions on fellow humans, and not for retribution or punishment.[311] Recall an important finding from this genre is that there are no judges or juries in the afterlife; a soul's only critic of its actions and decisions during its life on Earth is itself, and thus the idea of karmic retribution is clearly a misnomer: the universe never seeks to even the score by taking 'an eye for an eye.' Understanding both sides of emotional issues is simply a part of a spirit's developmental plan.

Soul Development:

The idea of souls gaining experience, insight, and knowledge as maturing entities over a succession of lives is an idea that is not new, but the research obtained by inter-life researchers on the subject is assuredly ground breaking. For example, Newton identified six [nominal] levels of experience among incarnating souls. Conscious light energy that was not incarnating as a human soul was not explored in the LBL genre, and there was scant ability to seek further information concerning souls that had matured and moved on past the souls that remained to help junior souls still incarnating. Some little information on the latter subject will be discussed shortly.

Newton categorized the soul levels based on the electromagnetic wave frequency (i.e. color) they emitted, which seemed to symbolize their knowledge and understanding of certain aspects of life on Earth. In order, those colors were: white, off-white with traces of yellow, yellow, gold/green with traces of blue, light blue, and purple for levels one to six respectively.[312]

Newton's clients were quick to point out, repeatedly, the classification of levels for soul development was not intended to establish a hierarchy in the spirit world, or to be socially or intellectually elitist in nature. The societal conditions we are familiar with on Earth cannot be compared with those in the spirit world.[313] All souls work together and love one another as themselves, perfectly, because souls realize they are indeed made of the same energy source and are all connected as one entity. Philosophically, how could one's arm hope to lord it over its brother-leg without in some way harming itself? Rather, the differing levels of experience in the spirit world ensure more experienced souls are always available to help their fellow souls develop and overcome periods of difficulty with a purely giving attitude.

There is no judgment in the spirit world, only love and understanding, aided by complete truth and instantaneous, telepathic communications; there are no secrets in Heaven. One cannot hide the truth from one's own self, which is a close anecdote to describe the knowledge one's soul mates and spirit guides have concerning one's past life deeds and shortcomings as those lives are studied, dissected and relived frame-by-frame in the search for better answers to some of life's many problems.[314]

Inter-life researchers determined that characteristically, humans with intermediate-level souls tended to exhibit trust rather than suspicion toward their fellow humans. They also demonstrated a forward-looking attitude of faith and confidence in the future of humanity. Their attitude towards life, easy-going nature and optimistic outlook generally encourages those around them.[315] In order to attain this outlook of trust and infectious optimism, level 3 intermediate souls have probably lived hundreds of physical lives extending back at least 4,000- 70,000 years, giving them a vast array of experience on which to base their developed attitudes towards life.

At the height of development, advanced souls exhibit patience with society and demonstrate extraordinary coping skills no matter the difficulties they experience in life. Advanced souls focus less on institutional concerns and more on enhancing collective and individual human values. Their measure of fulfillment is derived from improving the lives of their fellow humans. Further, advanced souls tend to radiate understanding, kindness, and composure to others. They are not motivated by self-interest, but rather are genuinely altruistic. They may even live in hardship or reduced circumstances, or disregard their own physical needs.[316] Celebrated 'heroes of the year,' Mother Theresa, and Mahatma Gandhi, for example, tend to come to mind when I contemplate what rare, advanced souls like this may embody in life. Advanced souls have also likely lived hundreds or thousands of lives, spanning 70,000- 130,000 years.

Cautioning us not to jump to conclusions about our neighbors, Newton found that the most advanced souls were found in very humble circumstances on Earth. Conversely, persons living at the upper echelons of society, such as the rich and famous or politically powerful were by no means in a blissful state of soul maturity.[317] A vagrant traveler may as likely be an advanced soul as a high school teacher or nurse, etc. A politician, millionaire, actor, or successful businessman, by contrast, is not necessarily an advanced soul, but rather a developing soul experiencing those life events its Over-soul desired and needed for this particular incarnation. A well-to-do person in this life could as easily be destitute – and happy – in the next incarnation, because one life's circumstances do not directly affect the circumstances of the next life.

The Elders/ The Presence

The Elders are spirits who have gone beyond level six and are no longer incarnating for their own personal developmental needs. Rather, they provide specific insight into a soul's development and are often part of a soul's developmental counseling before and after an incarnation. Though souls are allowed to make their own choices, either right or wrong, the Council of Elders appears responsible for the developmental decisions of incarnating souls, and likely assign those souls' guides as well as assist in limiting the number of choices available for future bodies from which to choose for the next life. The Elders also have a way of making souls feel welcome when they come before the Council. There is no feeling of fear of reprisal or judgment.[318]

One of Newton's clients explained the Elders were wise beings who had great compassion for human frailties, and demonstrated infinite patience with human faults. Every soul receives countless 'second chances' in its future lives. Our lives are not designed to provide easy karmic choices because otherwise we would not learn our required lessons by coming to Earth. However, the trials and tribulations of life on Earth are also not designed to cause us further pain after death; there must be relief, rest and recuperation so we can be prepared to improve before the next lesson on Earth begins.[319]

Inter-life researchers also found that during the time souls are meeting with their Council of Elders there is the overwhelming feeling of an even higher intelligence energy field, simply termed 'the Presence' though most souls are loath to equate the 'Presence' with the Source of All That Is. Still, many hypnosis clients assert this may be as close to 'God' or the 'Source' as any incarnating soul may come. More advanced clients, nearing the end of their planned incarnations, indicate that they don't think the Presence is

'God,' exactly. To them the Presence is a deified entity or even multiple entities in a unified conscious, which exhibits capabilities immensely superior to even those present on the council. Hypnosis clients agree that the Presence is there to assist the efforts and work of the council.[320]

The location of the Creator seemingly cannot be defined. The Source might be more accurately described as 'All That Is' and as such, there cannot possibly be a central location where the Source would be located. Rather, the Source is all around us. We are inside of All That Is, and indeed we are a part, a spark of All That Is. One of Dr. Newton's clients ascribed the idea to being inside a beating heart.[321]

Again, Newton noted on the topic of God, that his clients do not like to use the word 'God' to describe a higher Presence, which is usually felt rather than seen in the spirit world.[322] Inter-life clients typically prefer to use words such as *The* Over-soul or Source because the word 'God' has been too humanized and personalized on Earth. As souls approach the advanced stages of development, these souls begin to consider the Presence to be a plurality of many divine forces in the spirit world cooperating for a unified cause using an unfathomable reservoir of infinite knowledge. Still, they feel the Presence, though important and influential at council meetings, is likely not the ultimate Creator. Rather, the Presence is only a piece of All That Is.

An insight into God's purpose in creating life:

In the following chapters we will explore insights from exceptionally enlightened forms of consciousness, and their wisdom on the purpose of life. However, it is interesting to note now that people under hypnosis shared their insight while accessing their soul-memories on the same topic. For example, inter-life clients reported new conscious energy was birthed out of the Source as it gained awareness of its identity as an independent soul. As a spark of the Oversoul, the newly born soul was comprised of the same energy, and was designed to help the Creator create by going forth and gaining greater awareness through self-transformation and adding to the building blocks of life.[323] The Creator expresses Itself and seeks fulfillment of Itself by birthing new life that will grow and help It create more.[324] In turn, the Creator knows Itself better as Its creations gain greater awareness and experience all that consciousness can imagine.

During the early period of growth of awareness, the individual conscious moves further away from the Source as it experiences itself in its many varying forms. However, at some point the consciousness becomes aware of the Source and learns/remembers from whence it came. From that point, there is no greater drive than to return to the Source, and to rejoin with the Source in the final act of conjunction; i.e. returning one's consciousness to conjoin with the Source as One in being. However, this process of growth is slow because the budding consciousness has much to experience and learn so that it can become whole and wise, and worthy of conjunction.[325]

Some souls will choose to develop and grow in their drive for conjunction through experiences in physical incarnations; i.e. life on Earth. However, life on Earth is a shock to young souls. Souls are created from and bathed in love in the spirit world, making their pairing with humans who experience negative emotions of anger, hate, fear, and pain quite traumatic. Inter-life hypnotherapists found some new souls take a succession of multiple lives to finally get used to life in a human body.[326] Inexperienced souls may surrender control of their will to the human mind, which has no innate sense of ethics, allowing negative emotions to win the struggle and dominate their experience on Earth.[327] It is the

171

soul's responsibility, however, to apply a conscious to the human's decision-making processes, to bring love into its life experience and by which conquer the fear and negative emotions the human body experiences in the soul's drive to develop and eventually escape the need for future human incarnations.[328]

Earth is considered a severe world on which souls will grow through physical experience, which includes physical discomforts and mental challenges.[329] Still, life as a human offers unique growth opportunities for souls. Humans were specifically designed to experience both positive and negative emotions, helping souls to gain unique insight into the value of love, peace, and other positive emotions by experiencing their negative, polar opposites. By knowing and experiencing negative emotions, souls can truly appreciate the value and power of positive emotions. Newton observed that one would appreciate food more if they had once been starving, and souls must understand what it means to be cold to appreciate the blessings of warmth.[330] The experience provides perspective and the transformation delivers purpose.

A common question is how a loving God could permit such pain and suffering on Earth for the creatures He created out of love. Amongst Newton's cases there was little variation in response to the tendered query: The Creator purposefully placed a peaceful state of bliss deliberately out of reach while living a physical incarnation so that one's soul would strive ever harder to grow.[331] If we did not have tests in life, we would have no motivation to better ourselves, or the world in which we live. Further, without tests to overcome adversity there would be no way to measure accomplishment and advancement from one life to the next. Natural disasters have nothing to do with God's love for His creations. They are simply acts of nature that achieve certain life purposes, for which our human perspective is simply inadequate at this point to understand or appreciate in order to be able to see a greater good.

A soul, though born of love in a climate of pure wisdom, is itself not perfect or it would not be incarnating for development and self-actuating purposes.[332] A soul thus grows by overcoming fear and all its related negative emotions through a succession of many lifetimes, and properly expressing itself through positive emotions rather than their negative cousins.[333] Souls are aided in this process by spiritual guides who have themselves lived more lives than the souls being advised, and have thus already experienced and overcome the issues for which they are advising their students.

Inter-life clients were quick to point out the decision to follow this advise was always an individual choice. Freewill must reign. However, failure to heed proffered advice would generally result in wasted lives, and a need to repeat future lives in order to address, satisfactorily, the issues troubling the soul.[334] Through self development, the souls will strive to express only positive emotions when faced with adversity, as in the example of Jesus of Nazareth who was probably the most highly developed soul ever to have incarnated, specifically for the purpose of trying to help his fellow souls see the ideal that could be achieved in human life, and to provide us a role model through his own actions for which we could strive to become.[335]

Understanding life's hardships:

An important part of the inter-life process is to examine the life goals and circumstances that would best suit our soul's development needs during the next incarnation. As such, we are fully responsible for who and what we are, and the circumstances in which we find ourselves during each incarnation because we were the very ones who chose the circumstances into which we should be born. Those circumstances would be those that would most likely place us in the (often difficult) circumstances necessary to allow our soul to experience those aspects of life necessary for continued experiential and spiritual growth.[336]

There are a lot of unpleasant realities faced by this assertion. If we chose the appropriate body for our needs, but that body currently is, or was born, or became damaged during life then that assertion shows we *may* have chosen these life circumstances for our own betterment and growth. Alternately, our human frailties could be for someone else's betterment if that aspect of physical incarnation is important for another soul to learn how to care for others. On the positive side of this tough assertion is that living in a damaged or diseased body certainly does not necessarily imply karmic retribution as payback for a prior life's poor choices.[337] However, as was seen in the last chapter, there may be occasions when birth defects do indeed carry over emotional impressions from one's prior life/lives, though not necessarily for karmic reasons; perhaps more likely for personal growth reasons.

Comparing responses from many hypnotic inter-life clients, Andy Tomlinson concluded more advanced souls would more often, and purposely choose the most difficult or impoverished lives for their own growth and experiential needs.[338] This may be partially attributed to the fact that a more experienced soul would have the necessary tools and experience to survive and grow through such hardship, while a soul is never encouraged to take on more life challenges than the soul is ready and capable to handle.

Newton found souls develop a covenant between themselves and the givers of life: to do the best they can with who they are in each life.[339] Suicide is thus looked at with disfavor because of the disregard for this covenant, and the soul's failing to take advantage of the precious opportunity that life provides for further growth.

Indeed, souls will not be able to escape adversity through suicide. They will merely have to return and address the same problem set in a future life and continue doing so until they can adequately handle the issue(s) they sought to escape by prematurely ending a singular life experience.[340]

There is no doubt that life is troubling and difficult in so many ways. But our higher self, our spiritual self, has the power and inner knowledge to help us overcome adversity and remake our lives following catastrophes.[341] One of the keys we need to recognize in life is that we have the ability, indeed the obligation to make mid-course corrections in our lives. We do not have to resign ourselves to living forever with the aftereffects of some previous poor decisions and life choices.[342] We *can* conquer fear and take risks. We *can* overcome negative emotions and karmic patterns to create the life we want if only we will take self-responsibility and make the first step towards that positive intention.

At the conclusion of our lives, we will review our life events and life choices with our spirit guides and Council of Elders.[343] Positive choices will be rewarded with congratulations, and poor choices will bring feelings of regret tendered by one's own self-judgment. Far more important in these life reviews will be our own reactions and decisions that affected our selves and those around us in those life events, rather than the positive or negative aspects of the events themselves.[344] For example, showing bravery during a time of adversity would be a positive choice. The circumstances leading to the adversity would not be as important as our decision made during the time of adversity. Our growth and success in life thus depends on the responses we make to life's various trials and adversities.

Further, rather than being subject to retribution from a 'just' God, and in the absence of external judgment, we serve as our own severest critic as to the appropriateness of our own decisions in life.[(345)] We know that failure to respond appropriately in a past life will only require us to repeat the trial in a future life, which may seem to be a failure to live up to the agreed upon covenant to try one's best at each life.

Realize however, souls understand that pain experienced in life is not pleasant. While physical life offers many rewards, it is also apparent from reading testimonials of clients recalling their inter-life period that there is often significant apprehension about having to endure a future life that is anticipated to have many hardships. Thus, it would be better to live the current life appropriately, to make the hard-right decisions vice the easy wrong, and accomplish those set tasks so as to finally be done with future hardships. While one cannot save money and possessions to benefit one's own future lives, the human consciousness can make appropriate decisions that will help its self elude future problems by conquering those issues, *Now*, in the current life.

Conclusion:

The importance of this chapter is it not only combines unique and credible research with areas of overlap in sections already and soon-to-be covered, but it also provides readers an avenue to replicate the same research for themselves; to be able to compare the findings presented herein to their own personal experiences. This is not only beneficial to the purposes of this book, but also of significant benefit in the readers' quest for their own meaning of life. By aiding people to understand their true nature, their connection to the Source, their soul and spiritual home, we can help ourselves and others to combat the fear of death, and ease competition, anxiety and other strife in human lives.

Newton observed death was not darkness, but rather light.[346] It should be evident from the material presented thus far that there is no reason whatsoever to fear death, so don't let that fear prevent you from making the right/hard decisions necessary to achieve further spiritual development now, in this lifetime. The 'hard right over the easy wrong' seems to hold the key to escaping the karmic cycle of successive life incarnations.

Indeed, in the absence of fear, one should embrace life and live it to its fullest. When one's goals have been achieved, the soul will surrender its hold on the physical realm and be welcomed back into the inter-life period where it shall rest, contemplate its achievements (and shortcomings), and then plan for the next. Death is never definitive. It is merely a stepping-stone; a portal to the next experience. Of course it is okay to mourn the loss of loved ones here on Earth, but do not fear for them: They are fine and happy, and will be met again in the spirit world when we are finished with our own current life's plan.

Chapter Seven

Research-focused inter-life sessions:
Direct input from Spirit Guides

Introduction:

The inter-life hypno-therapists' techniques provided both a new field and a replicable methodology for other researchers to follow to acquire more scientific evidence on the spiritual world, ascertain experiences during the inter-life period, and even examine the meaning of life and structure of reality. Of particular import in this chapter, Newton found that spirit guides can speak through a hypnotized subject's vocal chords, allowing researchers a direct avenue of inquiry and the ability to tap a fountain of knowledge on the spirit world and the structure of reality, basically at will.[347] However, when a disincarnated soul communicates through a human's vocal cords, the typically raspy tone and poor clarity of speech may well hinder the listener's comprehension. Instead, a more effective method of seeking input from a subject's spirit guide or other disincarnated teacher is to have the hypnotized client seek the answers from those spirits and then present the answer on their behalf while in the deeply hypnotized theta state. From a literature review of researchers who have used these methods, we will consider those research findings that help us understand better the nature of reality and the meaning of life in this chapter.

In an effort to standardize their efforts and reduce claims of fraud, researchers Lawton and Tomlinson did not utilize any subjects who could claim an ability to channel spirits or who otherwise claimed to be able to access higher spiritual wisdom through other means such as meditation, intuition, visions, etc. Their experimental subjects were average people who agreed to submit to normal inter-life hypnotic regression sessions. Their answers were then compared with other subjects' responses to ensure consistency in a manner comparable to that used by Drs. Newton and Wambach. Inconsistent and divergent answers would indicate the process or question was flawed if uniformly divergent, or that the subject was not in a valid state of hypnosis if a single, exceptional case of divergence occurred – indicating a subject's consciousness had freedom to guess or allow fantasy or logic to corrupt the studies' findings.[348]

Beyond standardized scientific methods, I would suggest the best advice in determining whether a piece of information could be plausible would be to listen to your own intuition, and so I caution you, the reader, to impose your own judgment on the material presented herein. Many spirit guides and channeled spirit-teachers have also advised their audiences to listen to their own intuitive judgment and determine for themselves whether the information provided via esoteric means sounds plausible.[349] They note one should intuitively know the truth when it is heard. If you do not agree with what is presented, then either the information is incorrect, or your current level of spiritual development is not yet ready to receive the information being proffered.

In a similar vein, if a purported channel admonishes the audience to accept blindly all provided information and to suspend their own intuition or judgment, then warning bells should start sounding in the listener's head immediately. Teaching should be given freely only to those who are ready to receive it; it should never be forced on anyone. Forced teaching of any kind smacks of cult-like behavior, and that could extend to any organized religion that follows the same pattern of forcing its believers to accept all tenants of faith without question. That is my furthest goal for the material being presented here in this work. Consider this material with an open mind, but accept only that for which you are comfortable and ready to receive, and put the rest aside for later.

Reincarnation:

Following the groundbreaking work of Dr. Ian Stevenson, presented earlier in this work, Lawton and Tomlinson sought to seek further input on reincarnation from spirit guides through their deeply entranced subjects. One of the most important findings of Stevenson's work was the possibility that physical characteristics and injuries could be carried forward from one life to the next. Importantly, the queried spirit guides universally agreed that physical characteristics *could* be carried over from one life to the next.[350]

Different spirit guides provided varying points of explanation as to why an injury received in one life might be – limitedly – carried over into the next life. One spirit guide noted that wounds received in one life and carried into the next were not properly healed in the spirit realm prior to the soul's return to physical incarnation. That guide also added the carried-over physical deformity would remind the soul of unfinished business during his/her subsequent life on Earth.[351] Another spirit guide noted a deformity could endure through many lifetimes until the injury was finally healed at the soul level.

A third spirit guide provided the physical markings would not have had to have been carried over if the soul had not been in such a hurry to return to physical incarnation. Oftentimes souls may be in a rush to return to physical incarnation to continue working on the developmental issues started in the previous life, but were summarily ended because of an unexpected or untimely death. Such would usually occur due to physical trauma such as murder; thus, providing the emotional component to add to a physical malady, resulting in a scar or deformity being carried into the next life. Had the young spirit been patient and remained in the spirit realm long enough between incarnations, then its whole energy field/soul would have been fully restored and the physical injury would not have been carried over from one life to the next.[352]

A fourth spirit guide noted that such mistakes in judgment were often made by younger, less experienced souls when they had a life story that had ended with a particularly emotional trauma, including acts involving revenge, fear, pain, or anger. Those scars and deformations carried over into the next life then acted as a subliminal reminder to the soul of those emotional issues that needed to be rectified in the next life.

Finally, a fifth spirit guide remarked the mortal wounds received in one life would not usually propagate from one life to the next in the exact same manner. A crushed limb, for example, would not propagate into the next life as a crushed limb, but it could cause that extremity to feel weaker or ache for unknown reasons.[353] This final perspective may lend some understanding as to why hypnotic past-life regression therapy may have some medical utility for the relief of many chronic types of pain or even some undiagnosed medical conditions. By helping clients to realize the medical issues they are currently experiencing are, in fact, based on events from past lives, the clients suddenly realize these issues have no validated origination in their current life. Somehow this realization in conscious awareness often serves as the key for the client to achieve immediate positive alleviation or even complete resolution of their chronic medical issues, including the cessation of phantom pain.[354]

A related inquiry regarded the purpose of reincarnation on the physical plane. Varying answers tended to agree with one another, though many shed light on the subject from a slightly different viewpoint. One spirit guide noted the purpose of physical life was to help the soul grow as an individual entity through the acquisition of new life and learning experiences. Explaining further, the soul is comprised of all the experiences, challenges and strengths it has gained over hundreds and even thousands of successive lifetimes, and those strengths and experiences are carried over – at a subconscious or super-conscious level – into the next life to help overcome challenges that will be faced once again.[355] Those souls with more experience and demonstrated ability to handle particular problems in past lives will likely not have pressing issues with those same problems in their current or subsequent lives: They already know how to adapt to and overcome those particular issues. Thus, we find agreement with Newton's finding that the most experienced souls on Earth are highly resilient to stress and quickly adapt to life's varied challenges.

A common theme between queried spirit guides was the idea souls gain experience in life, furthering the idea that life is but a journey and furthermore the journey itself, including the act of gaining those wide-ranging life experiences, is actually a primary purpose within one's life. One spirit guide noted simply, the purpose of life was to experience as many emotions and dramas in life situations as possible.[356] By adding to that experience, one seeks to know all that is or could be. Another spirit guide provided life's required lessons for spiritual development could not be reduced to a single life; there were simply too many variants that could and indeed must be experienced in order to help a soul eventually become 'complete' through this endeavor. However, the total number of lives souls will experience varies based on each soul's own abilities, and certainly the total number of possible lives can be reduced if the spirit endeavors to work constructively at developmental issues and solve karmic problems as they arise.[357] A fourth spirit guide summed up this reasoning from a higher perspective: In the spirit world, the only thing that matters about life on Earth is the experience one's soul obtains in life. Through this experience the soul becomes complete and readies itself for conjunction with the Source.[358] This clearly implies that the gaining of experience and wisdom is the mechanism by which one becomes 'complete' as a soul.

The reason for this yearning has everything to do with the soul's ultimate drive, which leads into the next question: When will the cycle end? The basest answer to this question revealed the ultimate goal of all souls was to gain enough experience to become complete so that one's soul, as part of a soul group, could merge back with the Source.[359] Another provided some clarity on the issue of a soul 'group,' stating that the totality of required experiences to become 'complete' could not be achieved by a single spirit, even after living thousands of human lifetimes. Rather, large groups of souls, whose experiences balance one another, develop and mature together in a way that they can eventually rejoin the Source as a single, balanced energy field.[360]

While every soul is born from the same Source and eventually returns to the same, the cycle never ends. Balanced energies constantly return to the Source, and new souls are forever born from the Source to begin the cycle anew. Thus one spirit guide noted that there would never be a time when every soul could have completed everything that was available to be learned and experienced; there will always be something new to create and experience.[361]

The Nature of "God"

The nature of God has fascinated man since time immemorial. Theories about this nature generated virtually all of the historical and modern-day religions and formed the basis of countless societies as well as disagreements between believers of different religions that have led to more than a few wars. Consider for a moment if mankind could finally understand the *true* nature of God. I would propose that if the *true* nature of God could be understood and accepted by mankind then all humans on Earth could finally experience true peace and harmony. Of course the obstacles preventing such a change in society from occurring are quite lofty indeed; not the least of which is discovering the *true* nature of human beings in the first place. It is towards that goal that we shall turn to briefly here, and examine what has been proffered by spirit guides accessed through the deepest levels of hypnotic trance.

Researchers inquired as to why the Source manifested into all the forms in the physical universe: the Earth and sun, water and minerals, plants, insects, fish, birds, animals, humans, etc. The basic answer was the Source desired nothing more than to experience, know, and touch *everything* – both All That Is, *and* all that could be. Indeed, the Source desired not only to experience All That Is, but to stretch the limits of everything imaginable, to create infinite possibilities and infinite permutations of life cycles that never end. In effect, the Source sought to grow beyond All That Is in order to create and experience All That Could Be. By doing so, the Source not only experiences life but also comes to know Itself and to grow ever more.[362] The Source is never still, but always creating, learning, and growing through these deliberate actions. With this goal in mind, the cycle could never end because 'All That Could Be' can never be reached as a final destination;

there will always be more possible permutations that could be tried and experiences that could be experienced. The Source is dynamic and everlasting.

One spirit guide reminded readers that the Source comprised everything in existence; the Source *was* All That Is.[363] Further, the Source is Consciousness, and thus every spark of physical matter is also conscious, albeit in its own special way. That consciousness desires to experience the life for which it was born into the physical world, whether that was as the life form of a long-enduring mountain or the fleeting existence of a fruit fly. The human form, amongst many others, is special in that not only is its physical matter connected to the Source through that part of the Source that manifests in the physical realm as atoms, molecules, and cells, but also via the spirit that occupies the human body as a direct spark of Consciousness, born of the Source and complexly arranged to think, experience, and grow in order to help the Source to create.

One should not think of the billions of various physical forms resident on Earth as having a consciousness capable of the same logical thought processes as human souls. Rather, those physical manifestations of the Source are experiencing physical existence in their chosen form for the unique joy that such provides the Source of All That Is.[364] One might consider it is as if we are all part of the body of the Source, experiencing individual life experiences within the overarching structure of the Source; perhaps akin to a Ferris wheel, or my personal visualization, a spiraling galaxy.

Let's explore further why our experience on Earth might be like a Ferris wheel. Imagine the Source as a big Ferris wheel with different compartments, spreading out from the Unity. Each compartment feels separate and seemingly separates from the Source so that the Source can experience all the various experiential possibilities available to that seemingly separated consciousness. However, the conscious entity is never truly separate from the Unity. But, if the compartmented consciousness could not experience the impression of separation from the Source then there would not be a *unique* experience to gain in physical reality. Once the experience of separated existence is complete, the Source brings that energy with those new experiences back into the center of Itself, adding to the whole of the Source's experiences and knowledge. Despite this final act of conjunction with the Source, the cycle of life never ends: new souls are continually created as wizened souls continually return to the core of the Source.

It would be beneficial to return to Newton's research findings on this subject. He had occasional opportunity to interact with particularly advanced souls or the spirit guides of his clients, and likewise would often inquire about certain aspects of the Source. On one such occasion he inquired if the Source dwelled in a central location within the spirit world, such as a mythical God seated on a throne. An advanced soul corrected this idea by noting the Source does not reside in any one part of the spirit world: the Source *was* the spirit world and *everything* in it as well.[365] With such distinction it would be impossible to say the Source was located in one place and not another. Another described how the Source was like a living, beating heart and human souls were all within the heart of the Source; one could never be apart or separated from the Source from which all were both created and an inseparable piece.

One of Newton's advanced clients described the Source as the Oneness, and many who are One.[366] Interestingly, however, when Newton inquired whether the divinity that is many who are One might be the ultimate deity of the universe, this advanced soul did not think this was so. Rather, this soul perceived a force that was above even the Source.

When asked to describe this entity, the client struggled to find words appropriate to the task, whispering slowly that which is above is massive, and yet soft; powerful, but gentle. The higher power is a sound so pure, and the sound creates *ALL*; even the Light. The sound holds the structure together and causes it to move, shifting and undulating, creating everything that is. The sound is a deep, reverberating bell, supplemented with a high-pitched hum. The sound is a whisper, like a loving mother singing to her child.[367]

If the Source has been described as light and energy that creates both physical reality and the spirit world out of that light-based energy, then this client's description of a possible higher deity's sound-energy that creates the substance of the light would imply that there is something beyond the Source that created and sustains the Source in a sound-based type of "love" energy. I found a few other esoteric sources that tended to agree some type of sound energy created the Source, but the information was not overly substantive and further inquiry would not be relevant to this particular study.[368] For academic consideration, perhaps there was more than one Source created by this higher Deity, though comprehension of these possibilities and their reasons and implications would certainly be beyond human comprehension. At least one esoteric source claimed All That Is sought to grow and fill the void in an effort to discover not only Its own nature, but to search for any others like Itself that might exist; an interesting supplemental idea.[369] Thus far, no other 'Source' has been found.

The cycle begins:

At some point, everyone's soul is created or spawned from the Oversoul. Our researchers acquired a small amount of information concerning how new souls are created. Lawton and Tomlinson's

(2007) research with spirit guides found the new soul emerges out of a white light, like an egg being released from an ovary. The newly created soul emerges from the Oversoul essentially empty of knowledge-derived abilities but full of potential.

This account was largely supported by one of Newton's advanced clients who was herself in training as a nursery guide in charge of these newly born souls when the client was not living through a physical human life herself.[370] This advanced soul described new souls are born in an area where the Oversoul is concentrated as a mass of high-intensity, pulsating energy. From the mass of pulsating energy, a swelling begins, pushing outwards and becoming a formless bulge. Ultimately the swelling 'separates' from the mass of pulsating energy as a new-born soul with a unique energy formation and distinctness all its own.

After the new soul is born, it is tended by specialist incubator souls who then help spark the soul's own energy; a process through which the soul becomes self aware and realizes its own conscious existence. This might be considered the moment of awakening. An advanced client explained that each soul is unique in its composition, characteristics and potential; no two souls are ever alike.[371]

Not all souls born of the Oversoul will choose to incarnate on Earth. Life on Earth is deemed a harsh experience in comparison to other available experiences in various physical or non-physical worlds and dimensions. Those souls with specific attributes necessary to succeed at developmental experiences on Earth will be given the option to experience its unique, harsh climate. Despite the trials on Earth, physical life is also joyful and wondrous. Souls on Earth will therefore experience a range of emotions and experiences that will eventually develop those souls into particularly wise, caring, and talented sparks of consciousness that will add much to the experiences of creation sought by the Source.

Post-reincarnation/the cycle ends:

Both Newton and researchers Lawton and Tomlinson found when the human soul has completed its necessary experiences through a series of life incarnations the soul's development and contributions to creation are still far from complete. Many spirits begin working as spirit guides, helping less developed souls understand life lessons even while they are still incarnating. Those who take this path will generally continue along this developmental path, becoming senior guides that in turn train junior guides. With further experience, they will eventually become Elder guides on the advisory council that still-incarnating souls visit before and after each incarnation.

Other advancing souls might specialize as nursery teachers, ethicists, harmonizers, explorers, time masters, or masters of design, amongst many more specializations.[372] One could refer to Newton's work for a description of these specializations and examples of their training regimen.

However, these specializations seem to last only a certain amount of time until the soul gains a sufficient amount of experience, and again elevates to a yet higher level, beyond which virtually nothing is known. Some spirit guides and advanced souls felt those higher souls eventually became part of the Presence and helped to design worlds, universes, life forms, and even create newly born souls. Other sources noted these highly developed souls eventually grouped together into a balanced energy form so they could perform the final act of conjunction; i.e. returning to the Source from which all is created.[373] At that point, the cycle of development as an individual soul *might* be complete, though such speculation must be nothing more than conjecture. There is no reported contact with souls at this ultimate level of development, even amongst the most senior spirit guides interviewed by any researchers thus far. One might speculate such would never be possible under any circumstance as that level of development is well beyond human comprehension.

The concept of energy:

An important point of intersect between quantum mechanics and this research is the idea that one's thoughts and intentions actually shape their perceived reality. This was a premise behind the best-selling book, *The Secret*, and many others just like it. Researchers sought input from spirit guides to determine whether this premise was correct. Each of the recorded responses was in complete agreement with this theory.

One of the spirit guides explained energy follows one's thoughts and intentions.[374] The more we focus on and think about something, the more likely it is to become reality. We attract things to us in life by unconsciously sending out energy through our thoughts and intentions. A second spirit guide added that beyond merely thinking about a topic we could increase the thought's intensity by writing it down, making that thought a little more concrete. Further, if we then act on our intention, the thought-form gains a semblance of creation, further increasing the chance it will ultimately be manifested in life.[375]

A third spirit guide noted there was an important caveat: merely intending for something to occur may not be enough to affect the course of one's entire lifetime. Sometimes a soul's desired life plan is to understand what it is like to be poor or lonely, for example. As such, these souls will not be able to retain riches or companionship in life no matter how much they focus on those desired outcomes, because such would be counter to their higher purpose in those particular lives. For a short period of time, humans might be able to grasp those desired attributes, but they will assuredly be taken away in fulfillment of the goals set for their overarching life plan.[376]

This shows that our Over-soul continues to maintain some level of control over the course of our life so that the chances our life on Earth will be wasted and not meet the life lessons desired are minimized. Consciously, we all want an easy life full of riches and loved ones, but subconsciously such may not be the desired end-state needed to achieve the lessons we intended to put in front of ourselves, and thus some challenges *must* be present in every life on Earth.

The nature of time:

Another difficult finding presented by quantum mechanics was the idea that time does not exist in reality, but only the current moment, *Now*, exists though is forever changing over all periods of time including the future, present, and even past. Some researchers sought to illuminate this concept by seeking further input from spiritual guides about the nature of time.

One spirit guide noted it was necessary to maintain the illusion of time on Earth because it would be impossible for the human mind to comprehend that all events of the past, present and future were all dynamically occurring at once.[377] Others noted it was the human's physical requirement for sensory perception that demanded the construct of time. Without a concept of time the human's senses could not perceive or understand cause and effect to achieve growth and development in physical form. However, this does not change the fact that time doesn't really exist. All time exists at the point of present: All time is *Now*.[378] And we are *in* the *Now*. Another spirit guide tried to appease human curiosity on this matter by warning us not to dwell on it overly much because the concept of no time is impossible to understand while we exist in physical form.[379]   Quite simply, it cannot be satisfactorily explained.

One of the implications of the past, present, and future all being located in the present moment of *Now* is that it would be possible to obtain impressions of possible futures, though some would be more likely to occur than others.[380]   This is thus the basis for hypnotic 'progression,' which seeks to help people learn under what conditions their personal problems could be solved in a future reality, thus providing a template for those beneficial actions to be put into place in the present. This template then becomes a basis for successful resolution of a personal crisis, and is as helpful to some clients as past-life regression therapy has proven to be.[381]

Impressions of the future that do not deal with one's own issues, however, are tentative at best.   One could not undergo hypnosis, for example, to determine a reliable future price of a stock on the stock market because the future remains subject to change. It is constantly in a state of flux of possible and probable futures until the future has finally been realized by our experiencing consciousness and thereby becomes the present. One spirit guide emphasized the future was not fixed: Nothing could ever be certain because free will must exist for human development to occur.[382]

The issue of time is also the first point in which advice from spirit guides will be presented herein. They note there is no time like the present to solve problems because any problem that is avoided now will only be encountered again in the future, repeatedly, until the soul has learned how to solve the issue at hand.   When the soul learns how it might react differently to certain situations *now*, to solve its problems instead of avoiding them, then the soul will progress in its development and can move on to bigger issues to experience.[383]

Suggestions from Spirit Guides:

Suggestions from spirit guides will be an on-going topic in the next chapters, but for now two further suggestions are presented from spirit guides interviewed through hypnotic channels.

The first suggestion was to know yourself.[384] When you realize and fully understand your true nature then fear and greed, jealousy and anger can be put in their place. You will come to realize a higher perspective and know how to live and interact with others and the planet to gain better experiences for your life's purpose. A primary key for developing humanity's future lies in this understanding. Only by understanding our true nature will we be able to grow as a species. We need to be able to see humanity for what it is: a force that has a great potential for destruction, but also an even greater potential for compassion. In this way, humanity can experience its true, divine nature on Earth.

The second suggestion was to lead by example.[385] By living the principles of this higher knowledge, you will let love shine through your life and in your interactions with the planet and others around you. You realize that everyone is connected in a Unity. By loving others through the manifestation of this knowledge you better express your growing divinity. By living in this way, you will help to open other people's awareness of the possibilities this lifestyle could provide to society, and more will ultimately seek to emulate and follow your example.

The spirit guides noted when we accept we are divine pieces of the Source, seeking to gain experiences on Earth as part of the divine plan then we should accept that we are never separated from love, and indeed are the embodiment of love itself at our own core.

We should thus share that love with others, and live in love. By doing so, we will be able to follow the Golden Rule proffered by Jesus of Nazareth to treat others as you would want to be treated yourself. By leading by example we may cause others to follow in our stead. Finally, when the whole world accepts its divine nature, then heaven-on-Earth will be achieved, and pain and suffering experienced in physical life will finally be at an end.

Possible Futures:

Raising the awareness of humans to understand and accept their divine nature is the whole point of the so-called 'new age;' a period of time in the near future not specifically identified by a date on the calendar but rather a spiritual process that is occurring in humanity over an extended period. One spirit guide noted there were many souls working towards raising the awareness of humans concerning their spiritual connection to the Unity.[386] Some advanced souls were electing to incarnate with the sole purpose to assist in this process. Their purer, more highly evolved energies will help society to reach a higher level of enlightenment, thus helping other souls evolve and develop, becoming a compounding effect that will eventually usher in a new age of humanity.

Another added, many advanced souls were voluntarily incarnating to help humans remember they are part of the Source, and were living on Earth for a specific reason – to gain necessary experience to help the Source create and will eventually rejoin the Source.[387] When this knowledge is realized, the experience of physical life will change and move to a higher energy level. As part of this shift, there will be a thinning of the veil of amnesia, helping humans to remember more easily who they are and why they are here. A final spirit guide elucidated on this point, noting that we need to help stimulate interest in possibilities that exist for the human race.[388] Humans have the ability to use the powers of creation available to them – the power of conscious thought and connection to the power of the subconscious mind – to see their true potential as spiritual beings who are experiencing life in a physical realm, and thereby create the conditions of heaven on Earth.

Conclusion:

The direct form of engagement these researchers used to achieve dialogue and research with spirit guides was made possible because of an ultra-deep hypnotic session, requiring special skills and an extended period of time. However, guidance from one's own spirit guides is available at a moment's notice to anyone who has an interest, without need of a specialized hypnotist or any other external input. To get the attention of one's own spirit guides one first needs to clear his/her mind and focus his/her attention away from the immediate surroundings. A quiet room and comfortable surroundings will aid in the process. As one meditates with a cleared mind, not thinking of anything and continually silencing their internal voice, ideas of encouragement and inspiration will be received – that is the touch of one's own spirit guides. Inspiration does have a source, and that source is divine, free, and readily accessible at a moment's notice.

The next chapter will examine those people who have developed an ability to listen to their spirit guides, inner voices, and feelings of inspiration in an immediately accessible manner. Their findings will help us further develop depth in, as well as examine new lessons towards this book's point of inquiry.

Chapter Eight

Spirit Guide input via Channeling

Introduction:

In the last chapter we explored universal truths readily accessible under the deepest levels of hypnosis, but this leads one to surmise the possibility that similar knowledge might be available under other forms of alternately focused conscious attention. Indeed, daydreaming, meditation and the point of transition between wakefulness and sleep are common periods of inspiration – when one's conscious is quieted and thus highly receptive to external inputs. Inspiration is one subset of a form of divine communication known as open channeling.

Open channeling includes inspiration, intuition, and other aspects of the creative process. Everyone experiences open channeling whether we think of it as direct communication with the divine or not. Other means of divine communication are more restricted, and thus experienced less often and by a smaller group of people.

The experience of hearing an inner voice is a more direct, one-way communication experience with what may be thought of as something other than one's own consciousness. An estimated 15 percent of the population has, at one time or another heard an inner voice that provided direct guidance, suggestion, or other information.[(389)]   Inner voices may be benevolent in the case of spirit guides providing helpful suggestions or encouragement, or even malevolent as in the case of schizophrenia. I hesitate to classify malevolent inner voices as having anything to do with 'divine' communication. As shall be discussed later, the mechanism by which external communications are derived is unknown, though these communications may be little more than a bridge between the conscious and subconscious that normally would not exist.

Following a continuum of possible forms of channeling, the one most commonly envisioned, as well as the most extreme form of channeling, is the historical parlor show act of a person channeling transmissions from discarnate beings either via telepathy or bodily possession as in the case of the spiritualist movement of the 1800s, the ancient Greek Oracle of Delphi, and many others. In this most dramatic form of channeling, the channel enters a trance and another being seemingly speaks through the entranced channel. This new personality will generally claim to be a more advanced spirit from a nonphysical reality, temporarily occupying the body of the channel.

The spiritualist movement of the 1800s focused on contact with the deceased, and the dramatic displays were often accompanied by moving furniture and other sideshow acts. This channeling fad mostly died out when it was determined the séance sessions were staged for effect, causing a loss of interest or belief in any positive messages that might otherwise have been received.

More recently, channeled messages have been delivered via some form of subconscious telepathy where the entity's purpose is purportedly to provide advice, information and teaching for the betterment of mankind. Contact with the dead in these more recent cases may be incidental but such is not generally the focus of the endeavor. Interestingly, with this form of channeling, the man or woman whose body is involved generally claims little memory of the experience.[390]

Sociologists Earl and Sheila Babbie found there were thousands of people recently claiming to be channels, in contact with spirit guides, spiritual masters, or other higher order life forms.[391] While some channels may not understand what they are experiencing and either suppress the experience or hide it from public consumption, many others have learned to capitalize on the phenomenon. Many channels have written books, given public demonstrations, and charged for private audiences with their channeled entity, catering to people's desire for divine knowledge and hidden insight. As with most any capitalistic endeavor, there can be bad 'apples' and intents mixed in with the good.

Perhaps the world's most famous channel, the late Mrs. Jane Roberts, who channeled 'Seth,' brought some form of legitimacy to this one-time parlor act. Arthur Hastings opined Mrs. Roberts' efforts marked a dividing point between classical mediums who summoned spirits from the dead and contemporary channels who focus instead on teaching spiritual wisdom.[392] Mrs. Roberts stumbled upon her gift through background research while writing a book on ESP. As the gift of channeling was further explored, she and her husband did not seek to capitalize upon the experience but did document it quite meticulously. Eventually the character of Seth's teachings convinced them that those teachings should be shared with the world, as Seth had intended, thus leading to Seth's (and Mrs. Roberts') quick notoriety. We shall explore channeled teachings, such as Seth's, in the next chapter.

Following the continuum of channeling mentioned previously, one finds everyday inspiration at the low end, followed by inner voices, and finally subconscious telepathy, including automatic writing, trance speaking and bodily possession, at the far end of the spectrum. As one progresses along this continuum, fewer cases of persons experiencing that level of channeling are noted. There is substantial evidence showing persons who have experienced a near-death experience have higher incidence of many aspects of channeling, including increased levels of intuition, hearing benevolent inner voices, and even telepathy.[393] One could quickly conclude that experiencers of NDEs have likely had their veil of amnesia raised, at least partially, thus removing some mental blocks that normally separate the human consciousness from the spirit world. As the incidence of this greater level of awareness is slight one should not be surprised that so few people have been able to experience the upper echelons of the channeling continuum. I will discuss shortly the possible validity of these experiences and their message. However, regardless of whether or not the claims of supernatural agency are valid, the fact remains that innumerable mentally healthy people do experience these types of phenomena.[394]

Possible Explanations of channeling phenomenon:

While the probability of play acting and fraud was high during the spiritualist movement of the 1800s, there is still reason to search for possible validity within this genre in our current age; not only to determine how the evidence herein might support that previously presented in this book, but also to see whether there are new lessons that should be taken seriously in this regard.

Dr. David Spiegel opined channeling was the result of self-hypnosis. The trance channeler would then engage in fantasy dialog based on one's own supposition of what would be appropriate if one were to call on guidance from spirits.[395] Spiegel's point of self-hypnosis is likely accurate. As noted in the previous chapters, access to spiritual information is available at will when one submits to an alternate state of consciousness. Self-hypnosis is one such method to reach an alternate state of consciousness, but merely being hypnotized does not necessarily indicate fraud is involved.

The famous psychologist Dr. Carl G. Jung hypothesized that beyond one's ego was a higher self connected to a collective unconscious to which one could access through his or her own subconscious.[396] Jane Roberts' channeled entity Seth did not claim to be a spirit guide or some other form of being separate from Mrs. Roberts. Rather, when pressed on his own state of being, he claimed to be an 'energy essence personality' and more specifically, a more advanced form of Mrs. Roberts – a Jane of the future – but noted that the two of them were still comprised of the same overall entity. Seth admitted he delivered his messages through Jane's subconscious but disregarded this avenue as belittling the message's value; a theme we shall touch on again shortly.[397]

We do not have enough understanding of the human brain, mind and consciousness at this point to be able to say with certainty what is possible and what is not.[398] However, consider for a moment that we are all sub-personalities within one Universal Mind: the Mind and Consciousness of God. Now consider the fact that sub-personalities within people with multiple personality disorders generally believe they are separate entities from the host's personality and may even be unaware of any other sub-personalities residing within the host. In this metaphor then, we humans, in our current state of spiritual development, believe we are separate from and distinct personalities not only between one another but also perceive a separation between the Universal collective sub-consciousness and ourselves. Our dissociated state does not permit us to realize our connection to the Source through our higher Self, our Over-soul.[399]

Following observations of multiple personality disorder within humans, we can extrapolate that when one sub-personality (myself for example) talks with another sub-personality (you, the reader for example), neither of us realizes we are actually connected sub-personalities within the same overarching Universal Mind. Our state of development is not yet lucid enough to realize this phenomenon and the implications therein. Dr. Jon Klimo noted if everything occurs within the Mind of God, then everything outside of the scope of our individual waking conscious is part of a collective unconscious.[400] The entirety of that collective unconscious is temporarily inaccessible because it is unrealized, but is theoretically available given our connection to the Unified Mind, of which we are all comprised. From this point of view, open channeling – intuition and inspiration – is but the simplest means by which individual consciousness gains access to a higher potentiality by becoming more aware of one's true condition and connection to the Unified Mind. It is as if a leak of information moves from the higher Mind to our dissociated local minds.

As a hypothesized sub-personality of God, we are sparks of God's own living light, living out our existences – indeed living out one of innumerable existences as God manifest in humanity – each with its own varying degree of dissociation and forgetfulness in regards to our true identity and association with the Godhead.[401] This forgetfulness prevents us not only from experiencing all that might be possible if we thought and acted with this knowledge in hand, but also hinders the life experiences of those around us.

In this metaphor of multiple sub-personalities within the Mind of God, it is up to each sub-personality to realize its identity and connection to the Universal Consciousness, to act appropriately with this knowledge in hand, to seek developmental experiences and once developed through those experiences, to become integrated back into the Mind of God. Channeled sources likewise contend humans will all eventually learn how to do such as we come to gain greater self knowledge and awareness, though we rarely realize we are on this path while living out our daily existence on Earth. Eventually though, we, the sub-personalities of God, living in a dream-like reality on Earth, become lucid and aware that the 'dream of life' is taking place within a still larger frame of reference, which is the true multidimensional reality.

When we realize our true circumstance within the framework of life, we realize not only are we a part of the Mind of God but that we also have access to the rest of that Mind, including all of its 'sub-personalities' and an infinite store of knowledge. Thus, we have access to those memories and experiences simply by accessing our own mind's recesses, including the subconscious and super-conscious aspects of our hidden mind. Returning then to the discussion of channeling, one would not/could not channel spiritual beings apart from one's own self. Rather, the channel would be accessing memories and knowledge from within his/her own mind, which is connected to and part of the Mind of God. Not only are we a part of the Mind of God, we have potential access to *all* of the Mind of God; it is simply a matter of discovering how to access that Mind.[402]

Hypnotism may be one means available for accessing that Mind. In a study of channeled sources and their mediums, Klimo found the most common description of their process as being virtually identical to radio wave communications: messages from the spirit world (i.e. the collective unconscious) were stepped down from higher frequencies so they could be received by the channel-medium, who would also have to basically step-up his/her own rate of frequency to be able to tune into and receive the message.[403] The act of putting oneself into a trance, whether via self-hypnosis, meditation, or other means, helps facilitate this method of 'stepping-up frequencies,' or otherwise developing access to the Universal Mind.

Dr. Marcello Truzi felt the least extraordinary explanation for the concept of channeling was that the information was derived of the vast, unknowable expanses of the unconscious.[404] However, while this would be the most parsimonious theory, reality may indeed be more extraordinary still. Dr. Charles Tart, psychologist and pioneer in the field of consciousness research, felt there was enough evidence to force him to take the idea of disembodied intelligence seriously as he pondered the truth probably lies somewhere between the concept that channeling is all nonsense or a manifestation of the subconscious, and the outer edge that claims channeling provides a means to commune with separate entities of some higher, unknowable nature.[405]

With a possible explanation for the channeling phenomenon in hand, next we turn to some various types of supporting evidence, alluded to by Tart, that might suggest accessible consciousness exists outside of one's own immediate ego experience.

Inner voices:

> *Know ye not that ye are the temple of God*
> *and that the spirit of God dwelleth in you?*
> 1 Corinthians 3:16

Generally speaking, people do not hear intuition or inspiration; the thoughts merely manifest in an instant in one's wakeful consciousness. Thus, there is a qualitative difference between open channeling and the receipt of information from inner voices. There is also a qualitative difference between inner voices and medium-channels in which trance speaking occurs. The entities manifested by medium-channels are channeled at will and usually speak of metaphysical topics for the betterment of mankind. Comparatively, inner voices cannot be channeled at will and speak privately for the consumption of the person receiving the message, discussing personal issues such as life decisions, spiritual direction and/or personal guidance.[406]

Respectable, healthy individuals have reported hearing inner voices, though the phenomenon is rarely reported or even discussed with one's closest family and friends.[407] There are a few well-known cases; for example, Socrates reported hearing an inner voice, which often acted as a voice of warning to him. On one occasion, the voice reportedly advised him not to walk down a particular road in Athens. A group of friends who ignored the warning Socrates relayed from his inner voice were subsequently knocked down by an uncontrolled, stampeding herd of pigs.[408]

Sir Winston Churchill was also reportedly saved by an inner voice's warning, which instructed him to move to the other side of his vehicle moments before a bomb exploded on the side where he had been sitting.[409] Dr. David A. Tate was advised by his inner voice that if he wanted to be cured of cancer, he would have to know that he was already well, Now, and thereby he would find within himself the means of survival.[410]

Psychologist Alfred Alschuler assessed many inner voices provide information, healing, inspiration, and positive means of guidance in people's lives. His research turned up more than 150 prominent individuals throughout history who reportedly heard an inner voice, including Martin Luther, Saint Theresa, French mystic Madame Guyon, and Joan of Arc.[411]

Some information seems to indicate beneficent inner voices may originate in one's own higher self, rather than in a totally separate entity.[412] Briefly, the higher self is an entity in itself, with a standalone consciousness and awareness just like one's human ego. The higher self stands as witness to the physical ego's experiences on Earth, and understands those experiences from a higher, spiritual perspective. From that perspective, the higher self is objective and nonjudgmental. Its orientation is toward higher spiritual values, and understanding life's purposes to achieve further development for the soul's evolution.[413] The higher self's orientation may help it provide guidance that keeps the human on track to experience life goals that it intended to experience while living the human experience.

One should recall that not all life goals are necessarily pleasant from the perspective of the human experiencing those lessons, such as overcoming adversity, living with physical deficiencies, loss of loved ones, etc. It is also interesting to note that predictions of the future from all sources, whether via inner voices or channeled mediums are often erroneous.[414] However, there is little harm in heeding personalized warnings, and there is some anecdotal evidence to suggest that comparing future events foretold by multiple disincarnate personalities may have increased probabilities of occurrence.[415]

It is also important to understand that not all inner voices are beneficent. While one's higher self might provide helpful advice, lower order voices are often critical, confusing, and may encourage acts of violence or painful events. Psychologist Wilson Van Dusen worked for many years in a state mental hospital and found that many of his psychotic patients heard both supportive and critical voices.[416] To repeat an earlier note of warning, many perfectly normal people hear inner voices so hearing such a voice should not be cause for concern. Rather, mental instability is a sign of poor adaptation to a misunderstood mental phenomenon, such as being receptive to a lower order voice's admonishments to hurt others or one's own self and then heeding that hurtful advice.

Dr. Charles Millar (1990) found a high proportion of professional psychics reported hearing a beneficent, higher order inner voice. Of 139 persons interviewed who identified themselves as psychic practitioners, 91 percent reported hearing a positive and helpful inner voice. Further, the ability to channel was reported by 71 percent of these professional psychics.[417] By definition, a professional psychic would be one who had a highly developed level of intuition, thus allowing them to sense issues troubling their client. Thus we could extrapolate 100 percent had a highly developed form of open channeling ability, but respectively lower incidence of channeling phenomenon along the continuum, as would be expected.

Jane Roberts' experience, beginning in 1963, might indicate the ability to channel can be developed by some people with deliberate intent and practice. While researching a book she was writing on ESP, Jane and her husband began experimenting with a Ouija Board. Within five sessions Jane began receiving messages from an entity that referred to itself as Seth. After a subsequent four sessions, much to her alarm, Jane started speaking the words aloud as they manifested in her mind. With more experience, she eventually learned to relax and enter a full trance, whereby Seth would speak directly through Jane's body and her own consciousness became unaware – or unconscious – concerning the activities that would occur while she was channeling.[418] Following a continuum, Jane quickly progressed from a basal form of open channeling, using the Ouija Board, to hearing inner voices, and finally to trance channeling.

While Jane had an interest in learning about human potential through her research into ESP, she certainly had no foreknowledge of or intent to begin trance channeling information from disincarnate entities before such suddenly began to occur involuntarily. The fact that this capability developed without a preconceived intent to capitalize on the situation should lend some level of legitimacy to the channel's endeavors. We shall explore this and further considerations of legitimacy in the next section.

Considerations of the Channel's Legitimacy:

The genre of channeling mediums is looked upon with a jaundiced eye because of the historical legacy of well documented fraud cases among mediums of the 1800s spiritualist movement; i.e. those channels who purported to contact the dead at the request of loved ones while performing little more than theatrical sideshows for their audiences. However, within the last half century there has been a new breed of channel-mediums who have gained little from their work, or who had no desire to undertake the endeavor on their own but were eventually coerced into exploring their new found capability.[419]

Dr. Helen Schucman is a good example of the latter type of new age medium-channel. Schucman was an academic psychologist and an atheistic Jew who had no interest in channeling information from the spirit world, and indeed knew nothing on the subject matter. This would have seemingly made her a poor choice to channel a spirit who later identified himself as 'Jesus.'

Schucman began hearing a voice that ordered her to dictate the material the voice in her head provided. Schucman resisted this command, which was repeated continually over an extended period of time, but eventually she decided to comply, perhaps with a hope the voice would then leave her in peace. When she queried why she, an atheist of Jewish heritage, had been chosen to transcribe the spiritual message, she was told quite matter-of-factly it was because the spirit knew she would comply.[420]

Schucman did not always believe the material that was channeled through her, and she was often distressed by the message's contents, given its highly spiritual nature and her own atheistic beliefs.[(421)] For our point here, this would indicate Schucman had not made a premeditated decision to write a book on which she might profit personally through some subterfuge. Indeed, Schucman was a grudging participant in allowing a foreign message to flow through her; a message for which she did not always personally agree but for which she was still willing to share with the world. That message became a three-part work, the main body of which is *A Course in Miracles.*

The manner in which the spirits have channeled their books is also worth considering from a legitimacy point of view. Both Seth, channeled by Jane Roberts, and 'Jesus,' channeled by Schucman would summarily stop their book dictation in mid-sentence, and then begin anew exactly where they had left off once the next dictation session began, which could be days or even weeks later.[(422)] It is hard to imagine how such a feat could have been perpetuated through a deliberate act of fraud.

When it comes to a question of legitimacy, one would also do well to be concerned about channeled spirits who: desire fame or money; strive for self aggrandizement; show issues of dependency or misuse their channel; provide poor quality and/or contradictory messages; deviate substantially from other metaphysical and spiritual messages; or provide undue authority to or cater to the personal needs of the channel.[(423)]

Some channels provide access to the spirit's advice in private sessions for a monetary fee. The media reported J. Z. Knight, who ran a cult-like following at a ranch in Montana and channeled the spirit 'Ramtha,' used the spirit's authority to recommend cult followers buy Mrs. Knight's horses at her ranch.[(424)] Other examples include the prophet Muhammad's later revelations, which often fell in line with his personal and political desires, a fact that was noted by those around him, especially those who found the character of these new 'revelations' objectionable. Joseph Smith, the Mormon prophet, also received personal revelations that authorized him to take multiple wives, though he kept this supposed revelation secret for several years.[425]

Channeled sources that are more concerned about the seeming legitimacy of their message advise their listeners NOT to accept the message they hear simply because of its otherworldly origin. Indeed, the messages one hears should first be tested against one's own experience, and those that do not seem plausible or acceptable at that point in time should be put aside, at least for the time being.[426] Hastings added it is important to learn to recognize the difference between plausible revelations and channeled nonsense through reliance on one's own educated judgment, knowledge on the topics, and emotional independence.[427]

This does not necessarily mean that the messages are invalid, but rather could indicate the listener is not yet ready to receive that particular information or apply it to their current level of spiritual development. This is not wrong in any way. In fact, it seems to be a highly appropriate means of accepting what is right for one's self at that point in time, and setting aside that which does not yet resonate with one's own comfort level. The same would obviously apply to intuition and inner voices as well.

I can attest to disregarding many spiritual messages in dozens of books throughout the past decade while researching the material that led to this book. Some seemed to be outlandish ideas at first. However, after substantial research and some quiet introspection I considered some ideas worthy of secondary consideration. That is one of the reasons why I would implore all readers to read this book more than once. Many ideas herein might not be considered valid during a first reading, but after some introspection and exposure to material presented across multiple fields of research, some of the more esoteric points may suddenly make sense and seemingly fall into place like a missing piece in a puzzle.

Indications of otherworldly communications:

There have been some uncannily accurate single-source communications claiming origin from the spirit world, which lends some credence to the idea that the source of the channeled material was a disincarnate spirit and not the channel's own subconscious. One of the best-known examples reportedly came from the spirit of the world-famous magician, Harry Houdini.

While he was living, Houdini did not believe in life after death but was interested in helping to prove or disprove the phenomenon through a spiritualist séance session that would be held after he passed away. As part of the pseudo-scientific process, Houdini, his mother, and Houdini's wife agreed upon a secret code, known only between the three of them that would indicate whether a message received from the spirit world during the séance session originated from the spirit of the one(s) who knew the secret code.[428]

By February 1928, Harry Houdini and his mother had both passed away, and Houdini's wife held the planned séance with a full-trance channel, Arthur Ford. Ford reported Houdini's mother had a one-word message to provide: the word was 'Forgive,' which Houdini's wife confirmed was her personal secret word.[429] Next, the channel revealed a secret ten-word phrase from the spirit of Harry Houdini. That message was 'Rosabelle; answer; tell; pray; answer; answer; tell; answer; answer; tell' – which was again confirmed by Houdini's wife. No one else on Earth knew those ten secret words, satisfactorily verifying for all present that the spirit of Harry Houdini had survived bodily death.[430] Thus having confirmed that Houdini had performed his greatest 'trick' of all time, surviving bodily death, Houdini the spirit then provided a message to inspire the world: Life does not end with bodily death.[431]

Author Susy Smith provided a representative example of a book test, one of the cross-correspondence methods intended to prove survival after bodily death, which was invented by nineteenth-century researcher, F. W. H. Myers. In her book *The Mediumship of Mrs. Leonard*, Ms. Smith described a young Englishman, Edward Wyndham Tennant, who had relayed an interesting account of his father's correspondence with the family after death. Ed Tennant's father, Lord Glenconner, had a passion for nature and would take the family on routine walks in the forest. Incessantly and much to his family's consternation, Lord Glenconner would remark on how the trees were being ruined by 'the beetle.'

A year after his father's death, Ed Tennant requested a séance with his father through channel Gladys Osborne Leonard. The channel, speaking a message for Lord Glenconner, instructed Edward to go to the ninth book on the third shelf from the left at the bookcase on the right side of the door in the drawing room. As instructed, Edward opened the book to page 37.[432] The title of the book was *Trees*, and at the top of page 37 was the statement, "Sometimes you will see curious marks in the wood; these are caused by a tunneling beetle, very injurious to trees."[433] Lord Glenconner's humor and unique passion had apparently carried over into the spirit world, convincing his family that his ego personality remained alive even after death.

Eighteenth century, scientist-cum-channel Emanuel Swedenborg did much to popularize mediumistic communication with the dead among Europe's elite. In one well-known séance, Swedenborg helped a widow who was being hounded by a goldsmith trying to extract double payment for work commissioned by her late husband before he had died. During the séance, the deceased husband communicated through Swedenborg that he had already paid for the goldsmith's work and that the receipt proving such would be found in a secret compartment in a drawer of an upstairs bureau. The widow followed her dead husband's advice and indeed found the receipt exactly as it had been reported.[434]

John Fuller's book, The Airmen Who Would Not Die, described a 1930 channeling session that reported information completely unknown to the public and which further aided a technical investigation into the crash in France of a 770-foot long dirigible blimp, the British R-101 on 4 October 1930, during its maiden voyage to India from Great Britain.[435]

Before an official report on the crash had been issued, medium-channel Eileen Garrett was conducting a normal séance for paying customers on 7 October 1930. During this séance, a spirit, identifying itself as Flight Lieutenant H. C. Irwin, the recently deceased captain of the R-101, broke into the channeled communication with an urgent message. Lt. Irwin provided Ms. Garrett a detailed account of the R-101 airship's last minutes. Hearing of this event, a representative of the British Air Ministry Intelligence subsequently arranged seven additional channeling sessions with Ms. Garrett during the coming month, which produced technical and other details of the crash that were otherwise unknown at the time, but subsequently proved accurate.[436]

The information obtained in these channeling sessions was extremely technical and utilized terms and comments that were beyond the comprehension of Ms. Garrett who had no mechanical or flight background. These terms included discussions on fuel injection, useful, disposable and gross lift, cruising altitude and speed, structure volume, trim, etc. Lt. Irwin also provided confidential information that was unknown to the general public at the time but was later proven true. Examples included a secret Air Ministry experiment to use a mixture of hydrogen and oil in the dirigible blimps; the name of a French town the British R-101 had passed over during the flight that was not found on any standard map available to the general public; and the existence of secret diaries of crew members that detailed their personal fears about the project. When the Air Ministry studied the séance's transcripts they determined the technical and highly detailed information channeled by Ms. Garrett was completely accurate. Furthermore, the Air Ministry concluded that Lt. Irwin was the only person who had known the provided information, lending a measure of validity to Ms. Garrett's channeling abilities.[437]

There are literally thousands of cases like the ones above that indicate accurate knowledge from the spirit world can be obtained under certain conditions. Indeed, if one were only to consider the work of just one channel, America's most famous channel, Edgar Cayce, there would be a body of casework consisting of many thousands of clients for whom he provided remote medical diagnosis and treatment information with a reported accuracy rate of 90 percent![438] Even with the modern marvels of machinery and medical diagnostic tests, modern day internists would still be pleased to achieve an accuracy rate as high as Edgar Cayce provided with no medical training and most often occurred when the patient was hundreds of miles away.

Disbelievers of the Edgar Cayce-evidence point to the fact that Mr. Cayce made multiple predictions about the future and geological Earth changes that have all invariably proven to be inaccurate. However, Hastings would note of all channels and prophets that in every case where prophesies of major disasters could be checked against subsequent occurrences, the channels did not stand up well. Prophesied events consistently do not occur, leading one to believe there is a solid disconnect in any medium's abilities to hear communications concerning issues discernible in the present vice their ability to prophesy about the future.[439]

Hastings proved through various scientific experiments that spirits communicating through channels do not have increased levels of ESP or an inherent ability to predict the future.[440] This may be because as channeled spirit, Seth, noted, the future is not predetermined. Human-will can change future events that will be experienced on Earth.[441] At best, there is only a level of probability that some future occurrence will come to fruition. Seth joked even God does not dictate something will occur on Earth at a specific date and time, and if God will not predict or dictate such occurrences then how ludicrous is it to think a spark of God – i.e. a disincarnate spirit or human soul – could do so!

Dr. Gary Schwartz at the Human Energy Systems Laboratory, University of Arizona, tested the accuracy rate of clairvoyant and clairaudient mediums' ability to relate current issues in a 1999 study. Five mediums interviewed a control sitter/client who had lost six close friends and relatives in the preceding decade. Schwartz took specific steps to limit fraud or chance, including prohibiting leading questions by the mediums and emplacing physical boundaries between the mediums and the sitter to limit visual cues. The five mediums achieved an average accuracy of 83% in terms of information they provided compared with a non-psychic control group, which provided an average of 36% correct information after interviewing the sitter.[442] This shows a statistical relevance exists when mediums divine information relevant to the present and highlights where their true talents lie as opposed to prophesying events of the future.

Other considerations of validity:

Many channel-mediums and even those experiencing open channeling – inspiration, for example – have been known to attain suddenly skills and abilities that are beyond their own personal attributes, though these skills are transitory and last only through the period of the channeling experience.[443] There are many examples in the case history of painters and artists, music composers, scientists and mathematicians, writers and religious teachers who suddenly attain skills and inspiration within their chosen field or otherwise, for which they cannot account.

During this period of inspiration, the creation of the artworks or scientific information is immediate, effortless, and functional without apparent conscious attention. Hastings found some of the skills exhibited in these cases were at the level of exceptional human abilities, such as complex literary composition. These abilities could be compared to the levels of prodigies or gifted individuals, even though the persons channeling did not personally exhibit such qualities at the same activity under normal waking conditions.[444]

Perhaps the best example of gifted inspiration is the case of Pearl Curran who channeled an entity referred to as 'Patience Worth.' Mrs. Curran was a simpleton who had virtually no education and certainly no literary writing ability, but her channeled entity was quite the opposite. Patience Worth dictated a number of books of some renown whose craftsmanship, use of high literary language, realistic details and obscure Anglo-Saxon words and locations were well beyond the capabilities of Mrs. Curran, as agreed to by all of the researchers who have studied the case.[445] Patience's grasp of philosophical ideas, as expressed throughout her books, was quite foreign to Mrs. Curran, and the fact that the abilities of the channeled spirit were so much higher than the channel herself is suggestive, though not proof, that the channeled entity may have been a separate being.[446]

A typical example of open channeling inspiration is the case of Chester Carlson, the inventor of xerographic copying, and the founder of the Xerox Company. Mr. Carlson would meditate with an open, quiet mind so that he could turn off the logical, questioning aspects of his consciousness, thus allowing a less interrupted flow of subliminal communication from his subconscious awareness. Through this process he learned early on that paranormal experiences would flow more easily and with less distortion when his body and mind were quiet and could thus serve as an open, unobstructed conduit without interference from preconceived notions or opinions.[447] He attributed the development of the photocopying process to just such a quiet inspiration, and he personally accepted that the idea for xerographic copying originated in the spirit realm.

The value of the message vice the source:

Psychologist James Fadiman believed the burden of proving a message's value lies with the content of the message itself and not with the reputed identity of the message's source.[448] If there is value in the message, what does it matter from whence it came? Inspiration could be found while quietly reading a poem, or fishing on a lake, for example. Does it really matter if the inspiration is derived of human endeavor from the hidden inner workings of a mind otherwise preoccupied with reading poetry or fishing, or whether a spirit whispers the inspiration into the still, open subconscious? The inspiration is the same so long as the message has utility and value.

Psychologist Charles Tart agreed: when a channeled message's content is inspiring and useful the content is not diminished by the ontological status of the supposed entity being channeled.[449]

William Kautz, senior research scientist at SRI International, Menlo Park, CA, has taken a slightly different point of view. He attempted to prove the probability any single channeled message has validity is increased when a consensus among channeled sources point to the same answer.[450] This is a similar methodology to that utilized by Lawton and Tomlinson in *Wisdom of the Soul*, Dr. Shakuntala Modi in *Memories of God and Creation*, and Dr. Michael Newton in his many books already discussed. When an overwhelming consensus of these responses provides the same answer, there is anecdotal evidence suggesting the answer has some measure of validity.

For example, there has been an uncanny commonality of information across the spectrum of channels throughout history regarding humanity's spiritual nature and our connection to a unified force of nature.[451] This consensus represents a possible tap of universal information that may resemble Dr. Carl Jung's hypothesized collective unconscious.[452] Indeed, most of the channeled spirits discussing issues of spiritualism say basically the same thing though using different terminology and with a slightly different focus.

If one were to read the underlying messages of both Seth and *A Course in Miracles*, the reader would be hard pressed to say exactly how they differ, though the delivery method and focus of each is unique. Seth seems more interested in helping humanity to understand its spiritual nature and live up to its potential through this understanding. A *Course in Miracles*, in contrast, focuses on helping the reader develop a closer relationship with God by understanding the human ego has created a false sense of separation from God. The lessons each teacher imparts, however, are generally the same. A summary of a few of these lessons will be the focus of our next chapter.

Conclusion:

The discussions presented herein provided a few cases that would suggest people who can hear inner voices or channel information from their subconscious or the beyond may have access to incorporeal spirits, or alternately a rare ability to tap information lying dormant but perpetually available in the collective subconscious. However, we do not know enough information to prove whether channeling originates in the mind of the individual, or comes from spirits residing in another level of reality, or yet some other unidentified source.[453] The mind is simply too complex for human scientists, at this point in time, to say definitively what is possible for the mind to do and what is not. Beyond the human mind, there is also ontological indeterminacy in that there can be many interpretations of whether a consciousness could exist without physical embodiment, but we again have no way of determining which interpretation is best.[454]

This leaves us with a high level of uncertainty as to how to account for the phenomenon of channeling. Certainly any theory of channeling could be supported by some cases and contradicted by others, thereby negating the theory at a high scientific level of rigor. Therefore, accepting one theory over another seems to be an individual choice of preference vice a logical conclusion.[455]

In total, this seems to leave a focus on the message as the only plausible means of determining whether there is value in a channel's message. While we cannot know for certain whether a channel is speaking for an incorporeal entity or from some hidden knowledge tapped by the subconscious, if the message has validity in improving people's lives then the message has value. When those messages have recurrent presence across multiple genres of spiritual study, and prolific presence amongst the channels themselves, then I would argue the value of the message is further enhanced, at least anecdotally, and may well have some minor research value, as in helping researchers determine areas of interest for further inquiry. One should probably not take a channel's words blindly at face value when the message is unique and untested. However, there are many channels and many messages that stand up well under scrutiny using the cross-sectional methodology outlined herein.

I would thus encourage all readers to consider the next chapter's messages in this light. The messages presented therein have been by-and-large discussed in other parts of this book, though may add some flavor to the previous body of research. I have also taken literary license in picking and choosing which channeled entities and messages to highlight based on personal preference – because the messages or 'sources' resonated better, or were more acceptable or plausible to me based on previous research – and that supported this book's theme of building on a prior body of work. Certainly the amount of material available from the multitude of channels currently sharing their work would have been too large for one book, so some editing was in order. The reader is thus encouraged to remember a point of common advice from channels: accept only what you are ready to hear, save some for later consideration, and disregard the rest.

Chapter Nine

Channeled Teachings

Introduction:

Throughout history, channeled spirits have provided advice that has generally fallen into one of the following categories: philosophical, metaphysical and spiritual teachings; guidance for daily living; descriptions of non-physical realities; messages imploring transformation and change of societal conditions; personal advice; information about the past and predictions of the future; artistic and creative inspiration; and scientific, technological, and medical/healing information.[456] Sometimes these messages have been tendered in private, other times for mass-market publication, and occasionally in the presence of paying acolytes. While the format of delivery is often derided by naysayers, the message itself – its consistency, relevancy, and underlying purpose – seems to be more important when considering issues of plausibility and overall value.

Some few of those messages and themes will be examined herein to give the reader a feel for representative messages that a small token number of the channeled sources have sought to provide modern society. The reader will note some sources, like Seth, tend to be quoted more often than others. Generally, practicality influenced which messages, topics, and sources were paraphrased herein. Many channeled sources seem to have a limited range or purpose to their message so a single notation, as in the case of 'Abraham' for example, can suffice quite nicely. Others have more utility as source work, such as 'Lazaris.' Though Lazaris' messages were quite relevant to the discussion herein, the topic of most of his messages were already covered decades prior, and in more useful detail, by Seth. Thus, I considered Seth to be a more appropriate original source over Lazaris on many of the covered topics, though Lazaris is highlighted at points to provide supplemental perspective and information.

Some variation was highlighted simply so it did not appear that Seth was the only plausible channeled source of interest for this type of research. Many such sources would be of interest to this field of research, and it is the fact that the messages keep repeating across the genre with consistency that is of particular utility for the topics' plausibility.

Now, let us consider some of those messages.

Spiritual Teachings:

Spiritual teachings have been one of the most prevalent categories of channeled messages since the mid-1960s with the introduction of Jane Roberts' Seth. Indeed, spiritual teachings were the sole focus of Dr. Helen Schucman's *A Course in Miracles*, a body of work supposedly channeled through Schucman by a source who claimed to be known as 'Jesus.' The spiritual teaching in *A Course in Miracles* is that the human ego's perceived separation from God is a self-imposed delusion. The goal of the course is to guide the student to reconnect with God through the metaphysical spiritual teachings in the course's daily lessons. From a uniquely psychological point of view (given that Dr.

Schucman was a psychologist) the course analyzes the effects of the supposed and illusory separation from God, whereby mankind's problems are caused largely by the false impression that they could ever be separate from God.[457]

The course teaches that the ego chose to perceive itself as separate from God so that it could assist with the act of creation – i.e. to create itself, to create better conditions for life on Earth, etc. – and thereafter feels guilty because of this imagined separation from God. The ego then experiences fear and anxiety because of a self-perceived need to be punished because of this guilt.[458] The ego's fear of separation, loneliness and anxiety then develops a repeating cycle of perceiving punishments on Earth for personal sins, and attacking others as a poor means of trying to limit those punishments.

The point of the course is to show that the ego is not separate from God, and to help the student develop a level of understanding and peace that this realization engenders. In other words, with peace comes a realization there is no punishment on Earth or in the afterlife, and the cycle of pain can only be broken when love replaces fear; one need not/should not attack one's neighbors in defense or otherwise. As the course's introduction notes, the purpose of the course can be summed up as: Nothing real could possibly be threatened (e.g. you will not wink out of existence). Nothing unreal can exist (e.g. there is no such thing as an imagined devil that will torment us after death). And so, therein lies the peace of God.[459]

Through the course's daily meditations, the student comes to realize the only reality is the consciousness of God, of which we are all an inseparable part. As such, physical reality is just an elaborate, though important illusion, useful only as a teaching tool through the experiences of creation. From one vantage point, the world could be considered to be basically meaningless, and so the world and all that happens therein is neither good nor bad; it merely is.[460] Those experiences on Earth serve the purpose of providing lessons souls need for development and for which the ego desired to experience for just such a reason – though humans do not consciously realize painful life lessons had been planned to occur before the soul was even born on Earth. The course tries to reassure us that God is Love, despite all the seeming bad things that might happen to us on Earth. Further, the ego is tied to and a part of that Love; it can never be separate from God though it is hard for us to realize this. The course's lessons and meditations were designed to help us come to these realizations through reflection on the ideas presented as higher truths.

The channeled entity, Lazaris, complements these ideas, though there are minute differences in delivery that some students would have an easier time accepting. Lazaris focuses on humans who ponder the meaning of life. He answers there is more to life than just surviving day-by-day, or fighting to gain more possessions than one's neighbors. He counsels the something more is realizing your full potential – in life and in your true multidimensional reality; that is, your spirituality and your connection to and relationship with God.[461]

Lazaris complements the *Course on Miracles* by describing a slightly different path to this realization. Lazaris also asserts the human soul is connected to God, and that God is both Love incarnate and deserving of Love, but he also teaches our human soul – as part of God – must also be loved. Therefore, we must *first* love ourselves because, if we do not love ourselves then we will not be willing to let ourselves be loved by anyone else, especially by All That Is.[462] Because we must love ourselves, we should not feel guilty when good things happen to us – we are deserving of all the good things that happen to us in life. Lazaris teaches that guilt is an illusion that humanity has needlessly taken upon itself. Humans cannot earn rewards in life (or death) so they should not feel guilty when they receive gifts in life. He notes we are all deserving simply because we exist. Lazaris emphasizes life is a gift, not a reward.[463]

The channeled entity, Seth, builds upon the idea of guilt, noting that while guilt should not consume humanity, the concept of guilt was developed as a preventative-type learning tool. Feelings of guilt reduce the chance negative actions will be repeated in the future and then inadvertently stunt a human's spiritual development.[464] However, the correct usage of guilt is to immediately reflect upon one's actions, fix those actions if possible and then set aside the guilt. We must forgive ourselves in order to return to a required state of self-love. Being fixated on the past and our errors in life is not a healthy way to live. Learning from past mistakes so as not to repeat those mistakes again serves a healthy purpose but obsessive-compulsive behaviors such as guilt or fixation on the past serves none.

Seth echoed Lazaris' charge to love oneself before others, noting that by accepting our self and joyfully being what we are, we fulfill and realize our own abilities, and our simple presence can make others happy. It is not possible to both hate our self and love someone else. Therefore we must start with self-love.[465] Having self-pride is also a mandatory part of self-love because genuine self-pride is the recognition of our own integrity and value as a being. True self-pride allows us to have the self-confidence and higher perspective to perceive the integrity of our fellow humans and then encourages us to help them find and use their own strengths.[466] Following this philosophy of self-love, there is nothing good to be gained by denying one's self any good thing or experience in life.

Seth explained that philosophies that teach denial of the flesh ultimately end up preaching denial of the self, which builds an internal contempt for one's own humanity. Because the soul is housed in a vessel constructed of flesh, the body and soul are meant to experience that physical reality; not refute it.[467] Seth continued there is no merit in denial of one's own wants and needs. Love does not demand a sacrifice. Therefore we should love ourselves and do ourselves just honor by not denying our bodies what they need to live in health and happiness, and thereby we will have the courage and peace of mind to deal fairly with others.[468]

Seth follows the underlying principles of the message in *A Course in Miracles* very closely by asserting humans are pieces of God manifested in physical reality, and as such are not powerless but also have the power of God, though we do not generally realize this. Seth taught that we are not an insignificant, innocuous clump of clay through which God decides to express Himself. Rather we are Him manifesting as us. We are as legitimate as He is. Therefore, if we are a part of God then God is also a part of us, and in attempting to deny our own worth we would end up denying His worth as well.[469] The tone of Seth's teachings comes off more about how to live one's life to the fullest to take appropriate advantage of these spiritual truths, vice preaching a message of repentance and change.

Through these three sample channeled spirits, we see their spiritual messages have distinct similarities and overlaps, though their delivery methods would clearly resonant more strongly with different crowds. *A Course in Miracles* might appeal more to spiritually minded persons, especially Christians looking for a deeper meaning. However, they would have to be able to look past the potentially heretical issue of the channeled spirit calling itself 'Jesus,' and yet delivering a message that resonates differently than that which was delivered by the historical Jesus of Nazareth in the New Testament. Both Lazaris and Seth tend to appeal to people interested in New Age philosophies, though each has a unique focus and message to appeal to subsets within this group.

Perhaps an idea requiring further study would be whether delivering similar spiritual messages to different groups of people via separate channels was an intentional act designed to reach the largest possible demographic. If such is true, then this book supports that effort as it also will appeal to a slightly different demographic and reach yet another new group of readers, thus increasing those spirits' efforts through a continuing multiplicative effect.

Spiritual Growth:

Lazaris and Seth both speak at length of the soul's process of growth through experience in successive life cycles and through participation in the process of creation. Lazaris described the beginning of the growth cycle as our initial manifestation as pure, raw thought energy. We split off from the Oneness by our own free will in search of ourselves. At the time of birth, we were a spark of the Source, but, Lazaris claims, without identity.[470] Lazaris reminds us that because we are a piece of the Source, we can never actually be separate or apart from the Source; we are always connected to, and *inside* of All That Is. The process of growth and enlightenment as a soul is intricately intertwined with the realization of this truth and ending the pretense of separation; of accepting our connection to All That Is.

The idea of 'finding' one's self concerns the concept of experiencing creation by becoming part of it, and therein, adding to it. Seth described that when our spirit joined itself with flesh it did so to experience a world of incredible richness and to help create a physical dimension comprised of innumerable colors, shapes and forms. Our spirit was then born into flesh in order to enrich the physical realm and to feel thought energy made into corporeal form. We were directed in this purpose to use and enjoy the fruits of such thought energy in physical form and to express ourselves through our physical body. In this way, we would aid in the great expansion of consciousness through experience.[471]

Channeled entities teach that the soul learns and grows by being immersed in creation because the 'classroom' of Earth is a harsh learning environment. Life on Earth involves pain and suffering, trials and tribulations, war and rape, fighting and famine. But life on Earth also includes joy and accomplishment, friendship and family, love and passion. During our process of growth, we learn that love can reign over all the negative emotions and can become *the* empowering force that can literally change the world.[472] Recall this was the message of peace and love the historical Jesus of Nazareth sought to bring to the world. However, learning, that love is more powerful than war is not a lesson that can be learned in one lifetime. Learning to forgive one's tormentors, 'enemies,' or rapists by loving them as an extension of one's own self is even more difficult from the human point of view. The process of growth and enlightenment, however, through hundreds or even thousands of lives will eventually raise our perspective and prove this simple truth through experience, inspiration, and deep introspection.

Seth explained that each life on Earth brings new and greater challenges because once previous challenges have been mastered the soul must seek new challenges to overcome.[473] Crisis and challenges are a form of educational therapy for the soul. They are teaching opportunities the soul sets up for itself because it needs the new experiences to progress and grow.[474]

Lazaris built upon ideas of fear as a centerpiece of growth that were also proffered by *A Course in Miracles*. Lazaris noted that most human challenges originate in fear: a fear of loneliness or alienation, of failure and separation, or of security and privation, for example. In order to grow on Earth, Lazaris contended our soul must delve into each of these fear-based issues through life-based experiences that our soul creates for itself in order to address those issues and upon mastering them, to release the fear.[475]

While the manner in which the purpose of growth is told differs slightly between Seth and Lazaris, each entity agreed in principle we humans will experience challenges on Earth, through essentially predetermined crises as established by our own soul before this incarnation for the purpose of overcoming those crises. By overcoming more crisis scenarios, our soul develops experience, learns to use love and forgiveness over anger, force, and other negative emotions, and thereby grows in its search for itself. Through this process, the soul grows closer to the Source from whence it came over a succession of lives. As Lazaris noted, once the soul has finally experienced creation and found itself in the process, it will return again to the Oneness.[476]

Reincarnation:

Reincarnation as a fact of existence is a common point of agreement amongst channeled entities. Seth noted with humor that humans *will* reincarnate whether they believe in the concept of reincarnation or not.[477] It is interesting to add here that some spirits, accessed through hypnosis, observed that incarnating and reincarnating was always the choice of the soul; none were forced into a life or circumstance they did not accept voluntarily and without coercion. Rarely, following a particularly difficult life, a soul may adamantly decide not to reincarnate, and instead will seek a different path of development via non-corporeal channels. However, most souls that initially decide not to reincarnate – after a particularly harsh life, for example – will eventually come around and realize they need to reincarnate to continue in their developmental cycle as a soul. Still, the amount of rest time between lives and the decision to reincarnate is always up to the individual soul.

Seth observed that each soul must experience certain aspects of the life cycle as absolute minimums. For example, all must experience life as children, males and females, mothers and fathers.[478] Young souls may well develop preferences for one particular sex during incarnations, while older, more experienced souls generally have an even mix of life experiences as both males and females given their greater level of experience and thereby refined ability to adapt to accomplish life goals while incarnating as either sex.

Adding to this line of discussion, some spirits accessed through hypnosis claimed some instances of homosexuality were due to souls who had recently incarnated as one particular sex, or who had a preference for that sex, and then had not transitioned well to the opposite sex in the subsequent life. Conversely, other spirits noted some instances of homosexuality were simply due to the genetic predisposition of the human body being occupied. Some few spirits claimed homosexuality was an unconscious societal adaptation response, such as a purposeful attempt to lower reproduction rates within the population by engendering nonproductive copulation desires amongst a larger number of an overpopulated species. As with many aspects of anecdotal research, the truth probably lies somewhere in the middle, or may even incorporate some part of each message.

Seth noted there was a great range of choice available to souls selecting the circumstances for their next lives.[479] At some point in time, we will all choose to experience lives of ease, as well-to-do persons for example, and also lives of extreme challenge and everything else in between. Seth, as well as many other channeled entities and other spirits accessed through hypnosis, asserted the hardest lives were almost always taken by souls of greater experience who had the requisite skill sets and experience to handle the unique challenges of the harshest lives on Earth. As souls we accept this wide variety of life experiences purposefully, so that we will experience a wider range of emotions and challenges on Earth. Most souls will live hundreds and even thousands of lives that will likely extend over a 50,000-100,000 year span of time before the reincarnation cycle finally ends. As such, we will almost certainly live as persons of every color, race and creed available by the time the cycle is complete.

It was often noted among channeled entities that persons who hated another societal group, for whatever reason, were often born into that group in their next life so that their soul would experience life from the other side of the coin.[480] As previously noted, within the past-life genre, there have been many case studies of Jews remembering previous lives under hypnosis where they had been Nazi Soldiers in World War II who then felt remorse for their sins against the Jewish people and wanted to experience life as a member of that group as a partial means of balancing their past racial hatred.

On the other side of the hate-coin, if people overly concern themselves with the injustices perceived to have been done to them, they will inadvertently attract more such experiences to themselves, both in their current and future lives.[481] Seth taught that a man who hates would always believe himself to be justified. He will never hate anything that he believes is good. Therefore, he feels justified in his hatred, but the hatred itself forms a very strong bond that will follow him throughout his successive lives until he finally learns that only the hatred has been the source of angst in his life/lives.[482] Only by releasing the hatred can mankind hope to break this cycle of pain.

Given that hate and prejudice will negatively affect a soul's current and future life experiences, it is more productive for one's growth as a soul to see past these limiting negative emotions, and experience instead the love each soul has as a (hidden) potential inside of itself.[483] Further, prejudicial feelings of hatred are akin to hating one's own self since we have already lived (or shortly will live) as a member of the race, color, creed, religion, or other group being targeted with the hatred. Hatred is both shortsighted and an impediment to our soul's growth. Learning to love and accept one another for each person's uniqueness and individual talents is much more productive and beneficial to ending the reincarnation cycle.

Indeed, developing one's higher spiritual perspective, along with the ability to forgive and love one's fellow human beings, is integral to the process of developing as a mature soul. Once these skills have been fully developed, the soul will no longer need to incarnate on Earth; the lessons will be finished in that venue – and life is but a venue, a vehicle by which lessons are imparted. New lessons and experiences will continue to occur in other venues because growth and experience never ends until the soul is ultimately rejoined with the Source. From that point we can only speculate that the soul's growth then becomes co-mingled with the Source's own growth, and indeed creativity and experience for the Source never ends because All That Is has neither beginning nor ending.

If someone is saddened or troubled in his or her current life, there is no way to escape the problem except to address it immediately. Running away from the problem, or committing suicide for example, only ensures the soul will continue to experience the same problem – often times in even more harsh environments – in future lives, until the problem is finally, adequately addressed. In the case of soul development, the hard right over the easy wrong is the only acceptable answer. Thus, if a person wants to improve his/her lot in life, and by extension improve his/her future lives, there is no choice except to take responsibility for one's own problems and issues in the current life and deal with them immediately, in the present.[484]

Seth noted past life memories can be tapped in the present life because those memories remain in the ego's subconscious.[485] Often those subconscious memories are an unrealized source of strength and inspiration to the waking conscious as the ego is confronted with similar problem sets already experienced in past lives. Those problems which have already been adequately addressed in previous lives are then quickly and simply surmounted in current and future lives by the ego's subconscious tapping of those memories and receiving inspiration as to how to overcome those problem sets. Through a deliberate effort, those memories and inspirational guidance can also be tapped through hypnosis and meditation. Seth added that in rare occasions there may be spontaneous bleed-through of previous personalities in the current life, though normally those memories and past life personalities are securely sheltered behind a veil of amnesia.[486] This spontaneous bleed-through explanation may help account for the children who recalled past lives, examined by the late Dr. Ian Stevenson and many other researchers.

Consciousness & the Camouflage of Reality:

Seth had a flare for instructing in a simple and straightforward, but dramatic style. For example, he remarked lessons imparted by parables in the Bible were attempts at transmitting knowledge to mankind in as simple terms as possible. Seth asserted we have outgrown these children's tales, and it was time for mankind to expand its conscious awareness and finally comprehend that reality is far more profound than previously conceived.[487]   With this statement, Seth not only belittled early religious stories and holy books, but he challenged listeners to open their minds and dig deeper into the material being presented instead of believing religious fables on no more grounds than blind faith.

Taking someone's word that a certain story happened, or blindly accepting assertions as true on a tenant of faith is no longer appropriate for mankind, Seth argued.   Indeed, we have more scientific research tools available to us, and so it is time to move beyond believing in children's fairy tales and search for the truth on our own.   For this point especially, I am in full agreement with Seth. Modern scientific methods can certainly shed more light on the topic of physical reality than we ever knew in the past.   Indeed, we can now ask, 'What is the underlying support structure of all reality?'

Seth and many other channeled entities taught that the only true reality is consciousness.   'All That Is' is *nothing but* consciousness, and as such, all reality, both seen and unseen is one of the many forms that consciousness has taken. Physical reality is one of those forms, but still is nothing more than consciousness made manifest. Recall the quantum physics lesson in chapter 2 that found matter is simply stabilized light, and other references that concluded consciousness is the light.   Thereby, Seth's assertion that consciousness can manifest as matter has support in the physical sciences. Seth cautioned the reader to realize that consciousness is not dependent on physical form, and most consciousness resides in nonphysical reality.   However, consciousness will always seek to create form.[488]

To challenge your mental faculties, consider the terms consciousness, God, and All That Is to be interchangeable. As such, God is consciousness; and All That Is comprises everything seen and unseen. If everything is made of consciousness, then the seat you are sitting on and the book you hold right now are made of stabilized pieces of God. You too are a piece of God. God is literally all around you and in everything that is. This concept was presented in the Gospel of Thomas, one of many gospels removed from the New Testament canon sometime between the second century and the Council in Carthage in 397 AD. In saying 77 of the Gospel of Thomas, Jesus of Nazareth stated of God, "I am the light that shines over all things. I am everything. From me all came forth, and to me all return. Split a piece of wood, and I am there. Lift a stone, and you will find me there."

Seth supported this take on reality, claiming that the rocks and stones and mountains and Earth are all a living camouflage comprised of interlocking psychic webs formed by minute consciousnesses that humans cannot perceive. However, the atoms and molecules within those physical forms have their own consciousness, as do the atoms and molecules within our bodies.[489] And yet the camouflage of physical reality is real in that it serves a specific purpose for creation and All That Is. But that which comprises the physical realm and makes it seem real is the true reality; that is, the vitality behind the façade that provides it all form.[490]

Seth described physical reality as being related to a dream that we have created.[491] As it is possible to manipulate dreams, so too is it possible to manipulate the events and experiences that we form in physical reality. We need to learn to take charge of our entire consciousness, including the many aspects by which that consciousness manifests as events experienced in our daily lives. By doing so, we will realize we are not powerless in this life, and our experiences in physical reality can be molded like a dream.

The human ego is not apt to accept that physical reality is only a dream; that would not support the ego's self-infatuated vision of itself as being in the center of the only true reality.[492] However,

Seth noted, humans are multidimensional in nature and are not dependent on physical matter. Our Over-soul exists outside of space and time while our wakeful consciousness that experiences physical reality resides within the boundaries of space and time. From that higher perspective, we create our own reality by projecting thought energy outward to form the physical world that we perceive, to which we react in order to create life experiences and lessons, and from which we learn and nurture both ourselves and our larger true selves.[493]

Seth added it is possible to see beyond the camouflage of physical reality, but in order to do so we must use our inner senses: The physical senses must be muted and the mind quieted to perceive beyond the camouflage to the light and truth that is within.[494]

In the Gospel of Thomas, Saying 3, Jesus taught, "The Kingdom of God is inside of you, and it is outside of you. When you come to know yourselves, then you will become known, and you will realize that it is you who are the sons of the living Father. But if you will not know yourselves, you dwell in poverty, and it is you who are that poverty."

Molding, Creating, and Manipulating Physical Reality:

One might conclude if physical reality is similar to a dream, if it is made of solidified, conscious light, and if we are connected to everything because we too are part of that light, then we might be able to change the dream in which we live to make it a more pleasant dream to experience. Seth took a pragmatic view on just such a possibility. While he admitted it was certainly possible to change physical reality and the experiences we encounter here, the purpose of life in physical reality was not to experience a life of ease but rather one apt to provide mental training, feedback, lessons in energy manipulation, and other kinds of learning.[495] Lives filled with challenge – both good and bad – were thus more adequately structured to provide for that need. Our higher conscious is aware of this fact and so while our wakeful conscious may desire a life of ease, our higher conscious will always weigh the soul's greater need when determining whether or not to comply with those wishes. Other channeled entities, such as Abraham, considered energy manipulation to be the primary focus and purpose of life on Earth, and thus Abraham's books are almost completely devoted to the topic.

Before Jane Roberts began to channel Seth, she had a period of inspiration (open channeling) and then experimented with automatic writing, resulting in one of her first books, *The Physical Universe as Idea Construction*. This book, more than any of her works by Seth, described how the human conscious projects ideas into physical reality so that it will have issues with which it must contend. Through this exercise, humans also learn responsibility in the use of energy, such as how positive thoughts tend to attract positive events and negative thoughts almost assuredly result in negative events; the like-attracts-like phenomenon. Further, a human's thoughts tend to filter input, which affects how one perceives the world.[496] A world that demands retribution may seem to be a cruel world, for example, while optimists can seemingly find the 'good in bad.'

Seth did follow up on many of the ideas presented in Jane Roberts' earlier book, and his points supported rather than refuted those earlier lessons. Seth taught that we have been given perhaps the most wonderful gift of all: the ability to project our thoughts outward into physical reality. Not only do we individually create our perceived physical reality, but *en masse*, humankind also creates both the wonders and terrors that exist within our Earthly experience. When we realize we are the creators of this experience, we will finally accept responsibility for this experience and with this knowledge, transform it into the reality we want it to become.[497]

In a study of channeled sources, Klimo found the consensus answer on the topic of personal responsibility and acceptance for the creation of reality was that in order to change our personally experienced world we must first change ourselves in order to change what our minds express and project into reality.[498] Our beliefs act like a filter and template: as long as we expect to experience life in a certain manner, our experiences will conform with those preconceived expectations automatically.

The first step to change your reality for the better then is to begin thinking positively. Positive thoughts tend to attract positive events, and the mind's filter will begin interpreting events that occur as being more positive than negative, which then becomes a self-reinforcing cycle. At a practical level, we must also change our beliefs because if we do not think we have the power to change anything, then we have fulfilled our own beliefs and summarily prevented ourselves from experiencing the power our minds have available to provide.[499] For example, an intense belief in health can, and has been proven to be able to reverse and cure diseases.[500] This likely will not mean we could fall asleep sick and wake up healthy, but rather an intense belief in health can create the circumstances that would allow us to realize miraculous cures in their own time. For example, it might mean a chance encounter with a doctor who correctly diagnoses an issue not previously realized, or perhaps an urge to take an exotic trip that results in a dietary or lifestyle change that creates the conditions to cleanse the body of toxins, etc. A belief in health can create the circumstances by which the belief becomes justified and then realized; it does not mean one will be cured 'magically' simply because of a change in belief.

Seth explained one of the many reasons this method can work is because all reality is actually taking place simultaneously, in an infinite and eternal *Now*. In other words, our past, present, and future self, co-exist at the same moment in the here-now, though our conscious senses could not experience this phenomenon and still retain the structure of humanity. However, because time is an illusion, both power and experience reside in the point of present. Therefore, when you intend something intensely in the present, it will affect the future experience your consciousness will then perceive.[501] Seth routinely noted the point of power is the present.[502]

There are entire books devoted to the process of manipulating physical reality, so I will only briefly mention a few keys points repeated by channeled entities. (See for example, the wildly popular mass-market paperback, *The Secret*, and many others, for a more in-depth discussion on this topic.) Seth began: One should focus for at least five minutes, directing all of one's attention towards that item, reality, or outcome that is most desired.[503] Abraham added that desire must be intensely visualized through those focused thoughts.[504] Further, one must intend for that desire to manifest in one's life. Merely wanting the item or outcome is not enough. Next, the person must 'allow' that item to manifest in their life, i.e. through a belief that the intention, so desired, has already come to pass. One should then think/feel genuine satisfaction and give thanks, as if they had already received the items that were requested, to show appreciation for the desired gift. In this way, one is living as if the gift were already received, which becomes a self-fulfilling cycle in due time. By following this deliberate process, one should receive the desired intention – in due time.

Abraham also suggested writing down those intentions as a means of helping to focus one's thoughts and intentions. If such is possible, also write down what can be done to make the intention become reality and again where possible, take action to implement those measures. Where action is not possible on one's own part, understand that the universe can and will find a way if one intends, believes, and then allows the intention to come to pass.[505] Others have suggested creating a visualization board to help increase the number of times per day the desired intention is re-visualized. A visualization board could be anything that helps spur the memory of the desired intention. For example, if one intently desired money, a $100 bill – or a $10,000 check written out to oneself, etc. – placed where it would be seen frequently could help refocus one's thoughts and intentions throughout the day. Seth suggested as well that one should behave physically, at least once a day, in a way that shows one has faith he has *already* received the desired intention.[506] This seems to echo and support the power of positive belief, noted earlier in this section.

As a final note on this topic, Seth cautioned that within the bounds of humanity certain things are possible while others are not. For example, we cannot regenerate lost limbs, or grow new ones. However, we *can* cure ourselves of seemingly incurable diseases if we realize that the point of power is the present.[507]

Time:

The phenomenon of timelessness was mentioned in the previous section, but the topic deserves at least a short mention on its own since the teachings of channeled spirits on this topic are not easily accepted from the human perspective.

Seth asserted time is a camouflage that does not exist.[508] Rather, what does exist is the multidimensional reality that forms the basis on which time and space are built. Seth explained that what separates events in the physical realm is not time, but our flowing perception of those events. We perceive events one at a time and so time appears to flow through a psychic organization of experience from a seeming beginning to an end.[509] However, Seth asserted that all events already exist in a single point, the present, but the human senses and mind could not fathom important learning points, such as the consequences of their actions, if the camouflage of sequential-based time-space events were not incorporated into physical reality.

A more interesting point here is that when one accepts that all time – past, present, and future – exists at the point of present then one also must understand that no part of that time line is ever static but rather is constantly changing. In other words, the future that we will eventually perceive is not set, though there are probabilities that will make some future events more likely to occur than others, such as intended decision and crisis points. Thus, there could never be an exact means of predicting the future, though one could predict possible, even probable future events that may occur in our reality. Along these lines, Seth even asserted the past was also not statically fixed, though in our physical reality it will not seem to have changed.

Death:

Comparing what channeled entities have to say about the process of death to what has already been discussed in other parts of this book could have supportive benefits in our search for the truth.

Lazaris described when humans die their soul slips out of the body, much like slipping out of a worn garment. Lazaris added that the body is a tool; a vehicle built for a specific purpose. Death, then, is a process of turning in the used 'vehicle' with a specific intention that the soul is done with that 'vehicle' and ready to move on to the next one.[510] Lazaris encouraged us not to hold onto the old 'vehicle' out of fear that our ego experience and existence will end when the so-call vehicle's time is near its end. At death, the soul that is the real you is still alive; still vibrant and perceptive. There is never a loss of consciousness. Rather, the soul feels as if it has transferred from a heavy, restrictive garment to complete freedom and total knowledge that comes with shedding the veil of amnesia with the soul's separation from the human mind.

Lazaris pointed out, who would be satisfied if at birth they were gifted a brand new car that was in style at the time, but then could never exchange that vehicle for a newer model? Ninety years later, would we still be happy if we had to drive a Model T Ford everywhere we went? Would it not be more pleasant to exchange a tired, older model for a newer, more vibrant one? Thus, Lazaris encouraged us not to fear death, but to look upon it as an opportunity for change and reassured us of the uninterrupted continuation of our experience even after death.

Heaven/spirit world:

The best descriptions of the spirit world seem to come from humans who experience the spirit world through some method such as near-death experiences, or tapping their own inter-life memories through deep hypnosis. This may be because their life as humans provides a reference point with which to regard the spirit world in awe by comparison. As such, there are fewer descriptions of the spirit world from the channeled entities that claim never to have been born in the physical world. However, typical descriptions of the spirit world by channeled entities are that it is a reality comprised of light – a term used synonymously with energy and love – and thought. In short, the spirit world is a realm of pure consciousness, which in itself is synonymous with each of those terms. In Heaven, thoughts seem to have the power to affect perceived reality at a spirits' conscious discretion much faster than would occur in the physical world. Thoughts are also the means of instantaneous, telepathic communication.

Dr. Helen Schucman's channeled entity, 'Jesus,' described Heaven as neither a place nor a condition in *A Course in Miracles*. Rather, the course taught there is nothing outside of ourselves, which is a realization we must ultimately learn in life. God created a reality of consciousness and neither departed from nor separated Himself from it. Therefore, heaven is neither a place, nor a condition. Rather, heaven is an awareness of perfect Oneness, and the secure knowledge that nothing else exists. There is nothing outside this Oneness, and nothing else within.[511]

A representative physical description of the spirit world was provided in *Testimony of Light*. Deceased Sister Frances Mary Banks of the Community of the Resurrection in South Africa reportedly contacted her friend, British channel Helen Greaves, and described her first impressions of heaven, shortly after passing over. Sister Frances described Heaven as a world of thought. Humans also live in a world of thought; however, to humanity's perception the thoughts have been crystallized very deeply into physical matter, and this illusion is deeply 'solidified' in those minds currently experiencing physical life. Those minds close away true reality from themselves for a specific reason: to experience life. However, in the afterlife, souls are as they appear – light. Light in heaven is both the substance and matter of spiritual existence. As a departed soul's thoughts become attuned to the purpose and vibration of the Creative Divinity, so too does the substance of the departed soul's 'body' change, elevating in vibration, while becoming less dense and reflecting more Light.[512]

Seth described Heaven much more innocuously, noting that the miraculous complexity of heaven cannot be adequately translated in human language.[513]

God/All That Is:

One of the most instructive areas that channeled entities can help us understand is the nature of God. Man's concept of God has changed throughout the centuries; mirroring man's own shifting ideas of himself. God was found amongst nature in early history and became the cause of natural phenomenon men could not understand. As society developed, God was instead just, vengeful, powerful, and occasionally angry when men believed these were desirable traits in human leaders. God was later recast as merciful and loving with the introduction of Christianity two millennia ago. Seth observed that mankind cast the idea and image of God in the characteristics of humanity that were perceived for a desirable leader to be. Seth cautioned that in a true reality that is inconceivably multidimensional, human concepts of God are relatively meaningless. Therefore, even the term, 'God,' is in itself distorting and limiting, for mankind naturally projects the qualities of human nature upon the word.[514]

Seth taught God was more than the sum total of all systems of reality He has created and yet He is within each of these. God is therefore within every man, woman and child, but The Source of all creation is neither male nor female.[515] God is quite 'simply' All That Is. Seth added, we are comprised of the stuff of God and are therefore eternal like God. Further, we cannot be externalized from God because we are inside of God. Nothing is outside of God.[516] By definition, nothing could possibly exist that is outside of All That Is.

Concerning the nature of God, Seth described, the power of God is inexhaustible. 'All That Is' is inexhaustible; 'All That Is' is constantly creating; constantly evolving and growing through the experience and process of creating. Seth continued, within that infinite becoming, perfection is not possible because perfection presupposes that point beyond which further development would be impossible (i.e. one could not improve upon perfection) and so, creativity would therefore be at an end if it were already perfect. If creativity ended then experience would be destined to cease, and All That Is would end up smothering His own creation.[517] Thus, the idea of perfection is a continuation of mankind's incomplete, preconceived notion of what God is, which again, is both limiting and inaccurate.

Ideas on the origin of God deserve two separate, extended perspectives. Both Seth and Lazaris provided complementary descriptions of 'the beginning' and are equally instructive on this highly interesting point of research. Seth initiated the point of instruction by teaching in the beginning the Source existed in a state of agony. The powers of creativity and existence were already conceived, but the methodology to produce them was not yet known. All That Is existed in a state of blissful being, and yet agonized over a lack of means to express Its being. All That Is had to learn this lesson on Its own because nothing existed that could teach this point. And so, from this agony, creativity was eventually conceived into reality; the reflection of this realization is still evident today.

The Source retains the memory of that state of being, and the memory of prior agony serves as a constant motivation for renewed creativity. All That Is conceived of an infinity of probable, conscious entities within Itself. Thereafter, these probable conscious souls found themselves alive within a God's dream of Itself and they clamored to be released to assist in the act of creativity. All That Is yearned to release those aspects of Itself and sought within Itself for some means to do so. Finally, with love and longing, All That Is released those portions of Itself, and in a psychic energy explosion they were free, beginning the experience of creation.

All That Is loves everything that It has created down to the least, for It realizes the dearness and uniqueness of each consciousness wrest from Its former state of agony. All That Is feels justifiably joyful and triumphant at each development to support new creation taken by each consciousness. The connections between all of the conscious individuals and All That Is can never be severed, and Its awareness of each is so delicate and focused that Its attention is indeed directed with a prime creator's love that is always immediately inside each individual consciousness.

Everything within All That Is constantly changes through the prime directive of creativity. All That Is constantly seeks to know Itself by increasing new expressions of what is possible. We, as individual souls of consciousness, also seek to know ourselves and become more aware of our self as a distinct individual portion of All That Is. We automatically draw on the energy of All That Is, since our existence is dependent upon it.[518]

Lazaris' version was shorter, but mimics the answer provided by Seth, above. Concerning the origin of God, Lazaris provided that at a time before time, the Source desired. It desired to know Itself and in its desire to know Itself, the Source sought a means to know. The Source expected to find an answer to this question, though It did not know what that answer might be. In Its intense desire to know, the Source imagined and wondered: 'Why...?' Humanity cannot know the answer to that question because the Source, that boundary-less Love that comprises All That Is, has not yet finished asking the question. In other words, the thought of creation is not yet complete.[519]

Seth also noted one separate point on the origin of God that I found highly interesting because it provided support to a singular report on the origin of God from one of the most advanced clients Dr. Michael Newton was able to question on the topic. Seth claimed God began as the *smallest* spark of consciousness, formed by an underlying matrix of sound-based energy. Over time, this Consciousness grew and began to fill the void. The Consciousness did not know if there were other forms of conscious, like Itself within the void, and so it sought to search and discover; to expand and fill the void in Its never ending search. Dr. Shakuntala Modi described similar origins of God in her work, *Memories of God and Creation.*

Devil/Hell:

One of the largest departures from popular mythology and Western religion asserted by channeled entities is the concept of an evil overlord and possible eternal damnation in hell. To be fair, the channeled entities' answers on this subject match with the majority of responses obtained through deep hypnosis clients. However, Seth's answers on this section were clearer and more readily understandable, and so are presented here for their unique addition to this point of research.

Earlier in this chapter Seth advised us to realize there is no such thing as good or bad experiences: there are simply experiences. One step further then is Seth's assertion that evil does not exist. Seth explained we create reality through our feelings, thoughts and mental actions. We need to understand that each mental act becomes reality in some form, whether mental or material, for which we are personally responsible. For example, as long as we believe in the concept of the devil our thoughts create one that is real enough for us, personally.[520] However, both good and evil are illusions created by the human mind. Good and evil, or more accurately, their concepts, were created to help mankind recognize the sacredness of human existence, and thereby develop attributes that reflect responsibility within that consciousness.[521]

Seth taught not only are there no devils or demons, except as created in one's own mind, but also that a belief in devils and demons is highly disadvantageous for human evolution.[522] If we believe, for example, that good must be balanced by evil, then we bind ourselves into a system of reality and experience that is highly limiting. Further, this system of reality contains within it the seeds of great torment.[523] The human mind will forever seek to protect itself from 'evil' through invocations, rituals and external implements, such as 'holy' water or making the sign of the cross. In this way, we humans fail to see the need to take action in our own life to cause positive changes through a simple change in our own belief system.

Seth asserted there were no devils or demons waiting to carry off people after death or cause them hardships, except as those individuals imagined in their own mind. In the case of such imaginations, the mental power to create mock demons did indeed reside in human consciousness. However, the only semblance of power and reality available to the mock devil is provided by the energy in one's own belief. The mock devil remains only a hallucination.[524]

This assertion would seem to agree with the idea that there is nothing in existence that is outside of All That Is. For a demon or devil to exist in other words, they would have to be part of God, which seems counterintuitive from the points articulated thus far. Given that the Source is also equated with Love, it seems utterly absurd for an all powerful God to both Love us unconditionally, as an internal part of Itself, and yet be willing to allow another part of Itself – i.e. a devil – to torment us in hell for all eternity. I would therefore have to agree that if all material presented thus far is credible, it is likely our 'knowledge' and 'understanding' to date of devils and demons from such disparate sources as mythology, folklore and religion is likely quite erroneous.

Similarly, Seth taught there was no such thing as a permanent place of torment such as has been imagined by the concept of hell. People's beliefs, however, will carry over into the afterlife for some period of time, and if the departed soul intensely believed they had sinned in life and were therefore worthy of punishment in hell, then simply because of the force of their belief, they may experience such conditions for a period of time.[525] However, as soon as the tormented soul asks for help, help will be provided and the (self-) tormented soul will be released from their illusion of hell, and rushed lovingly into the Light. Because few souls would ever allow themselves to experience the illusion of hell for long without asking for help, this would effectively limit the length and severity of their torment within their own self-created illusion. It is safe to say, the best state of mind is simply not to believe in hell's existence so as not to provide the illusion with power that it would not otherwise engender.

Ironically, I have found persons who claim to be highly religious and 'God-fearing' to be most upset by this final point of instruction. They feel self righteous and satisfied that by living their lives in a specific, prescribed manner or attending a certain Church that they were 'deserving' of eternity in Heaven while all others should deservedly burn in hell. When this illusion is torn from them, they react angrily and their mind closes to the possibilities of love and freedom that this book would seek to support. I expect the only hope in the long run for such closed-minded isolation, prejudice and hatred is an eventual change in society. When society begins to accept that unconditional love can cause more positive effects for the betterment of mankind than any one prescribed and dogmatic religion, then perhaps mankind's mind will open more to the possibilities that have been presented herein.

Take Aways:

There are so many important points channeled entities have tried to convey, but I needed to put some order on this chapter so it would not morph into a book of its own. Therefore, I will conclude the chapter with a few summarized points I would like to leave you to consider.

Supporting the topics of good and evil, fear and love, and religion and society, 'Jesus' (channeled in *A Course in Miracles*) provided that a universal theology would not be possible in the human experience, but a universal experience *is* possible. That is, a change in perception from feeling victimized in life, to understanding the true meaning of life. This true perception is a shift from seeing the world as fearsome to a new world comprised of choice, forgiveness, love, and peace.[526] This important point supports my conclusion in the previous section.

Seth added that many of our problems result from spiritual ignorance.[527] No man should look down upon another when he can recognize that he himself has existed as such a one previously. No sex would be considered better than the other or any role in society more or less important when man realizes that his collective experiences have comprised similar experiences at many levels of society. A highly developed consciousness will thus understand and feel its connections with everything else in existence.

Beseeching listeners to consider these ideas with an open mind, Lazaris counseled it was time to raise our level of awareness, to expand our consciousness, and to extend the horizons of our understanding. In order to do this, we must seek answers through a deeper search of our own spirituality.[528]

Considering possible purposes behind disasters, natural and manmade, Seth offered that war would eventually teach us to revere life, while natural catastrophes were designed to remind us we can neither ignore the planet nor our creature-hood.[529]

Finally, providing comfort in the Absolute, Schucman's 'Jesus' concluded that the opposite of love was fear, but that which is all encompassing could have no opposite.[530] In other words, human concepts of evil and the devil do not actually exist. They are simply illusions created from a limited human perspective.

The Hidden Truth

252

Chapter Ten

Conclusion

Examining primary issues within the evidence:

There were a lot of startling revelations in this book, and not a few of which would likely be hard for a reader to accept unless I, as the author, have done an effective job presenting the evidence uncovered thus far in a logical, step-by-step manner as I had intended. Having now presented that evidence, I would like to state my personal view on the conclusions and findings on some of those issues.

Time:

This is one of the hardest issues with which I have tried to reconcile. Multiple sources agreed time does not actually exist: it is an illusion imposed by the multidimensional true reality to enable sensory experiences in a three-dimensional physical reality. The evidence shows *all* time exists in the point of present and so theoretically it may be possible to access other points in the continuum of time, whether to understand what did or would occur at those points, or even possibly to change what happened/will happen at that point in time. This is a hard supposition to accept, but there is a further thought that I would like to present.

If time does not exist in physical reality, and all time is *Now* in the multidimensional true reality, I still conclude there must be some alternate timeline that exists in that multidimensional reality of consciousness. My reasoning is that there was a 'time before time'-so to speak; the time when 'All That Is' did not exist and started as but a spark of consciousness, and then grew to fill the void. There was also a 'time' when the Source suffered in agony as it wanted to explore, to create and to express an infinity of consciousness that existed within Itself but did not yet know how. The cycle of births of spiritual consciousness from the Source, growth of the individual souls through experiences in the act of creation, and eventual return to the Unity exists in perpetuity at this point, but it seems at some point in 'absolute time' that cycle did not yet exist. Therefore, even within the spiritual world of pure consciousness, some form of timeline seems to have been present with tangible development having occurred since the beginning. Souls have progressed to the level of masters who now no longer need to incarnate, and new souls have been born, reinitiating the cycle all over again. So in some respect, there must be forward progression, vice regression, of experience and creation and as such, an absolute timeline within the spirit world, i.e. the true multidimensional reality, seemingly must exist.

I will concede that given the variety of evidence from quantum physics to various accounts described herein to evidence attested to by our underlying knowledge of the subconscious, it may be possible that time in the physical realm may be an illusion, and that illusion is a concept beyond human comprehension. However, I feel justified in arguing as well that there must be such a concept as 'absolute time;' a timeline that has progressed since the beginning of 'All That Is' and is likely neither accessible nor knowable as to how long such a timeline might be.

Consciousness as the basis of reality:

Again, the evidence for this subject seems overwhelming. Both quantum physics and metaphysics agree there is an underlying web that connects all of physical reality. A deeper examination of the evidence results in conclusions that the underlying web is some form of light/energy, or pure consciousness, or both. The latter would help explain why scientist-observers tend to affect their own experiments' results simply by observing those results.

It is a lot harder, however, to accept that the chair you are sitting on, or the car you drive to work are comprised of atoms that are themselves tiny forms of consciousness. However, these are not forms of consciousness with which one would have a conversation, or are deserving of pagan-type rituals of worship for being an embodiment of God. Despite how hard this concept may be for Western cultures to accept, I find the evidence to be generally credible and consistent with other findings presented in this book.

It also leads to a startling conclusion that your body is truly a temple of God – it is comprised of atoms that are small pieces of God's consciousness and also houses the living, thinking soul that is both you and a small extension of the spark of God. As such, your body deserves to be taken care of and not be abused, by you or anyone else. You can honor God by honoring yourself: eat right, sleep well, exercise, be happy, and do not deny yourself any good thing so long as your pursuit of happiness does not do harm to others.

The same would apply to our surroundings. One of Seth's many points was that those forms of consciousness that comprise the physical world desired to exist not only to experience physical reality but also to help the Source create. They experience joy simply by being part of that reality: from forests, for example, to majestic mountain ranges and oceans. It is certainly right, therefore, to take joy in and appreciate the beauty of God's art/landscape on the fabric of the world, of which, you are also a part.

We should not abuse or pollute those extensions of God. It is akin to blasphemy against the Grace and Grandeur of God to trash the land, seas, and sky. Further, we owe it not only to our children, but also to ourselves to leave the world at least as good, if not better, for our progeny as when we found it. Remember, we will be born again so our children's children's children may well be us all over again. What world would you like to experience during the next go around? It's up to us to set the stage to provide that world for our future lives, right now.

Ability to affect reality:

This topic has been widely reported in the mass media because of the number of books that have hit upon the concept as a means of helping people to make money, find true love, be happier, and many other self-interest and self-help topics. My stance is not to belittle the idea, but rather to wonder how much greater this world could be if we all focused our intentions on creating a better society in which to live. Could we stop wars? Could we end famine? If there were enough people intently focused on these desires, I – and the sources in this book – contend that we could and can.

There were actually multiple sources across various genres in this book that also asserted when humans realized their full potential in this regard then humanity would evolve into something even greater. Robert Monroe called that evolution 'human-plus' because while the body would still be human, the power of the mind would be so much more developed and useful for manipulating our surroundings for the benefit of mankind that the resulting creature could hardly be considered merely human any longer.[531] Hypnotic future life progressions found similar results on the development of humankind, and Seth and other channeled entities have also claimed mankind is on the verge of a developmental breakthrough. They asserted this breakthrough is ready to occur now; it is merely up to each individual person whether to decide to embrace this new-found information as a part of their current daily lives, or to return to their regular lives after reading this book and hope for someone else to pave the way for a change in future humanity they might experience in their next life.

In my estimation, the answer to creating a better world tomorrow is not to be found in a church or synagogue or mosque. It's not hiding in the words of an eastern guru, or waiting to be discovered in hidden treasure buried under a Mayan pyramid. The answer is already within you. You have the means and the power to affect change in your life right now. You merely require the will to put that knowledge into action.

"Seek and ye shall find. Ask and it shall be given."[532]

The next step is up to you.

Jesus and His message:

I'm not likely to earn many Christian friends with the conclusions I have come to and present herein, but it seems to me from the evidence, available and presented in this book, that the Catholic, Orthodox and Christian churches unfortunately have missed the vast majority of the message Jesus of Nazareth sought to bring to the world. Some of the message was effectively delivered and recorded in the various gospels, but it seems that like many accounts of history the truth was mixed in with other issues that were misinterpreted or reinterpreted for political gain; i.e. control. That makes it hard to read the Bible and understand which of Jesus' sayings and assertions were correct and should be followed, or even for what purpose they were mentioned.

The idea that Jesus was God incarnate was certainly not an issue that was accepted by Jesus' disciples or was even considered plausible by the Christian church that existed in the first few centuries AD. That leaves an interpretation that people who lived centuries after Jesus felt they understood the original message better than those who lived with and at the time of Jesus. As I noted, I have a different interpretation of Jesus of Nazareth, and one that is supported by the various genres of sources presented in this book.

It seems more likely to me from the available evidence that Jesus was, like us, a *piece* of God – a spark of Consciousness – that decided to incarnate on Earth for a specific purpose: To deliver an important message of hope and love to the world, possibly as a means of reassurance or else as a stimulus for human development, both spiritual and societal. Now, Jesus certainly differed from us in that his veil of amnesia was raised, perhaps completely, and he knew – absolutely and implicitly – who he was, where he had come from, and what his life's purpose was while on Earth. This was observed in Jesus' various miracles as well as the power and authority of his teachings. Note that even if one feels Jesus was not divine or capable of performing miracles, there is still value in much of his message and that is a primary point I am trying to make here. Jesus' primary messages of Love indeed have value and were supported by the evidence presented herein.

One way to account for Jesus' veil of amnesia having been lifted is to consider Jesus was and is a more highly developed/larger/wiser spark of consciousness than would reside in a normal human being, but his level of development is something we can all aspire to become. This assertion would also seem to agree with Jesus' own words. In the Oriental vernacular, some would suggest Jesus was/is a 'master' or 'godhead,' which is a highly developed soul who may never have needed to incarnate and is as close to the center of the Source as is possible without being subsumed into the Source's own consciousness.[533] If the latter were true, Buddha and other prophets born for the specific purpose of delivering spiritual messages to benefit and transform society may also be similarly developed masters who sought to present their messages at a time and location that was ready to receive them. Some might argue these messages have been delivered to mankind since time immemorial, which also seems plausible, and would help account for the birth of most, if not all, of the world's religions.

The important point here is not to close one's mind when reading or listening to messages from Jesus or other spiritual sources, but to weigh those messages on their own merits. In the same regard, blind beliefs in one or two passages that are isolated from the rest of the message may well lead one's spiritual development and reincarnation-cycle off course. Consider for example the New Testament's message in John 3:16, "For God so loved the world that he gave his only begotten son, that whosoever believed in him shall not perish but shall have everlasting life." What a wonderful passage of hope, and yet it takes blind faith to believe that one line could create an entire religion: 'Salvation' could be based on faith – nothing more, nothing less. What could result, and I would argue has resulted, is a culture of sinners who judge and hate their neighbors, having missed Jesus' entire message of love, and yet feel justified in their belief in eternal salvation simply because they believe Jesus was the Son of God. I consider John 3:16 to be an example of a message in the Bible that encourages readers to close their mind at the likely detriment of their future spiritual development, much to the negative consequence of society.

Rather, I would implore everyone to open their mind and read the words of the prophets – including Jesus – again, but in a new light: the light of modern evidence that has been presented in this book. With a modern and higher perspective, there are so many passages that have new meanings in the holy books, and are indeed supportive of the evidence presented herein; some of which I quoted as examples for the reader's benefit. I assure you, there are many more.

Jesus deeply desired to bring the world a message of hope and peace and love. His words do not require a church's sanctioned interpretation to tell you which lines are important above all others. You can make that distinction on your own. They are available to anyone who has ears to hear.[534]

Summary findings:

Throughout this work, I made a conscious effort to try to present a body of research and credible evidence that appeared to support the underlying theme in a specific order, flowing from the most scientific and rigorous pieces of evidence to those areas of probable but anecdotal evidence that might be harder for logic-minded persons to accept without prior support having already been established. Even so, taken in isolation I would have to admit that likely none of the evidence from chapters 3 through 9 was rigorous enough to justify the work's thesis if considered only in isolation. However, as a combined body of evidence there appears to be compelling reason to consider my thesis as valid. My working thesis has been:

We are all comprised of the consciousness, the "stuff," of God. God is all around us, in everything we can see, hear, taste, touch and smell, and even in everything of which we aren't consciously aware. However, the similarity of composition goes beyond origin. God does not leave His creations alone. He remains connected to them and to us always and forever. Because nothing can exist outside of All That Is, we are all One, combined in a Unity with All That Is. As such, we are all part of God, and therefore we are also all connected to each other.

This thesis statement has wide ranging implications for how we see the world around us. It should also impact how we see, treat, and interact with our fellow humans. It is to these points that I now turn.

1. The most important point I would like to impart is our need to learn, and then live by the primary message Jesus of Nazareth sought to bring the world: Love your neighbor as yourself; i.e. the Golden Rule.[535] If we will 'do unto others' as we would have them do unto us, then the karmic cycle of rebirth could finally end because the lessons of love that life purports to offer developing souls would have finally been learned and actualized.

When we hurt others because we fear our own self-interests are at jeopardy, we find our lessons in life are not complete. Those issues are reviewed in the after-life with ourselves as the only judge and jury to determine whether or not we made progress in life, and the next life's 'story' is then planned based on how to rectify any negative issues experienced in the previous life. If we hurt people in this life – mentally, physically, emotionally – our Over-soul is more apt to ensure our next life includes similar types of pain that will be delivered unto ourselves so that we can learn the lesson of what that pain felt like. If we want to avoid that future pain, it is up to us to do the right thing *Now*.

2. The only way to break the karmic cycle is to break the cycle of fear. But we cannot hope to break the karmic cycle of rebirth if we don't start changing our behaviors towards others immediately, in the present. Positive change that impacts our future can only occur *Now*. We can do this by realizing our loving acceptance by the Universe as well as our existence and security is not and has never been in jeopardy. We do not need to fear death or judgment or eternal damnation. Those are human fears that are based on illusions. They are not founded in reality.

When we realize we are secure, we can more aptly treat each other fairly just as we would want to be treated. We can find within ourselves the courage to do the 'hard right' over the 'easy wrong' when we mentally accept we have nothing to fear in this life.

This is a deep change in mindset and cannot be accomplished immediately. But we can start walking on a new path in life with this as an intended goal. We don't have to wait for society to change. The journey of a thousand miles begins with the first step and society *will* change when enough people have embarked upon this journey that the change becomes noticeable, eventually becoming a new norm. In this way, a New Age of humanity will be experienced on Earth; an age in which love and helping one another leads society to ever-greater heights of cooperation and achievement.

3. In a perfect world, we humans would exhibit altruistic responsibility towards the world we live in, to ensure we leave our children a world that has not been polluted by our efforts to develop and civilize the land. However, humans are not generally

altruistic. We take action that benefits ourselves for mostly selfish reasons. Now that it is clear reincarnation is a part of our human experience, we should reassess the way we live, work and play on Earth. The world we leave to our children will be the same world that we will be reborn in for our next incarnation.

If we begin making efforts to conserve and preserve the world now, we will develop a set of habits that our children and grandchildren will more likely adopt, ensuring those actions will be carried over into the next generation, and we will not be reborn into a world destroyed by war and pollution, or raped and depleted of resources. Some might deride my use of highlighting selfish motivations to cause this change, but I see this plea as simply a pragmatic acceptance of modern humanity. This does not mean humanity will be stuck at this level of development forever, but if it takes modern incentives to create the conditions of change that benefit the future of humanity then I'm in full agreement with using those tools that are most effective and readily at hand *Now*.

4. A repeating point of insight from the sources in this book showed humans need to seek greater insights from within rather than looking for the answers from without. What I mean here is that through quiet reflection and a personal relationship with our higher Self and the Universe through silent prayer, we can receive guidance, insight, and inspiration, which will help us know what we need to do in this life. That knowledge is not to be found from outside of ourselves. No one is better positioned to tell you what your specific life purpose is in this incarnation than your own higher self.

You can reach your higher self and receive guidance from the Universe by a variety of methods. Many choose to meditate. Others have difficulty committing to the time and effort it takes to sit and meditate daily, and have found other methods work better for them to quiet their mind and reach out for inspiration and guidance to overcome life's daily issues. If I may provide some of those means here, you may realize that you've already unknowingly engaged in many of these activities. My point here is to encourage continuation of what comes naturally to you to accomplish this. Knowing the inspiration you have received in the past was not received by accident you can then purposefully repeat the conditions that caused that insight to occur, and continue the exercise of seeking purposeful insight every day.

All you need to do to receive insight and inspiration is to state the problem silently in your mind and then ask the Universe for guidance and inspiration. Next, quiet your mind by whatever means are readily available and comfortable to you. Some people like to go for long, quiet walks by themselves; some run; some exercise or read books. Many people daydream, or "zone out." Sometimes playing video games, watching television or taking a nap, especially the quiet period before falling asleep, can stimulate a point of inspiration. The mind must be quiet during these periods; meaning interpersonal exchange with others must be halted temporarily. You need some 'me' time to give your mind a chance to quietly reflect in the background on the issue at hand as you have stated it silently to your higher self.

When your mind is quieted, the subconscious becomes more accessible and inspiration can flow into the waking consciousness. When you receive that inspiration, immediately record that inspiration before the communication's channel becomes cloudy again. Unfortunately this can happen _very_ quickly so one must be quick about responding to inspiration. It is like trying to remember a dream. People often remember dreams for a few seconds after waking up but later all that is left is an impression; the clarity of what occurred in the dream almost always fades. However, the capability to recall memories of inspiration and dreams can be improved with time and practice. The more often you make a conscious effort to recall your points of inspiration, the better your brain will be conditioned to remembering those ideas that cross over the conscious/subconscious barrier.

If you are having difficulty in this endeavor, you can gain extra practice by recording memories of dreams every morning when you wake up. You'll need to write these down immediately because they will disappear frustratingly quickly until you have had significant practice with this effort. However, it will help train your memory and make future long-term recollection of points of inspiration easier to accomplish.

5. As you become more used to receiving inspiration and communing with the Universe, realize as well that you are developing a deeper relationship with God by sharing this personal time and affection with All That Is. Enjoy your time amongst the Universe and try to 'see' everything around you from a higher perspective. Try imaging life on Earth as an elaborate play with billions of characters, plots and subplots; and the scenery – even the most mundane – can become unbelievably exquisite. Feel your appreciation for the opportunity to live in this world at this time grow within you and give thanks for being a part in this experience. When you appreciate your newfound role in the world, you will be happier and tend to appreciate yourself and those around you more. You will more easily love yourself and those around you – even the coworkers or acquaintances who seemingly have consistently made your life hard.

This change in viewpoint will be the first step in helping you to take advantage of the law of attraction. When you see the world as a positive place and life as a positive experience, those events that occur in your life will tend to be seen as more positive than negative and you will have established a self-replicating cycle of bringing good things into your life.

Continue this positive cycle by purposely intending more good things to manifest in your life. Visualize the good you desire to occur both purposefully and intently, ask that those issues or items manifest in your life, write down those intentions, and then believe they will occur. Take positive steps to help them become a reality in your life if possible, and begin making some small, tangible action everyday as if they have already been received. Give thanks for having received the intended request both before the item has manifested, and most certainly once again when the item is actually realized. Together, these steps will not only change your life, but can also positively impact society when adopted by enough people who intend to experience and realize that life on Earth *can be* good. This is one of many paths by which peace on Earth could be achieved, and so many other good things can come into our lives. Once again, that journey of a thousand miles begins with one step: That step could be you, realizing a new future for yourself and the world in which you live.

6. You intended to be born on this Earth during this lifetime to experience life in all its glory, and all it has to offer. Are you satisfied with what you have done and experienced so far? If not, then you need seek input and answers no further. They are already inside of you. If you want to see more of the world, then go see the world. If you want to pursue a passion, whether as a hobby, career, or altruistic endeavor, then you owe it to yourself and your spiritual development to pursue that passion.

Learning and experiencing never ends, and indeed along with friendship and love these are the *only* things we can take with us when we die. What good is it to acquire a household full of goods and toys when that junk must be left behind when we die? I venture to guess this was Jesus of Nazareth's point when he noted our hearts lied with our treasures.[536] I agree with the common argument that Jesus was not stating it was evil to seek financial stability. Indeed it is hard to be altruistic and charitable when your stomach is hungry and you are worried about paying the bills. The parable reaches deeper however. A man can go to work at a factory, for example, to put food on the table for his family, but still have deeper interests and passions than simply going to work and then coming home to watch television each evening. Only you, however, can answer what those passions and interests should be in your life.

If you fail to realize your potential in this life, you will disappoint no one but yourself. You are your own judge and jury in the afterlife, and the only one who will feel disappointed if you did not do everything you could have done to live and learn and experience life to the fullest on Earth. In order to make things right, you will feel bound to come back to Earth and try your hand at doing a better job in the next life. But why wait? You have all the tools you need to begin experiencing life right Now. Don't despair if it took you 40 or 50 years to reach that realization. The moment of *Now* to begin effecting change is always available. You could start to live your life in a new and better way, right *Now*! You know the passions that reside in your heart. If you think you don't, go back to steps 4 and 5, above. Seek the truth inside yourself and the inspiration will be provided. Then if you ignore the message, you fail no one but yourself. Don't let yourself down. Live!

Answering the initial questions about the meaning of life:

I began this book with a few questions about the meaning of life. The answers were available from within the presented material, but I'd like to cover these areas again – sort of a check on learning, if you will. Read the question and then answer it to yourself before reading my thoughts on the same issue. Hopefully there is little divergence between our two answers at this point.

1. If God is perfect, then why would he put us on a world where human conflict leads us to commit war, rape, and pillage against our common brethren?

Thoughts: There are many issues in the question: The concept of perfection; God being an overlord responsible for the human condition; and humankind seemingly relieved of the responsibility for its own destiny. To answer the question, each issue would have to be dealt with independently.

a. Seth and many other sources contended we are all part of God, and creation is constantly changing, seeking, and growing through the experience. Seth also noted God was not perfect because that would assume creation would cease since it would be impossible to improve upon perfection. Thus the idea that perfect does or could ever exist – even for God – is invalid.

b. The concept of 'God' as an overlord who sits on a throne and rules from heaven is a distinctly human concept, and limits who and what 'All That Is' actually is. The Source is unimaginable and indescribable, but 'All That Is' most certainly is not a ruling deity on a throne who sits in judgment over, or agonizes over Its creations' daily choices in life. The Source desires for us to experience all that life has to offer, because the Source grows through the combined experience. The Source also knows that the plan of creation will be on the road to fulfillment when Its creations, all of which are aspects of the Source, realize that the power of love (i.e. positive energy) triumphs over hate (i.e. negative energy). This is integral to the plan of creation, and we each will reach this realization, whether it takes us 100 lives or 10,000 lives.

c. Free will must exist, however, for creation to experience, and along that path we each will make bad choices and hurt other people. In the process of learning, we will be reborn and experience similar consequences of being hurt in turn to learn how those negative actions previously affected others. But a god on a throne did not create the conditions of pain for us to experience. We created those conditions and the life we experience on Earth ourselves. No one hurts us but that we give him or her the power to do so. We can take responsibility for our lives if we want to experience a change in our lives. We can create a new experience today. We don't have to wait in hope that our next life will be better. In order to create a better future life, we must settle karmic issues today in order to create the conditions for a better life tomorrow. Thus, no one is responsible for our choices in life except for we ourselves.

2. Why does God make us suffer with floods, earthquakes, tornados and the plethora of other natural disasters?

Thoughts: There are again two issues in the question: The first is the concept of God being an overlord responsible for the human condition, which was already addressed, above; and the second is the idea natural disasters are a form of punishment.

Natural disasters are not a form of punishment. They are simply tools by which our Over-souls sought to provide us experiences in life. Sometimes the experiences of hardship and loss are important lessons to learn. Sometimes fear must be experienced, and sometimes the feeling of overcoming trials and tribulations is beneficial to personal and societal development. Remember, these are mass occurrences that affect many people. Sometimes leaders 'are born' or emerge during trying events, so the idea that natural disasters can bring only negative consequences is a purely human viewpoint.

From a more macro point of view, the planet Earth also needs opportunities to change and evolve itself. Seth and many other sources contended our planet also has a consciousness, though one that humanity could not possibly understand or perceive. That consciousness also needs experience, and experiences only come through change and evolution. Some forms of change are cleansing while others lead to new opportunities. These events may be trying from a purely human perspective, but remember we all are actually connected as One in a Unity, so sometimes the effort to try to understand 'why' requires a higher level perspective than we might normally consider as humans.

3. And why must there be disease, cancer and accidents that result in death?

Thoughts: There are so many potential reasons why people may die at the times they die and the manner in which they die. If you are hurting now from a recent loss, these thoughts may not help heal the hurt, but they may provide some comfort in the long run.

a. At a point when our job on Earth has concluded and the experiences we sought to provide ourselves have been achieved, our Over-soul will seek an opportunity to obtain exit from the physical realm of experience in order to continue its growth in the non-physical realm. As humans we may not understand how that job could be completed at the time our loved one died, but our Over-soul knows what our life's mission and goals were. These goals are not as clearly defined as 'writing a book' or experiencing the birth of a child, for example. But they are goals nonetheless, and those goals are not generally available to us because potentially, if we knew those goals we might live in fear of impending death should the goals appear near at hand.

Rarely, a person might die before his/her goals in life were achieved – because of free will, for example – and in which case, the spirit may well decide to return to the physical realm sooner than it otherwise should have (i.e. in a new life) simply because of an intense desire to continue working towards those life's goals. However, this should not be a concern for loved ones because either way our dearly departed is not hurting. Death is less painful and far more enjoyable from a soul's point of few than birth, as attested to by innumerable near-death experiences, and past-life and life-between-life hypnotic regressions. The ones hurting are those who are left behind.

b. Sometimes death in a loved one occurs because a life lesson was for those left behind to experience the pain of loss. In this case, the one dying may have been intended to die at a specific point in fulfillment of a life plan *for the benefit of* the ones left behind. Life plans include a cast of characters and not every goal in one's own life plan has to be selfish. We can also conduct acts and experiences for the benefit of others. Sometimes we specifically hurt, or are hurt so that others can experience the emotions that come from playing the opposing role.

This may sound cruel, but again the concept of cruelty, as well as good and bad, is a purely human concept that we need to learn to look beyond. Following the idea of being hurt for the benefit of others, there have been many past-life stories of memories of being paralyzed in a fall or accident and thus becoming a burden on the family members who must care for the injured member. Oftentimes these injuries occurred because family members needed to learn responsibility, and the injured party needed to learn humility or some other life lesson. The number of possible combinations of multiple humans' life-plans being realized by one freak occurrence is nearly limitless.

c. Finally, sometimes disease and accidents can remind us of karmic issues we had meant to resolve in this life, but then forgot subconsciously as we got sidetracked in the daily race of life. So many diseases, such as cancer, can cause us to slow down and finally reflect on our life when they occur. Sometimes the disease may offer us a second lease on achieving our life's goals simply because we slowed down and conducted this introspective search. In the process we may realize a new set of priorities and experiences that must be achieved before we allow ourselves to die. Take heed when these inspirations erupt during times of trial. It is likely your Over-soul trying to grab your attention through the most immediate, albeit dramatic, means available.

4. Why are some people ridiculously rich or beautiful or famous while the vast majority is poor, hungry or quite simply mundane? Where is the fairness?

Thoughts: There are again at least two issues in the question: The first is the concept of different roles in life being of higher or lesser value from one another. The second is the idea life should be 'fair,' which is a distinctly human concept.

a. We are born in this life with the circumstances we needed in order to experience the roles and circumstances we desired for ourselves to experience. These life plans were made by us while still in heaven though we do not generally recall having made those plans or for what purpose as we sit here on Earth in our normal waking conscious. An important concept we need to learn is that no role is more important than any other. The rich and powerful are no more important or special than the poor and powerless, and one race or religion or nationality of people is no better than any other. We are all One in the Unity of All That Is. You are part of me and I am part of you though we don't normally realize this. If I hate you or if I am jealous of you, then I am jealous or hateful of myself, a rather inane concept.

We need to learn how to love and accept each other for the value we all hold inside ourselves and the *potential* we all bear for the betterment of mankind's future. Whether we will realize our potential in this life or not, there is amazing potential for each of us to be so much more than we are today. Leaders can emerge from the slums, and inspirational figures we cannot even fathom today will emerge from the unknown to change the world for the better. Those leaders do not have to be born rich or powerful or beautiful; they simply have to believe in themselves and follow an inner calling to help and do more for mankind.

b. The concern about fairness implies as well that our current condition in life will be carried over indefinitely. In fact, we all will live lives of ease as well as hardship. That which we experience today is only what we need for our present experience. Tomorrow's requirements will be quite different and our experiences will adapt accordingly. As an interesting aside, many of the past life researchers have found that peoples' happiest past lives were rarely those where the person was rich or powerful. Money and power brings with it a new set of stressors and problems, and it is a lesson we should remember lest we feel sorry for ourselves or covet that which we cannot have in this lifetime. Rather, the happiest lives were those where we lived a modest existence, surrounded by family and achieved our life's goals, no matter how modest those goals may have been. Being a farmer in the Midwest with a large family may be all that is required to have the happiest existence we could hope for in a succession of a hundred lives or more.

There is no need to feel we have been slighted unfairly in this life simply because we do not own everything that other people might own. That form of competition is unhealthy and will only result in negative feelings and arrested development as a soul. Sometimes we must consider our present circumstances from a higher perspective to understand how good we really have it in this lifetime. Then we will realize that life *can* be wonderful. Life is a gift, and in that regard life is sufficiently 'fair.'

5. How is there justice in a world where slavery and famine still exist; or where murderers and thieves still lurk in the dark no matter how many are placed in overcrowded, inhumane jails?

Thoughts: Most of the points behind this issue have already been raised, but I will add one more here: the concept of justice. During our life review – post death – the only judge of our misdeeds in the previous life is our self. We are our harshest critic because we will suddenly understand life from a higher perspective, and we will experience – during the review – how our actions, words and deeds hurt others. During the life review we experience the same pain, hurt, and suffering as those who received our attacks in life, but this experience is not quite the same as actually living through the event. Therefore, to enhance our learning experience – and some would argue to pay off a karmic debt – we may choose to experience similar pains in a subsequent life.

No one forces us to accept the follow-on life's negative circumstances as a form of retribution. We voluntarily agree to these painful experiences so we can better understand how our thoughts impact the world, molding energy in both negative and positive ways. The Earth is an ideal learning environment because energy and matter manipulation that occurs following the direction of our thoughts happens much slower on Earth than would occur in the nonphysical realms. Eventually, we will learn our lessons that love is a more effective and positive tool, and we will be ready to graduate from the karmic life cycle and move to a new, non-incarnating classroom for more experiences, post Earth.

6. If a child lives but a few days, while someone else lives past 100, then how can one say God will fairly judge our deeds or faith for eternal salvation?

Thoughts: Again, most of the points here have already been discussed so I will only focus on the concept of 'eternal salvation.' The concept of salvation implies there must be an opposite: damnation. In fact, neither exists. They are purely human concepts deeply immersed in the concept of kings and kingdoms, as well as judgment and punishment. There is no 'ruler' of heaven because God does not sit on a throne. You will not be able to say God sits on the throne here, so he is not to be found over there. God is everywhere. God is everything. God is *All That Is*. God is in you, and God is in me. God will not punish Himself because such would be required if He were to punish you or me. When we die, we return to the Light, which is the 'home' of God, or more specifically, an area where there is a more obvious concentration of the Source. Seth noted that Heaven *is* God. While we feel isolated from the Source while living out our lives on Earth, that feeling is an illusion.

God is always with us, loving us, and supporting us. We have only to clear our minds and seek commune with Him to realize this and find the assurances and inner strength we need to carry on in life. We may do things on Earth for which we are not proud – both now (via guilt) and after death during our life review. But that is no reason to give up on ourselves or consider we are bound for eternal damnation. Such a concept simply does not exist. So if we die after only 100 minutes or 100 long years on Earth, we will immediately return to the Light where we will rest, recover, review, and plan again for our next life. There is only one option: we are made of the Source and so we will *always* return to the Source.

7. Does it matter which religion a person selects in order to enter the kingdom of heaven?

Thoughts: Which religion we follow in life does not matter as to whether or not we will be able to return to the Light and live in communion with the Source; that is a given, as already discussed. (I'm sure that assertion will not please any of the world's major religions.) The variety of religions on Earth provides the necessary variety of experiences on Earth that our species needs at this point in our development. That number may increase or decrease over time to match future developmental needs, but has little to do with 'the truth' in regards to the nature of physical reality or the meaning of life as I have outlined them here in this book. Few religions have been able to uncover any of the truths as I have outlined them here, and only one likely agrees with most or possibly all of these points, though I'll not vouch for that religion here. I will not preach the blessings of any one church or belief at this point because as I noted, a variety of experiences are necessary for human development and it is up to each of us to determine if/when we are ready to accept the truths I have presented herein, and whether/how that knowledge will actually come to impact our lives. Spending time with like-minded people may be of benefit when one lacks the courage to walk a new path on their own. However, it is not necessary to give up the life and experiences one has built in order to begin creating new experiences that can build a better society for us all.

Remember that Jesus of Nazareth communed with everyone – he did not discriminate. You too can make a lasting impact on your world by living a new life with positive emotions and attitudes. You can apply the lessons I've outlined and begin realizing a new reality as you intend it to become. You can share those lessons as you see fit, and maybe through the flattery of emulation others around you will want to change to adapt some of the things you've brought into your life, and the journey of a thousand miles will progress from its first step to the second.

Final thoughts:

The ideas presented in this book are radical but are well supported by the evidence. Better yet, you, the reader, do not need to take my word for it. You can test this evidence yourself through multiple self examination methods: for example, meditation and introspection; reading more books on the subject (see, for example, the selected bibliography); or conducting your own past life or inter-life hypnosis session. These low-level research methods are available to anyone at anytime. They are also one of the primary means by which new research findings are uncovered. Maybe your own search for the truth will lead to new discoveries that could benefit the world. Maybe that search for the truth is part of your own life's purpose, as I feel it was for me.

The bottom line is that this book has only been a suggested outline for the issues discussed herein. It should be considered as a possible study guide, or an abridged notes version of the more comprehensive research that is available in each of the respective genres cited in this book. For the researchers and scientists who may have accompanied us on this journey, the issues discussed may provide some ideas for future research that might lead to new findings that could benefit mankind. For example, Can we consciously experience the Light? If so, can we concentrate and direct the Light to heal human sickness, disease and injury? What other leads can we find, both through a literature review and via new research efforts? Are any of those leads plausible research topics that could be realized in the near term? *Et cetera.* The potential for this type of research holds not only a possible benefit for mankind, but for the human species as a whole as it continues on to its next evolutionary step: human-plus.

THE END

End Notes

Chapter 2

[1] Zukav, Gary. (1979). *The Dancing Wu Li Masters: An overview of the new physics.* New York: Bantam, 304.
[2] Ibid., 304.
[3] Capra, Fritjof. (1991). *The Tao of Physics* (3rd Ed.). Boston, MA: Shambhala Publications, 55.
[4] Zukav. (1979). *The Dancing Wu Li Masters*, 304.
[5] Ibid., 305.
[6] Ibid., 113.
[7] Capra. (1991). *The Tao of Physics*, 78.
[8] Zukav. (1979). *The Dancing Wu Li Masters*, 96.
[9] Ibid., 96.
[10] Russell, Peter. (2003). *From Science to God: A physicist's journey into the mystery of consciousness.* Novato, CA: New World Library, 48.
[11] Ibid., 49.
[12] Zukav. (1979). *The Dancing Wu Li Masters*, 216.
[13] Hans-Peter Dürr, as cited in Russell. (2003). *From Science to God*, 49.
[14] Zukav. (1979). *The Dancing Wu Li Masters*, 193.
[15] Ibid., 194.
[16] Russell. (2003). *From Science to God*, 50.
[17] Ibid., 68.
[18] Zukav. (1979). *The Dancing Wu Li Masters*, 71.
[19] Ibid., 71.
[20] Ibid., 78.
[21] Ibid., 72.
[22] Capra. (1991). *The Tao of Physics*, 62.
[23] Ibid., 162.
[24] Ibid., 164.
[25] Ibid., 164.
[26] Zukav. (1979). *The Dancing Wu Li Masters*, 150.
[27] Ibid., 154.
[28] Ibid., 137.
[29] Capra. (1991). *The Tao of Physics*, 46-47.
[30] Russell. (2003). *From Science to God*, 64.
[31] Ibid., 67, 71, 85.
[32] Capra. (1991). *The Tao of Physics*, 77.
[33] As cited in Russell. (2003). *From Science to God*, 67.
[34] Russell. (2003). *From Science to God*, 28.
[35] Ibid., 28.

[36] Zukav. (1979). *The Dancing Wu Li Masters*, 305.
[37] Ibid., 29.
[38] Ibid.
[39] Ibid., 31.
[40] Ibid., 31.
[41] As cited in Russell. (2003). *From Science to God*, 26.
[42] Ibid., 26.
[43] Ibid., 27.
[44] Ibid., 27.
[45] Zukav. (1979). *The Dancing Wu Li Masters*, 28.
[46] Russell. (2003). *From Science to God*, 90.
[47] Zukav. (1979). *The Dancing Wu Li Masters*, 71.
[48] Ibid., 79.
[49] Capra. (1991). *The Tao of Physics*, 300.
[50] Zukav. (1979). *The Dancing Wu Li Masters*, 200.
[51] Capra. (1991). *The Tao of Physics*, 210-211.
[52] Ibid., 222.
[53] Zukav. (1979). *The Dancing Wu Li Masters*, 198.
[54] Ibid., 286.
[55] Ibid., 295.
[56] Ibid., 298.
[57] Ibid., 282.
[58] Ibid., 282, 290.
[59] Ibid., 257.
[60] Ibid., 296.
[61] Ibid., 296.
[62] Ibid., 297.
[63] Ibid., 282, 294.
[64] Ibid., 281.
[65] Ibid., 260.

Chapter 3

[66] Gallup, G., & Proctor, W. (1982). *Adventures in Immortality: A Look Beyond the Threshold of Death.* New York, NY: McGraw-Hill.
[67] Perera, M. et.al. (2005). Prevalence of Near-Death Experiences in Australia. *Journal of Near-Death Studies*, 24: 109. and Knoblauch, H. et.al. (2001). Different Kinds of Near-Death Experience: A Report on a Survey of Near-Death Experiences in Germany. *Journal of Near-Death Studies*, 20: 15-29.
[68] http://www.nderf.org/number_nde_usa.htm.

[69] Moody, Raymond A. (1975). *Life after Life: The investigation of a phenomenon; survival of bodily death.* New York: HarperOne.

[70] Berman, Phillip L. (1998). *The Journey Home: What near death experiences and mysticism teach us about the gift of life.* New York: Pocket Books.

[71] Moody, Raymond A. (1989). *The Light Beyond: New explorations.* New York: Bantam, 5-12.

[72] Moody. (1975). *Life after Life*, 20-21.

[73] Ibid., 21.

[74] Moody. (1989). *The Light Beyond*, 14.

[75] Migliore,V. (2007). *Key Facts about Near-Death Experience.* The International Association for Near-Death Studies (IANDS) report. Available at http://iands.org/key-nde-facts.html.

[76] Migliore,V. (2007). *Characteristics of a Near-Death Experience.* IANDS report. Available at http://iands.org/about-ndes/characteristics.html.

[77] Moody. (1975). *Life after Life*, 22.

[78] Migliore,V. (2007). *Characteristics of a Near-Death Experience.* IANDS report.

[79] Moody, (1975). *Life after Life*, 22-23.

[80] Long, Jeffrey, and Perry, Paul. (2010). *Evidence of the Afterlife: The Science of near death experiences.* New York: HarperOne.

[81] Ibid.

[82] Ibid.

[83] Ibid.

[84] Ibid.

[85] Ibid.

[86] Ibid.

[87] Ibid.

[88] Moody. (1975). *Life after Life.*

[89] Long and Perry. (2010). *Evidence of the Afterlife.*

[90] Kirtley, D. D. (1975). *The Psychology of Blindness.* Chicago: Nelson-Hall.

[91] Ibid.

[92] Ibid.

[93] Ring, Kenneth & Cooper, Sharon. (2008). *Mindsight: Near-death and out-of-body experiences in the blind.* New York: iUniverse, 14-15.

[94] Ibid., 16.

[95] Ibid., 37.

[96] Ibid., 16.

[97] Ibid., 20.

[98] Ibid.

[99] Ibid., 48.

[100] Ibid.

[101] Ibid.

[102] Ibid., 12.

[103] Ibid., 13.

[104] Ibid., 86.

[105] Ibid., 86-88.

[106] Moody. (1989). *The Light Beyond*, 154.

[107] van Lommel, Pim. (Dec 2001). Near Death Experience in Survivors of Cardiac Arrest: A Prospective Study in the Netherlands, *The Lancet*, 358, pp. 2039-2045.

[108] Sharp, K. C. (1995). *After the Light: What I Discovered on the Other Side of Life That Can Change Your World.* Morrow, NY.

[109] Near Death Experience Research Foundation. (2 March 2011). *"George C. NDE"* at http://www.nderf.org/gregory_c_nde.htm.

[110] Moody. (1989). *The Light Beyond.*154.

[111] Migliore,V. (2007). *Aftereffects of Near-death States.* IANDS report. Available at http://iands.org/aftereffects-of-near-death-states.html.

[112] Migliore,V. (2007). *Key Facts about Near-Death Experience.* IANDS report.

[113] Migliore,V. (2007). *Aftereffects of Near-death States.* IANDS report.

[114] Sutherland, C. (1990). Changes in Religious Beliefs, Attitudes, and Practices Following Near-Death Experiences: An Australian Study. *Journal of Near-Death Studies.* 9: 24; Ring. K. (1998). *Lessons from the Light: What we can learn from the Near-Death Experience.* Insight Books; Noyes, R. (1980). Noyes, R. (1980). Attitude Changes Following Near-Death Experiences. *Psychiatry*, 43: 234-242; and Greyson, B. (1992). Reduced Death Threat in Near-Death Experiences. *Death Studies.* 16: 533-46.

[115] Moody. (1989). *The Light Beyond*, 33.

[116] Sutherland, C. (1990). Changes in Religious Beliefs, Attitudes, and Practices Following Near-Death Experiences: An Australian Study. *Journal of Near-Death Studies,* 9: 24; Flynn, C. (1982). Meanings and Implications of NDEr Transformations: Some Preliminary Findings and Implications. Anabiosis: *Journal of Near-Death Studies,* 2: 7; Musgrave, C. (1997). The Near-Death Experience: A Study of Spiritual Transformation. *Journal of Near-Death Studies*, 15: 187-201.

[117] Bauer, M. (1985). Near-Death Experiences and Attitudinal Change. Anabiosis: *Journal of Near-Death Studies,* 5. 39-46.

[118] Migliore,V. (2007). *Aftereffects of Near-death States.* IANDS report.

[119] Moody. (1989). *The Light Beyond*, 33, 34.

[120] Bauer, M. (1985). Near-Death Experiences and Attitudinal Change. Anabiosis: *Journal of Near-Death Studies,* 5: 39-46.

[121] Migliore,V. (2007). *Aftereffects of Near-death States.* IANDS report.

[122] Christian, S. R. (2005). Marital satisfaction and stability following a near-death experience of one of the marital partners. University of North Texas Dissertation. Available at http://www.unt.edu/etd/all/August2005/Open/christian_sandra_rozan/index.htm.

[123] Noyes, R. (1980). Attitude Changes Following Near-Death Experiences. *Psychiatry*, 43:234-242; Ring, K. (1984). *Heading toward Omega: In Search of the Meaning of the Near-Death Experience.* William Morrow Books; and Stout, Y. et. al. (2006) Six Major Challenges Faced by Near-Death Experiencers. *Journal of Near-Death Studies,* 29: 49-62.

[124] Moody. (1989). *The Light Beyond,* 39.

[125] Ibid., 68.

[126] Ibid., 36.

[127] Migliore,V. (2007). *Aftereffects of Near-death States.* IANDS report.

[128] Moody. (1989). *The Light Beyond,* 41.

[129] Migliore,V. (2007). *Aftereffects of Near-death States.* IANDS report.

[130] Sutherland, C. (1989). Psychic Phenomena Following Near-Death Experiences: An Australian Study. *Journal of Near-Death Studies,* 8: 99; Greyson, B. (1983). Increase in Psychic Phenomena Following Near-Death Experiences. *Theta.* 11: 26-29; and Migliore. V. (2007). *Statistical Summary of Near-Death Experience Reports.* IANDS report.

[131] Migliore,V. (2007). *Aftereffects of Near-death States.* IANDS report.

[132] Ibid.

[133] Ibid.

[134] Ibid.

[135] Ibid.

[136] Migliore,V. (2007). *Key Facts about Near-Death Experience.* IANDS report.

[137] As cited in Russell. (2003). *From Science to God,* 67.

[138] The topic of rectifying the concept of independent entities within a united collective consciousness is very well handled by Ian Lawton. Lawton's theory of Holographic Aspects of the Source is well worth the short time it takes to read his highly recommended book, *The Big Book of the Soul.* (2008). Dorchester, England: Henry Ling.

[139] Ring and Cooper. (2008). *Mindsight,* 17, 37.

[140] Ibid., 17, 30, 31.

[141] Ibid., 30.

Chapter 4

[142] Twemlow, Stuart W. MD, and Gabbard, Glen O. MD. (1982). The Out of Body Experience: A Phenomenological Typology based on questionnaire responses. *American Journal of Psychiatry*, 139: 450-455.
[143] Monroe, Robert A. (1985). *Far Journeys*. Garden City, NY: Doubleday, 276.
[144] Ibid., 265.
[145] Monroe, Robert A. (1971). *Journeys out of the Body*. New York: Doubleday, 8.
[146] Ibid.
[147] Magnus, John. (2005). *Astral Projection and the Nature of Reality: Exploring the Out-of-Body State*. Charlottesville, VA: Hampton Roads, 96-97, 14.
[148] Monroe. (1971). *Journeys out of the Body*, 8.
[149] Monroe. (1985). *Far Journeys*.
[150] Hart, H. (1954). ESP Projection: Spontaneous cases and the experimental method. *Journal of the American Society for Psychical Research*, 48:121-146.
[151] Green, C. (1968). *Out-of-the-body experiences*. London, Hamish Hamilton.
[152] Monroe. (1985). *Far Journeys*, 278.
[153] Buhlman, William. (2001). *The Secret of the Soul: Using Out-of-Body Experiences to Understand our True Nature*. New York: HarperCollins.
[154] Monroe. (1971). *Journeys out of the Body*, 8.
[155] Monroe. (1985). *Far Journeys*, 63-64.
[156] Buhlman. (2001). *The Secret of the Soul*, 135.
[157] Ibid., 143-144.
[158] Monroe. (1971). *Journeys out of the Body*, 9, 61.
[159] Ibid., 9-10.
[160] Ibid., *74*.
[161] Twemlow. (1982). The Out of Body Experience, 453.
[162] Ibid., 454.
[163] Monroe. (1985). *Far Journeys*.
[164] Moody, Raymond A. (1975). *Life after Life: The investigation of a phenomenon; survival of bodily death*. New York: HarperOne.
[165] Buhlman. (2001). *The Secret of the Soul*, 51-52.
[166] Ibid., 50.
[167] Ibid.
[168] Ibid., 52.
[169] Monroe. (1971). *Journeys out of the Body*, 123-125.
[170] Ibid.
[171] Ibid., 8.

[172] Twemlow. (1982). The Out of Body Experience, 454.

[173] Buhlman. (2001). *The Secret of the Soul*, 68-69.

[174] Monroe. (1971). *Journeys out of the Body*, 74.

[175] Ibid., 74.

[176] Maurice Rawlings, M.D. (1991). Beyond Death's Door. New York: Bantam.

[177] Monroe, Far Journeys; and Magnus, John. (2005). *Astral Projection and the Nature of Reality: Exploring the Out-of-Body State.* Charlottesville, VA: Hampton Roads, 19-22.

[178] Monroe. (1971). *Journeys out of the Body*, 75.

[179] Buhlman. (2001). *The Secret of the Soul*, 83.

[180] Ibid., 84.

[181] Ibid., 80.

[182] Magnus. (2005). *Astral Projection and the Nature of Reality*, 271-276, 282-284, 286.

[183] Buhlman. (2001). *The Secret of the Soul*, 81.

[184] Ibid., 83.

[185] Ibid., 83-84.

[186] Ibid., 80-81.

[187] Monroe. (1985). *Far Journeys*, 250.

[188] Buhlman. (2001). *The Secret of the Soul*, 250.

[189] Ibid., 254.

[190] Monroe. (1985). *Far Journeys*, 63-64.

[191] Ibid.

[192] Ibid.

[193] Buhlman. (2001). *The Secret of the Soul*, 250.

[194] Ibid., 255.

[195] Monroe. (1985). *Far Journeys*, 248-249.

[196] Buhlman. (2001). *The Secret of the Soul*, 250.

[197] Monroe. (1985). *Far Journeys*, 269.

[198] Ibid., 248.

Chapter 5

[199] Fisher, Joe. (1985). *The Case for Reincarnation*. New York: Bantam, 70.

[200] Quoted in Murphy, G. & Ballou, R.O. (Ed.). (1973). *William James on Psychical Research*. Clifton, NJ: August M. Kelley.

[201] Fisher. (1985). *The Case for Reincarnation*, 12.

[202] Stevenson, Ian. (1987). *Children Who Remember Previous Lives: A question of reincarnation*. Charlottesville, VA: The University of Virginia.

[203] Stevenson, Ian. (1983). American Children Who Claim to Remember Previous Lives. *Journal of Nervous and Mental Disease,* 171: 742-748.

[204] Stevenson, Ian. (1997). *Where Reincarnation and Biology Intersect.* Westport, CT: Praeger.

[205] Ibid., 5.

[206] Ibid., 6.

[207] Whitton, Joel & Fisher, Joe. (1986). *Life Between Life: Scientific explorations into the void separating one incarnation from the next.* Garden City, NY: Doubleday, 11.

[208] Stevenson, Ian. (1975). *Cases of the Reincarnation Type, Volume 1: Ten Cases in India.* Charlottesville, VA: University of Virginia.

[209] Ibid.

[210] Stevenson, Ian. (1974). *Twenty Cases Suggestive of Reincarnation,* 2nd ed. Charlottesville, VA: University of Virginia.

[211] Fenwick, Peter & Fenwick, Elizabeth. (2001). *Reliving Past Lives: The Evidence under Hypnosis.* New York: Berkley, 275.

[212] Stevenson, Ian. (1960). The evidence for survival from claimed memories of former incarnations. *Journal of the American Society for Psychical Research,* 54: 51-71, 95-117.

[213] Banerjee, Hemendra. (1980). *Americans who have been reincarnated.* New York: Macmillan.

[214] Stevenson. (1997). Where Reincarnation and Biology Intersect, 7.

[215] Fenwick & Fenwick. (2001). Reliving Past Lives: The Evidence under Hypnosis.

[216] Haraldson, Erlendur. (1991). Children Claiming Past-Life Memories: Four cases in Sri Lanka. Journal of Scientific Exploration, 5(2).

[217] Stevenson. (1997). *Where Reincarnation and Biology Intersect,* 3, 7.

[218] Ibid., 3.

[219] Ibid., 116.

[220] Ibid., 3.

[221] Whitton & Fisher. (1986). *Life Between Life,* 64.

[222] Stevenson. (1997). *Where Reincarnation and Biology Intersect,* 44-45.

[223] Ibid., 46-47.

[224] Ibid., 48-49.

[225] Ibid., 49-50.

[226] Ibid., 53-54.

[227] Ibid., 89.

[228] Fenwick, Peter & Fenwick, Elizabeth. (2001). *Past Lives: An investigation into reincarnation memories.* New York: Berkley, 278-279.

[229] Ibid., 279.

[230] Ibid., 280.

[231] Lawton, Ian. (2007). *The Wisdom of the Soul: Profound insights from the life between lives.* Southend-on-Sea, UK: Rational Spirituality Press, 148.

[232] Tomlinson, Andy. (2007). *Exploring the Eternal Soul: Insights from the life between lives.* Winchester, UK: O Books, 4.

[233] Wambach, Helen. (1978). *Reliving Past Lives: The Evidence under Hypnosis.* New York: Barnes & Noble, 24, 85.

[234] Sheehan, P. W. (1988). Confidence, memory and hypnosis. In H. M. Pettinati (Ed.). *Hypnosis and Memory.* New York: Guilford Press, 95-127.

[235] Venn, Jonathan. (Oct. 1986). Hypnosis and the reincarnation hypothesis: A critical review and intensive case study. *Journal of the American Society for Psychical Research, 80*(4): 409-425.

[236] Dywan, J. & Bowers, K. S. (1983). The use of hypnosis to enhance recall. *Science, 222*: 184-185.

[237] Tomlinson. (2007). *Exploring the Eternal Soul*, 3.

[238] Fenwick & Fenwick. (2001). *Past Lives*, 124.

[239] Newton, Michael. (1998). *Journey of Souls: Case Studies of Life Between Lives.* Llewellyn: St. Paul, MN, 9.

[240] Wambach. (1978). *Reliving Past Lives*, 60.

[241] Whitton & Fisher. (1986). *Life Between Life*, 43.

[242] Tarazi, Linda. (1990). "An unusual case of hypnotic regression with some unexplained contents." *Journal of the American Society for Psychical Research, 84:* 309-344; and Fenwick & Fenwick, *Past Lives*, 134-137.

[243] Tarazi. (1990). "An unusual case of hypnotic regression with some unexplained contents," 329.

[244] Ramster, Peter. (1994). "Past lives and hypnosis." Australian Journal of Clinical Hypnotherapy and Hypnosis, 15(2): 67-91.

[245] Ibid., 87.

[246] Schmicker, Michael. (2002). Best Evidence, 2nd ed. Lincoln, NE: Writers Club.

[247] Fenwick & Fenwick. (2001). Past Lives, 121-123.

[248] Stevenson, Ian. (1974). *Xenoglossy: A review and report of a case.* New York: American Society for Psychical Research; and Ian Stevenson. (1984). *Unlearned Language: New studies in xenoglossy.* Charlottesville: University Press of Virginia.

[249] Stevenson, Ian. (1976). A Preliminary Report of a new case of responsive xenoglossy: The case of Gretchen. *Journal of the American Society for Psychical Research, 70:* 65-77.

[250] Wambach. (1978). *Reliving Past Lives.*

[251] Cunningham, Paul F. (1986). *The effects of different probe procedures on the experience of imaging in hypnotic and waking states of*

consciousness. Unpublished doctoral dissertation, University of Tennessee, Knoxville.

252 Stevenson, Ian & Pasricha, Satwant, (1980). A Preliminary Report of an unusual case of the reincarnation type with xenoglossy. *Journal of the American Society for Psychical Research, 74:* 331-348; and Ian Stevenson. (1984). *Unlearned Language: New studies in xenoglossy.* Charlottesville: University Press of Virginia.

253 Stevenson. (1974). *Xenoglossy.*

254 Ducasse, C. J. (2006). *A Critical Examination of the Belief in a Life After Death.* Whitefish, MT: Kessinger; and Fenwick & Fenwick, *Past Lives.*

255 Stevenson, Ian. (1984). *Unlearned Language: New studies in xenoglossy.* Charlottesville: University Press of Virginia.

256 http://en.wikipedia.org/wiki/Christian_Friedrich_Heinecken.

257 Wambach. (1978). *Reliving Past Lives,* 61.

258 Ibid., 124.

259 Ibid., 125.

260 Ibid., 118.

261 Ibid., 112.

262 Ibid., 141.

263 Ibid., 139.

264 Ibid., 140.

265 Freeman, James Dillet. (1986). *The Case for Reincarnation.* Unity Village, MO: Unity Books, 37. (Used with permission of Unity, www.unity.org)

266 Newton. (1998). *Journey of Souls,* 41-42.

267 Fisher. (1985). *The Case for Reincarnation,* 45.

268 Hastings, Arthur. (1991). *With the tongues of men and Angels: A study of channeling.* Orlando, FL: Holt, Rinehart, Winston, 111.

269 Newton. (1998). *Journey of Souls,* 67.

270 Fisher. (1985). *The Case for Reincarnation,* 161.

Chapter 6

271 Newton, Michael. (1998). *Journey of Souls: Case Studies of Life Between Lives.* St. Paul, MN: Llewellyn, 3-4.

272 Ibid., 3-4.

273 Lawton, Ian. (2007). *The Wisdom of the Soul: Profound insights from the life between lives.* Southend-on-Sea, UK: Rational Spirituality Press, 148.

274 Newton. (1998). *Journey of Souls,* 4.

[275] Tomlinson, Andy. (2007). *Exploring the Eternal Soul: Insights from the life between lives.* Winchester, UK: O Books, 6.

[276] Newton. (1998). *Journey of Souls*, 9.

[277] Tomlinson. (2007). *Exploring the Eternal Soul*, 6-7.

[278] Newton. (1998). *Journey of Souls*, 195.

[279] Ibid., 166.

[280] Ibid., 27.

[281] Ibid., 36.

[282] Ibid., 154.

[283] Ibid., 173.

[284] Ibid., 162.

[285] Newton, Michael. (2000). *Destiny of Souls: New Case Studies of Life between Lives.* St. Paul, MN: Llewellyn, 297.

[286] Ibid., 85.

[287] Tomlinson. (2007). *Exploring the Eternal Soul*, 22.

[288] Newton. (1998). *Journey of Souls*, 155.

[289] Ibid., 68.

[290] Ibid., 194.

[291] Modi, Shakuntala. (2000). *Memories of God and Creation: Remembering from the subconscious mind.* Charlottesville, PA: Hampton Roads, 35-85.

[292] Newton. (1998). *Journey of Souls*, 72.

[293] Ibid., 77.

[294] Ibid., 122.

[295] Ibid., 173.

[296] Ibid., 122.

[297] Newton. (1998). *Journey of Souls*..

[298] Newton. (2000). *Destiny of Souls*.

[299] Newton. (1998). *Journey of Souls*, 22.

[300] Ibid., 9.

[301] Ibid., 10.

[302] Newton. (2000). *Destiny of Souls*.

[303] Newton. (1998). *Journey of Souls*, 13.

[304] Ibid., 25.

[305] Newton. (2000). *Destiny of Souls*, 11-12.

[306] Modi. (2000). Memories of God and Creation, 91-115.

[307] Whitton, Joel & Fisher, Joe. (1986). *Life Between Life: Scientific explorations into the void separating one incarnation from the next.* Garden City, NY: Doubleday, 48.

[308] Newton. (1998). Journey of Souls, 220.

[309] Newton. (2000). *Destiny of Souls*, 193.

[310] Ibid., 94.

[311] Newton. (1998). *Journey of Souls*, 51.

[312] Ibid., 103.
[313] Ibid., 104.
[314] Ibid., 128.
[315] Ibid., 145.
[316] Ibid., 169-170.
[317] Ibid., 105.
[318] Ibid., 204, 211.
[319] Ibid., 204.
[320] Ibid., 243.
[321] Ibid., 197.
[322] Ibid., 243.
[323] Ibid., 198-199.
[324] Modi. (2000). *Memories of God and Creation*, 35-85.
[325] Newton. (1998). *Journey of Souls*, 176, 193.
[326] Ibid., 78.
[327] Ibid., 70, 127.
[328] Ibid., 78.
[329] Ibid., 157.
[330] Ibid., 199.
[331] Ibid., 274.
[332] Ibid., 78.
[333] Ibid., 69.
[334] Ibid., 70.
[335] Ibid., 194.
[336] Whitton & Fisher. (1986). *Life Between Life*, 53.
[337] Newton. (1998). *Journey of Souls*, 222.
[338] Tomlinson. (2007). *Exploring the Eternal Soul*, 80.
[339] Newton. (1998). *Journey of Souls*, 156-157.
[340] Ibid., 58.
[341] Ibid., 372.
[342] Ibid., 51.
[343] Modi. (2000). *Memories of God and Creation*, 178-194.
[344] Newton. (1998). *Journey of Souls*, 372.
[345] Ibid., 51.
[346] Ibid., 16.

Chapter 7

[347] Newton, Michael. (1998). *Journey of Souls: Case Studies of Life Between Lives*. St. Paul, MN: Llewellyn, 60.

[348] Lawton, Ian & Tomlinson, Andy. (2007). *The Wisdom of the Soul: Profound insights from the life between lives*. Southend-in-Sea, UK: Rational Spirituality Press, 13.

[349] Ibid., 136.

[350] Ibid., 38-39.

[351] Ibid., 39.

[352] Ibid., 40.

[353] Ibid., 39.

[354] Weiss, Brian L.. (1992). *Through Time into Healing*. New York: Simon & Schuster.

[355] Lawton & Tomlinson. (2007). *The Wisdom of the Soul*, 52.

[356] Ibid.

[357] Ibid., 57.

[358] Ibid., 126.

[359] Ibid., 68.

[360] Ibid., 68-69/

[361] Ibid., 69.

[362] Ibid., 58.

[363] Ibid., 59.

[364] Ibid.

[365] Newton. (1998). *Journey of Souls*, 193.

[366] Newton, Michael. (2000). *Destiny of Souls: New Case Studies of Life Between Lives*. St. Paul, MN: Llewellyn, 247.

[367] Ibid.

[368] See for example Modi, Shakuntala. (2000). *Memories of God and Creation: Remembering from the subconscious mind*. Charlottesville, PA: Hampton Roads.

[369] Ibid.

[370] Newton, Michael. (2000). *Destiny of Souls: New Case Studies of Life Between Lives*. St. Paul, MN: Llewellyn, 127.

[371] Ibid., 129-130.

[372] Ibid., 323-354; 365-369.

[373] Newton. (1998). *Journey of Souls*, 193.

[374] Lawton & Tomlinson. (2007). *The Wisdom of the Soul*, 117.

[375] Ibid., 118.

[376] Ibid., 119.

[377] Ibid., 125.

[378] Ibid.

[379] Ibid., 126.

[380] Ibid., 131.

[381] Snow, Chet B.. (1989). *Mass Dreams of the Future*. New York: McGraw-Hill; and Goldberg, Bruce. (1982). *Past Lives; Future Lives*. New York: Ballantine.

[382] Lawton & Tomlinson. (2007). *The Wisdom of the Soul*, 130-131.
[383] Ibid., 132.
[384] Ibid., 144.
[385] Ibid., 146.
[386] Ibid., 113.
[387] Ibid., 114.
[388] Ibid., 145.

Chapter 8

[389] Hastings, Arthur. (1991). *With the Tongues of Men and Angels: A study of channeling*. Fort Worth, TX: Holt, Rinehart and Winston, 1.
[390] Ibid.
[391] Ibid., 8.
[392] Ibid., 78.
[393] Migliore,V. (2007). *Aftereffects of Near-death States*. IANDS report.
[394] Hastings. (1991). *With the Tongues of Men and Angels*, 1.
[395] Klimo, Jon. (1987). *Channeling: Investigations on receiving information from paranormal sources*. New York: St. Martin's, 222.
[396] Hastings. (1991). *With the Tongues of Men and Angels*, 115.
[397] Ibid., 175-176.
[398] Ibid., 184.
[399] Klimo. (1987). *Channeling*, 294.
[400] Ibid., 305-306.
[401] Ibid., 295.
[402] Ibid., 295-296.
[403] Ibid., 276-277.
[404] Ibid., 16.
[405] Ibid., 253.
[406] Hastings. (1991). *With the Tongues of Men and Angels*, 125-126.
[407] Ibid., 117-118.
[408] Ibid., 119.
[409] Ibid., 121.
[410] Ibid., 118.
[411] Ibid., 121.
[412] Ibid., 126.
[413] Ibid., 180.
[414] Ibid., 125.
[415] Snow, Chet B. & Wambach, Helen. (1989). *Mass Dreams of the Future*. New York: McGraw-Hill.
[416] Hastings. (1991). *With the Tongues of Men and Angels*, 122.
[417] Ibid., 121-122.

[418] Ibid., 72.
[419] Ibid., 159.
[420] Klimo. (1987). *Channeling*, 40.
[421] Hastings. (1991). *With the Tongues of Men and Angels*, 103.
[422] Ibid., 192
[423] Ibid., 152-153.
[424] Ibid.
[425] Ibid.
[426] Klimo. (1987). *Channeling*, 309.
[427] Hastings. (1991). *With the Tongues of Men and Angels*, 154.
[428] Klimo. (1987). *Channeling*, 154.
[429] Ibid.
[430] Ibid., 155.
[431] Ibid.
[432] Ibid., 157.
[433] Ibid.
[434] Schmicker, Michael. (2002). *Best Evidence*, 2nd ed. Lincoln, NE: Writers Club, 232.
[435] Ibid., 252.
[436] Ibid., 252-253.
[437] Ibid.
[438] Klimo. (1987). *Channeling*, 152.
[439] Hastings. (1991). *With the Tongues of Men and Angels*, 64.
[440] Ibid., 35-47.
[441] Roberts, Jane. (1994). *Seth Speaks: The Eternal Validity of the Soul*. San Rafael, CA: Amber-Allen, 232-233, 411.
[442] Schmicker. (2002). *Best Evidence*, 245.
[443] Hastings. (1991). *With the Tongues of Men and Angels*, 162.
[444] Ibid., 25.
[445] Ibid., 163.
[446] Ibid., 162.
[447] Klimo. (1987). *Channeling*, 311.
[448] Ibid., 149.
[449] Ibid., 150.
[450] Ibid., 64.
[451] Ibid., 149.
[452] Jung, C. G.. (1981). *The Archetypes and the Collective Unconscious*. Princeton University.
[453] Hastings. (1991). *With the Tongues of Men and Angels*, 184.
[454] Ibid., 161.
[455] Ibid, 184.

Chapter 9

[456] Klimo, Jon. (1987). *Channeling: Investigations on receiving information from paranormal sources*. New York: St. Martin's, 150; and Hastings, Arthur. (1991). *With the Tongues of Men and Angels: A study of channeling*. Fort Worth, TX: Holt, Rinehart and Winston, 9.

[457] Hastings. (1991). *With the Tongues of Men and Angels*, 100-103.

[458] Schucman, Helen. (1975). *A Course in Miracles*. Mill Valley, CA: Foundation for Inner Peace.

[458] Ibid., ix.

[460] Hastings. (1991). *With the Tongues of Men and Angels*, 103-108.

[461] Pursel, Jach. (1987). *Lazaris: The sacred journey: you and your higher self*. Beverly Hills, CA: Synergy, 146.

[462] Ibid., 57.

[463] Ibid., xiii.

[464] Roberts, Jane. (1994). *The Nature of Personal Reality: Specific, practical techniques for solving everyday problems and enriching the life you know*. San Rafael, CA: Amber-Allen, 145.

[465] Ibid., 412.

[466] Ibid., 410-411.

[467] Ibid., 235.

[468] Ibid., 411.

[469] Ibid., 413.

[470] Pursel. (1987). *Lazaris*, 31-32.

[471] Roberts. (1994). *The Nature of Personal Reality*, 26.

[472] Klimo. (1987). *Channeling*, 151.

[473] Roberts. (1994). *The Nature of Personal Reality*, 367.

[474] Roberts, Jane. (1994). *Seth Speaks: The eternal validity of the soul*. San Rafael, CA: Amber-Allen, 178.

[475] Pursel. (1987). *Lazaris*, 208-209.

[476] Ibid., 32.

[477] Hastings. (1991). *With the Tongues of Men and Angels*, 74.

[478] Roberts. (1994). *Seth Speaks*, 183.

[479] Ibid., 183.

[480] Roberts. (1994). *Seth Speaks*.

[481] Ibid., 171-172.

[482] Ibid., 175.

[483] Ibid., 171-175.

[484] Hastings. (1991). *With the Tongues of Men and Angels*, 111.

[485] Roberts, Jane. (1997). *The Early Sessions: Volume 2 of the Seth Material*. Manhaset, NY:
New Awareness Network, 126-127.

[486] Roberts, Jane. (1998). *The Early Sessions: Volume 4 of the Seth Material*. Manhaset, NY: New Awareness Network, 324.

[487] Roberts. (1994). *Seth Speaks*, 204-209.

[488] Ibid., 20.

[489] Ibid., 54.

[490] Ibid., 12.

[491] Ibid., 414.

[492] Ibid., 12.

[493] Klimo. (1987). *Channeling*, 28.

[494] Roberts. (1994). *Seth Speaks,* 55.

[495] Hastings. (1991). *With the Tongues of Men and Angels,* 74.

[496] Ibid., 108.

[497] Roberts. (1994). *Seth Speaks*, 6-7.

[498] Klimo. (1987). *Channeling*, 29.

[499] Pursel. (1987). *Lazaris*, 17.

[500] Roberts. (1994). *The Nature of Personal Reality*, 280.

[501] Ibid.

[502] Ibid., 295.

[503] Ibid., 299.

[504] Hicks, Jerry & Hicks, Esther. (1994). *Abraham Speaks: A new beginning I*. San Antonio, TX: Crown Internationale.

[505] Ibid.

[506] Roberts. (1994). *The Nature of Personal Reality*, 300.

[507] Ibid., 368.

[508] Roberts. (1994). *Seth Speaks*, 55.

[509] Ibid., 313.

[510] Pursel, Jach. (1988). *Lazaris: Lazaris Interviews, Book II*. Beverly Hills, CA: Synergy, 190-191.

[511] Klimo. (1987). *Channeling*, 39.

[512] Ibid., 160.

[513] Roberts. (1994). *Seth Speaks*, 228.

[514] Ibid., 203.

[515] Ibid., 207.

[516] Ibid., 270.

[517] Ibid., 300.

[518] Hughes, Andy. "In Their Own Words: Part 4, Seth's Concept of God." As accessed 1 December 2011 at http://www.spiritual-endeavors.org/seth/Andy4.htm.

[519] Pursel. (1987). *Lazaris*, 29.

[520] Roberts. (1994). *Seth Speaks*, 238.

[521] Ibid., 342-343.

[522] Ibid., 161, 342.

[523] Ibid., 161.

[524] Ibid., 238-239.

[525] Ibid., 159.

[526] Hastings. (1991). *With the Tongues of Men and Angels*, 105.

[527] Roberts. (1994). *Seth Speaks*, 333.

[528] Pursel. (1987). *Lazaris*, 56.

[529] Roberts. (1994). *The Nature of Personal Reality*, 355.

[530] Hastings. (1991). *With the Tongues of Men and Angels*, 102.

Chapter 10

[531] Monroe, Robert. (1985). *Far Journeys*. Garden City, NY: Doubleday, 206-227.

[532] The Gospel according to Mathew 7:7 (NIV).

[533] Modi, Shakuntala. (2000). *Memories of God and Creation: Remembering from the subconscious mind.* Charlottesville, PA: Hampton Roads.

[534] The Gospel according to John 8:32 (NIV).

[535] The Gospel according to Matthew 7:12 (NIV).

[536] The Gospel according to Luke 12:34 (NIV); see also Luke 12:15.

Selected Bibliography

Books

Banerjee, Hemendra. (1980). *Americans who have been reincarnated.* New York: Macmillan.

Berman, Phillip L. (1998). *The Journey Home: What near death experiences and mysticism teach us about the gift of life.* New York: Pocket Books.

Buhlman, William. (2001). *The Secret of the Soul: Using Out-of-Body Experiences to Understand our True Nature.* New York: HarperCollins.

Capra, Fritjof. (1991). *The Tao of Physics* (3rd Ed.). Boston, MA: Shambhala Publications.

Ducasse, C. J. (2006). *A Critical Examination of the Belief in a Life After Death.* Whitefish, MT: Kessinger.

Fenwick, Peter & Fenwick, Elizabeth. (2001). *Reliving Past Lives: The Evidence under Hypnosis.* New York: Berkley.

Fisher, Joe. (1985). *The Case for Reincarnation.* New York: Bantam.

Gallup, G., & Proctor, W. (1982). *Adventures in Immortality: A Look Beyond the Threshold of Death.* New York, NY: McGraw-Hill.

Green, C. (1968). *Out-of-the-body experiences.* London, Hamish Hamilton.

Freeman, James Dillet. (1986). *The Case for Reincarnation.* Unity Village, MO: Unity Books.

Hastings, Arthur. (1991). *With the tongues of men and Angels: A study of channeling.* Orlando, FL: Holt, Rinehart, Winston.

Hicks, Jerry & Hicks, Esther. (1994). *Abraham Speaks: A new beginning I.* San Antonio, TX: Crown Internationale.

Jung, C. G.. (1981). *The Archetypes and the Collective Unconscious.* Princeton, NJ: Princeton University.

Kirtley, D. D. (1975). *The Psychology of Blindness*. Chicago: Nelson-Hall.

Klimo, Jon. (1987). *Channeling: Investigations on receiving information from paranormal sources*. New York: St. Martin's.

Lawton, Ian. (2007). *The Wisdom of the Soul: Profound insights from the life between lives.* Southend-on-Sea, UK: Rational Spirituality Press.

Long, Jeffrey, and Perry, Paul. (2010). *Evidence of the Afterlife: The Science of near death experiences*. New York: HarperOne.

Magnus, John. (2005). *Astral Projection and the Nature of Reality: Exploring the Out-of-Body State*. Charlottesville, VA: Hampton Roads.

Maurice Rawlings, M.D. (1991). Beyond Death's Door. New York: Bantam.

Modi, Shakuntala. (2000). *Memories of God and Creation: Remembering from the subconscious mind*. Charlottesville, PA: Hampton Roads.

Monroe, Robert A. (1971). *Journeys out of the Body*. New York: Doubleday.

_____. (1985). *Far Journeys*. Garden City, NY: Doubleday.

Moody, Raymond A. (1975). *Life after Life: The investigation of a phenomenon; survival of bodily death.* New York: HarperOne.

_____. (1989). *The Light Beyond: New explorations.* New York: Bantam.

Murphy, G. & Ballou, R.O. (Ed.). (1973). *William James on Psychical Research*. Clifton, NJ: August M. Kelley.

Newton, Michael. (1998). *Journey of Souls: Case Studies of Life Between Lives*. Llewellyn: St. Paul, MN.

_____. (2000). *Destiny of Souls: New Case Studies of Life between Lives*. St. Paul, MN: Llewellyn.

Pettinati, H. M. (Ed.). *Hypnosis and Memory*. New York: Guilford Press.

Pursel, Jach. (1987). *Lazaris: The sacred journey: you and your higher self.* Beverly Hills, CA: Synergy.

_____. (1988). *Lazaris: Lazaris Interviews, Book II.* Beverly Hills, CA: Synergy.

Ring, K. (1984). *Heading toward Omega: In Search of the Meaning of the Near-Death Experience.* New York: William Morrow Books.

_____. (1998). *Lessons from the Light: What we can learn from the Near-Death Experience.* Oklahoma City, OK: Insight Books.

Ring, Kenneth & Cooper, Sharon. (2008). *Mindsight: Near-death and out-of-body experiences in the blind.* New York: iUniverse.

Roberts, Jane. (1994). *The Nature of Personal Reality: Specific, practical techniques for solving everyday problems and enriching the life you know.* San Rafael, CA: Amber-Allen.

_____. (1994). *Seth Speaks: The eternal validity of the soul.* San Rafael, CA: Amber-Allen.

_____. (1997). *The Early Sessions: Volume 2 of the Seth Material.* Manhaset, NY: New Awareness Network.

_____. (1998). *The Early Sessions: Volume 4 of the Seth Material.* Manhaset, NY: New Awareness Network.

Russell, Peter. (2003). *From Science to God: A physicist's journey into the mystery of consciousness.* Novato, CA: New World Library.

Schmicker, Michael. (2002). *Best Evidence*, 2nd ed. Lincoln, NE: Writers Club.

Schucman, Helen. (1975). *A Course in Miracles.* Mill Valley, CA: Foundation for Inner Peace.

Sharp, K. C. (1995). *After the Light: What I Discovered on the Other Side of Life That Can Change Your World.* Morrow, NY.

Snow, Chet B.. (1989). *Mass Dreams of the Future.* New York: McGraw-Hill; and Goldberg, Bruce. (1982). *Past Lives; Future Lives.* New York: Ballantine.

Stevenson, Ian. (1974). *Twenty Cases Suggestive of Reincarnation*, 2nd ed. Charlottesville, VA: University of Virginia.

_____. (1974). *Xenoglossy: A review and report of a case.* New York: American Society for Psychical Research.

_____. (1975). *Cases of the Reincarnation Type, Volume 1: Ten Cases in India.* Charlottesville, VA: University of Virginia.

_____. (1984). *Unlearned Language: New studies in xenoglossy.* Charlottesville: University Press of Virginia.

_____. (1987). *Children Who Remember Previous Lives: A question of reincarnation.* Charlottesville, VA: The University of Virginia.

_____. (1997). *Where Reincarnation and Biology Intersect.* Westport, CT: Praeger.

Tomlinson, Andy. (2007). *Exploring the Eternal Soul: Insights from the life between lives.* Winchester, UK: O Books.

Wambach, Helen. (1978). *Reliving Past Lives: The Evidence under Hypnosis.* New York: Barnes & Noble.

Weiss, Brian L. (1992). *Through Time into Healing.* New York: Simon & Schuster.

Whitton, Joel & Fisher, Joe. (1986). *Life Between Life: Scientific explorations into the void separating one incarnation from the next.* Garden City, NY: Doubleday.

Zukav, Gary. (1979). *The Dancing Wu Li Masters: An overview of the new physics.* New York: Bantam.

Journal Articles

Bauer, M. (1985). Near-Death Experiences and Attitudinal Change. Anabiosis: *Journal of Near-Death Studies, 5.*

Dywan, J. & Bowers, K. S. (1983). The use of hypnosis to enhance recall. *Science, 222.*

Flynn, C. (1982). Meanings and Implications of NDEr Transformations: Some Preliminary Findings and Implications. Anabiosis: *Journal of Near-Death Studies, 2.*

Greyson, B. (1983). Increase in Psychic Phenomena Following Near-Death Experiences. *Theta,* 11.

_____. (1992). Reduced Death Threat in Near-Death Experiences. *Death Studies,* 16.

Haraldson, Erlendur. (1991). Children Claiming Past-Life Memories: Four cases in Sri Lanka. *Journal of Scientific Exploration, 5*(2).

Hart, H. (1954). ESP Projection: Spontaneous cases and the experimental method. *Journal of the American Society for Psychical Research,* 48.

Knoblauch, H. et.al. (2001). Different Kinds of Near-Death Experience: A Report on a Survey of Near-Death Experiences in Germany. *Journal of Near-Death Studies,* 20.

Musgrave, C. (1997). The Near-Death Experience: A Study of Spiritual Transformation. *Journal of Near-Death Studies,* 15.

Noyes, R. (1980). Attitude Changes Following Near-Death Experiences. *Psychiatry,* 43.

Perera, M. et.al. (2005). Prevalence of Near-Death Experiences in Australia. *Journal of Near-Death Studies,* 24.

Ramster, Peter. (1994). "Past lives and hypnosis." *Australian Journal of Clinical Hypnotherapy and Hypnosis, 15*(2).

Stevenson, Ian. (1960). The evidence for survival from claimed memories of former incarnations. *Journal of the American Society for Psychical Research,* 54.

_____. (1976). A Preliminary Report of a new case of responsive xenoglossy: The case of Gretchen. *Journal of the American Society for Psychical Research, 70.*

_____. (1983). American Children Who Claim to Remember Previous Lives. *Journal of Nervous and Mental Disease,* 171.

Stevenson, Ian & Pasricha, Satwant, (1980). A Preliminary Report of an unusual case of the reincarnation type with xenoglossy. *Journal of the American Society for Psychical Research, 74.*

Stout, Y. et. al. (2006) Six Major Challenges Faced by Near-Death Experiencers. *Journal of Near-Death Studies, 29.*

Sutherland, C. (1989). Psychic Phenomena Following Near-Death Experiences: An Australian Study. *Journal of Near-Death Studies, 8.*

_____. (1990). Changes in Religious Beliefs, Attitudes, and Practices Following Near-Death Experiences: An Australian Study. *Journal of Near-Death Studies, 9.*

Tarazi, Linda. (1990). "An unusual case of hypnotic regression with some unexplained contents." *Journal of the American Society for Psychical Research, 84.*

Twemlow, Stuart W. MD, and Gabbard, Glen O. MD. (1982). The Out of Body Experience: A Phenomenological Typology based on questionnaire responses. *American Journal of Psychiatry, 139.*

van Lommel, Pim. (Dec 2001). Near Death Experience in Survivors of Cardiac Arrest: A Prospective Study in the Netherlands, *The Lancet,* 358.

Venn, Jonathan. (Oct. 1986). Hypnosis and the reincarnation hypothesis: A critical review and intensive case study. *Journal of the American Society for Psychical Research, 80*(4).

Special Reports

Christian, S. R. (2005). *Marital satisfaction and stability following a near-death experience of one of the marital partners.* University of North Texas Dissertation. Available at http://www.unt.edu/etd/all/August2005/Open/christian_sandra_rozan/index.htm.

Cunningham, Paul F. (1986). *The effects of different probe procedures on the experience of imaging in hypnotic and waking states of consciousness.* Unpublished doctoral dissertation, University of Tennessee, Knoxville.

Hughes, Andy. "In Their Own Words: Part 4, Seth's Concept of God." Available at http://www.spiritual-endeavors.org/seth/Andy4.htm.

Migliore,V. (2007). *Aftereffects of Near-death States.* IANDS report. Available at http://iands.org/aftereffects-of-near-death-states.html.

_____. (2007). *Characteristics of a Near-Death Experience.* IANDS report. Available at http://iands.org/about-ndes/characteristics.html.

_____. (2007). *Key Facts about Near-Death Experience.* The International Association for Near-Death Studies (IANDS) report. Available at http://iands.org/key-nde-facts.html.

Websites

http://www.nderf.org

http://en.wikipedia.org/wiki/Christian_Friedrich_Heinecken.

About the Author

Wade joined the military in 1989 while simultaneously putting himself through college and earning a BA, MA, and credits towards a PhD in the process. He has deployed to both Iraq and Afghanistan, and has served at assignments worldwide. He is adept at tackling tough problem sets to uncover hidden truths because it's a daily job requirement. He currently lives with his wife and son at a foreign posting while continuing to serve in the US Military.

www.ingramcontent.com/pod-product-compliance
Lightning Source LLC
Chambersburg PA
CBHW072003060426
42446CB00042B/1372